Murder and Its Consequences

MURDER AND ITS CONSEQUENCES

ESSAYS ON CAPITAL PUNISHMENT IN AMERICA

Leigh Buchanan Bienen

Northwestern University Press
Evanston, Illinois

Northwestern University Press
www.nupress.northwestern.edu

The following articles were previously published and are reprinted by permission of the journals in which they appeared: "A Good Murder," *Fordham Urban Law Journal,* vol. 20, no. 3 (Spring 1993): 585–607; "Anomalies: Ritual and Language in Lethal Injection Regulations," *Fordham Urban Law Journal,* vol. 35, no. 4 (2008): 857–81; "The Quality of Justice in Capital Cases: Illinois as a Case Study," *Law and Contemporary Problems,* vol. 61, no. 4 (Autumn 1998): 193–217; "The Proportionality Review of Capital Cases by State High Courts After *Gregg:* Only 'the Appearance of Justice.'" *The Journal of Criminal Law and Criminology,* vol. 87, no. 1 (Fall 1996): 130–314.

"Not Wiser After Thirty-Five Years of Contemplating the Death Penalty" was previously published in *Studies in Law, Politics and Society,* vol. 42 (2007): 91–133. Copyright © Emerald Group Publishing. Reprinted by permission of Emerald Group Publishing.

Printed in the United States of America
10 9 8 7 6 5 4 3 2 1

Library of Congress Cataloging-in-Publication Data

Bienen, Leigh B.
Murder and its consequences : essays on capital punishment in America / Leigh Buchanan Bienen.
p. cm.
Includes bibliographical references.
ISBN 978-0-8101-2697-8 (cloth : alk. paper)
1. Capital punishment—United States. 2. Murder—United States. I. Title.
KF9227.C2B54 2010
364.660973—dc22

2010010448

∞ The paper used in this publication meets the minimum requirements of the American National Standard for Information Sciences—Permanence of Paper for Printed Library Materials, ANSI Z39.48-1992.

For Henry and our lovely daughters, Laura, Claire, and Leslie, and their wonderful families. Without you, what is the point?

Contents

Foreword by Deborah W. Denno ix

Acknowledgments xv

Introduction: Murder, the Rule of Law, and the Tale of the Little Red Hen xvii

Chapter 1
"A Good Murder" 3

Chapter 2
Not Wiser After Thirty-Five Years of Contemplating the Death Penalty 23

Chapter 3
Anomalies: Ritual and Language in Lethal Injection Regulations 59

Chapter 4
The Quality of Justice in Capital Cases: Illinois as a Case Study 75

Chapter 5
The Proportionality Review of Capital Cases by State High Courts After *Gregg:* Only "the Appearance of Justice" 91

Notes 143

Foreword

Deborah W. Denno

I vividly remember the moment I first met Leigh Bienen so many years ago. It seems odd in retrospect to recall the rather low-key impetus for our introduction, given the impact that Leigh would later have on my career. But like many aspects of people's lives, big things happen when we least expect or even welcome them. So let me tell you my story about Leigh—a tale of law, statistics, and the death penalty, not to mention serendipity and heart. Colleagueships may often be complicated but my tie to Leigh, which spans a quarter-century, is as straightforward as they come.

In 1984 I was a senior research associate at the Sellin Center for Studies in Criminology and Criminal Law at the University of Pennsylvania. My mentor, Marvin Wolfgang, was the center's founding director. At the time, I was heading a massive study of biological and sociological predictors of crime as well as contemplating going to law school. My days were full but, as I would soon find out, they would become fuller still.

One afternoon Neil Weiner, a Sellin Center colleague, stopped by my office with what seemed to be a minor request. Would I be willing to attend a meeting with Leigh Bienen, a lawyer from the Office of the Public Defender in Trenton, New Jersey? Leigh was in charge of the Special Projects Unit at the office; she wanted to begin a statistical analysis of all the homicides processed in New Jersey starting in 1982, when New Jersey reenacted the death penalty. Neil had initially agreed to work on the project alone but was already sensing that the task would be a bit more daunting than predicted. He asked me to help him—just for a couple of weeks, he said.

With that explanation, I was impressed with Leigh even before I had met her. Clearly, she was not your typical lawyer. Those drawn to the legal profession commonly shun working with the sciences or even with numbers, not to mention the heavily quantitative kinds of modeling that Leigh had in mind. Leigh was also sufficiently discerning and sophisticated to know that the Sellin Center would be a good place to come for assistance. While many professionals called or relied on our center, surprisingly few were lawyers, despite Marvin Wolfgang's remarkable ability to bridge both law and criminology. After all, the *British Journal of Criminology* had pegged Marvin as "the most influential criminologist in the English-speaking world." No small part of that clout derived from Marvin's research on the death penalty, which, among other contributions, was used in the Supreme Court's 1972 decision in *Furman v. Georgia. Furman* had held that the death penalty as applied by states was unconstitutional.

I was proud of the Sellin Center's focus on the death penalty and most particularly Marvin's critical revelations that the penalty was disproportionately applied to poor African Americans. At the same time, however, it was depressing to contemplate working on a death penalty study. I had avoided researching the area, far preferring to spend my time explaining why people committed crime, not why people were executed. Besides, I wondered, what could realistically be discovered about the death penalty process in New Jersey? Like Marvin, some years earlier other researchers—especially the renowned University of Iowa law school professor David Baldus—had revealed the death penalty's racially disproportionate application in southern states. Leigh and her colleagues wanted to study the death penalty in a northern state in the 1980s. Surely, I thought, their research would be barren.

So when Neil asked me that day to come to the meeting and help out, he and I agreed that the deal would really be for just two weeks—simply to get the data set started and the preliminary steps out of the way. I attended the meeting with Leigh and one of her colleagues, along with Marvin and Neil. Leigh was clearly on top of the discussion, given her knowledge of data management. I would later learn that she had a history of conducting sociological and statistical research as well as a professional connection to Marvin because of it. I could think of no one more uniquely fitted for the New Jersey project than Leigh, both in terms of background knowledge and expertise. And Leigh and her colleague were very dedicated to the enterprise. But my mind was still set on only short-term involvement, given my reservations about the subject matter.

Those two weeks I volunteered would quickly turn into years and, ultimately, along with law school and other interests, a career-long intrigue with the death penalty. Because of Leigh's sway, I began a trajectory I would never have predicted. Of course, show a criminologist a nice bit of data and he or she can be instantly hooked; statistics can create a mesmerizing story of their own that can be impossible to put down. Yet the New Jersey data set was like none I had ever seen. One look at even the preliminary statistics showed how serious the problems were even within a northern state. As Leigh documents so compellingly in "A Good Murder," the New Jersey study found a greater likelihood that prosecutors would seek death in white-victim cases, along with an inordinate death-seeking disparity between different New Jersey counties. Other discoveries included the effects of inadequate counsel and discriminatory decision-making throughout the many steps of the process for determining who would be deemed death-eligible.

But the draw for me was not just the shocking statistics. Within months of the start of our project, two others came on board to create a team: Doug Mills, a Princeton University computer and data expert whom Leigh brought on, and Paul Allison, a revered University of Pennsylvania sociology professor and statistical maven. With Leigh at the helm, our group worked hard but we played hard too. Our in-person gatherings and phone calls would be a source of lightning-rod productivity and group creation. But they were also incredibly fun. Along with a superb intellect, Leigh has a wonderful sense of enthusiasm and merriment. Her frequent trips to the University of Pennsylvania to work with Neil and me were bonded by healthy bouts of laughter—all the better to see us through the dismal statistics we were researching. These were my good friends as well as my colleagues; I felt lucky to be part of our warm little cluster.

Almost immediately, Leigh assured that our findings would be put to good use, and they were. Indeed, the third enticement for me to join in was seeing how pragmatically powerful our results could be. With some regularity we met with public defenders and other members of the New Jersey bar. Many seemed hungry for our discoveries, and they were rewarded with good outcomes when they used them in court. But the years were passing. By the time Leigh had arranged for our first set of findings to be published in the *Rutgers Law Review* in 1988, I had completed two years of law school at the University of Pennsylvania. With law school now dominating much of my time, Leigh, Neil, Paul, and Doug moved on without me to publish on the disparities evidenced by proportional review of New Jersey's death penalty cases. Those proportionality review results were striking. They prompted the New Jersey Supreme Court to appoint David Baldus as special master so that he could examine whether in fact the New Jersey death penalty was being implemented arbitrarily—a conclusion that he would later definitively confirm.

Indeed, the accumulation of death penalty research—starting with Leigh's project at the University of Pennsylvania—would reveal so many problems that it would forever change New Jersey's death penalty world. In 2007 the state ultimately ended its death penalty entirely; not one person had been executed post-*Furman.*

From 1988 on, Leigh, Neil, and I would all continue with our own individual death penalty projects as well as other interests and personal commitments. Until Neil's sudden and untimely death last year, he was actively involved in the death penalty arena—a path I know he would never have taken without Leigh as a catalyst and her years-long support. My own involvement with Leigh and the New Jersey project would also have career-long implications. After graduating from law school in 1989, I soon became a professor at Fordham Law School, where I have engaged in a range of different issues associated with the death penalty, but most particularly the constitutionality of execution methods.

During these years my professional and personal links with Leigh have never wavered. Leigh has been the most supportive cheerleader I could possibly have wished for. At the same time, Leigh's own death penalty career began soaring, as the few selected articles she has provided in this volume demonstrate. I was delighted to learn that Leigh included two articles that were first published in the *Fordham Urban Law Journal:* "A Good Murder" and "Anomalies." "A Good Murder" provides an insightful account of Leigh's death penalty work in New Jersey, while "Anomalies" depicts her textual focus on the rituals surrounding lethal injection. According to Leigh, the protocols for lethal injection executions exist more as a symbolic effort to appease any concerns witnesses may have about the process rather than to ensure that the executions are humane. This view is distinctly convincing in the way that only Leigh can present it.

Leigh's other articles in this volume represent just some of her publications that took place while she was at the Northwestern University School of Law. Her article on "The Proportionality Review of Capital Cases" puts her groundbreaking New Jersey proportionality review work in the context of other such efforts that were mushrooming nationwide. It is this kind of comparative analysis that demonstrates the strength of the empirical research and explains its effect on the New Jersey legislature. But Leigh hardly stopped with New Jersey. As soon as she landed at Northwestern she dove into all of the many extraordinary developments in Illinois, a point of focus in her piece on "The Quality of Justice in Capital Cases: Illinois as a Case Study."

Leigh reflects on all these matters in "Not Wiser After Thirty-Five Years of Contemplating the Death Penalty"—a retrospective based on her decades of death penalty research and all the trials and tribulations accompanying them. There is no question that Leigh ranks among the top death penalty scholars; her commitment and devotion, not to mention her spunk and ingenuity, have set new standards and heights.

A foreword of this sort is not so much about the substance of Leigh's work as it is her personal impact. For Neil Weiner and me, that influence has no parallel. And anyone who knows Leigh Bienen would know that any association with her goes well beyond the doorstep of statistics or the death penalty. Leigh's passion for the arts is boundless—for music, theater, you name it. To be Leigh's friend and colleague is to have accompanied her to countless performances—at the Metropolitan Opera House or on Broadway and anywhere in between—often with packs of other friends that she has brought together. It is the rare e-mail from Leigh that is not followed by detailed recommendations of all that is going on in the cultural community of New York, or accounts of a play she has just seen or music she has just heard. "Life is too short not to enjoy the opera!" is a common Leigh refrain. On this level and many others, she is among the most extroverted and generous people I have ever known. The richness in Leigh's life is reflected in the thrill of her work: it accounts for much of her academic style, as well as her perception of the death penalty world. While Leigh is an impeccably thorough and careful researcher, she also has the gifts of clarity and creativity—resources that bring together the law and statistics so that they make sense in a way that no one else would have ever considered. Along with her dedication and heart, her work moves just right. Readers will be enthralled and will learn from the pages that follow as I have done for twenty-five years.

Acknowledgments

The author gratefully acknowledges the continued support of many, including those at the Northwestern University School of Law: Dean David Van Zandt, Christine Rosso, Esq., librarians Marcia Lehr and Pegeen Bassett, Juana Haskin, Cecilia Torres, and my research assistants and students over the years, as well as the many, many others at Northwestern and elsewhere who have assisted and supported this research.

Introduction: Murder, the Rule of Law, and the Tale of the Little Red Hen

The test of the integrity, the authority of a society, its core identity, is its legal system: the government's ability to control violence, to impose order over lawlessness. There is killing among all men, in all societies. War seems to be endemic. Whenever men have enough to eat, they kill one another, hoard wealth, and build larger, more intricate and expensive weapons, what we now call weapons of mass destruction. The old ways of killing are not good enough for modern societies, although the old ways were sufficient for the most recent genocides in Africa and Asia. The new technologies have raised the stakes for diplomacy and statecraft, and instant communication and the universal spread of old and new weapons offer fresh challenges to the establishment of the rule of law. Or perhaps that is just how it seems to us, at this time.

The essays in this book are about the punishment of small-scale murder, old-fashioned murders, garden-variety murders: mostly young men killing other young men in disputes defined by the style of the community and the times, an outburst over a gang symbol; a gun; a car. For the family murders, it is usually men killing their wives or other women over real or imagined issues of sexual domination; or some women killing children; or occasionally women killing men. This is what murder looks like in state courts across the country. It is the revenge murders over a perceived slight or insult, the drunken slashings, the murder during a burglary or robbery, the drive-by shootings, the killings over territory or drugs; the senseless beating to death of a child or woman. This is lowercase justice. State courts in America do not ordinarily address issues of genocide or civil war. They do thrive on drama: the drama of a capital prosecution; the drama of seeing an accused who is facing the death penalty; the drama of the witnesses; the drama of waiting for the jury verdict; the drawn-out drama of the appeals; and then the final vigils on both sides as the death penalty is administered, or not.

Where did capital punishment come from? The first criminal laws enacted by the colonies, for example, the Crimes Act of March 18, 1796, in New Jersey, were simply modeled upon the British common and statutory law which provided death as the penalty for all felonies, with the benefit of clergy.[1] So inequity in the application of punishment in the common law dates from our earliest heritage. When New Jersey and Illinois and Connecticut passed statutes saying the common law of Great Britain was in effect in those states, they enacted the death penalty.[2] This book looks at how capital punishment has played out recently in a few state jurisdictions over the recent past. For fifteen years I was a defense attorney in New Jersey helping to develop a system for the proportionality review of capital cases before the New Jersey Supreme Court.[3] Basically, proportionality review asks whether this death sentence is imposed fairly or proportionately in comparison to the sentence in other murders in the same jurisdiction where the death penalty was imposed or not imposed. Several of these essays describe how proportionality review evolved or was implemented in New Jersey. It was a long commitment by a principled and intellectually powerful court to the meaningful review of the capital cases which came before it after reenactment of the death penalty in New Jersey in 1982. No other state high court has made that commitment. The U.S. Supreme Court has steadily backed away from its previous willingness to find constitutional infirmity in the arbitrary and capricious application of the death penalty by the states.

In 1995 I came to Illinois and thus was witness to an extraordinary development in capital punishment jurisprudence, as is described in several of these chapters. The commutation of 167 death sentences by then Governor George Ryan was unprecedented in the history of American law. Fittingly, it was announced in Lincoln Hall at the Northwestern University School of Law. It would not have happened without the way being paved by years, decades of work by lawyers, faculty members at many universities, students, journalists, nonprofit groups, and so many others in Illinois and around the country. A groundswell of support for the commutations crested at a propitious moment with the cascading revelations of case after case of men on death row in Illinois for murders they did not commit.[4] And the commutations might have been derailed by one atrocious murder with a sympathetic victim hitting the front pages of the newspapers at the same time. And then there was the national movement which accompanied what was happening in Illinois. The commutations would never have occurred without the unpredictable coming together of specific groups of people, events, and institutions, such as the *Chicago Tribune,* the American Bar Association, university students in legal clinics and journalism classes, and many institutional actors capable of playing an influential role behind the scenes over a period of years. At the end of the day, however, the historic decision to empty death row, to declare the system in Illinois unjust, was made by a person, the governor leaving office, with the political power to do it, not by a court, not by a federal or state judge.

It is a strange and contradictory world, the world of capital punishment jurisprudence in America. The total number of executions since 1976 is 1,136, of which 11 were women; 78 percent were for the murder of a white victim; 13 percent for the murder of a black victim, the rest being Latino, Asian, and other.[5] Of those now on death row, 45 percent are white; 42 percent are black. Most states, 38 out of 52 jurisdictions, have capital punishment; there is huge variation in the way the death penalty is applied, between states and within a single state, as is described in these chapters. Some states execute persons sentenced to death; some execute few, or none.[6] Some states have a much higher rate of imposing the death penalty than others, some counties within a state have a significantly higher rate or probability of imposing the death penalty than others. There are vast disparities in who gets prosecuted and who gets convicted and executed, and these disparities are uncomfortably linked to race, socioeconomic status, and geographic region.[7]

At the end of the day, however, the death penalty is not about the statistics or the evidence of racial or socioeconomic discrimination, although many who observe and work within the system believe such discrimination exists and is both predictive and explanatory. The criminal justice system, and especially the death penalty, have always been about morality, about what is right and what is wrong. No one disputes that there are guilty persons on death row who have committed murders so vicious that in terms of individual responsibility they deserve to pay for the crime with their lives. That has always been the case and always will be the case. And for some that is enough.

Perhaps maintaining the rule of law in a large, complex society has always been difficult, ambiguous, slippery. Not to imply that meting out justice is simple in any society. If punishment is an important aspect of the rule of law, which it is, and if capital punishment is the most extreme form of punishment a society can impose, then one test of the rule of law in any culture is the society's success in the imposition of death as a penalty. What does "success" mean in this context? In America we point to societies where women are stoned to death in the street, without trial or appeal, and we condemn those acts as characteristic of a society not governed by the rule of law. In America summary justice is against the law, no matter how heinous the offense. And if summary justice takes place, the executioner is subject to prosecution. One characteristic of our modern society is supposed to be our open and principled form of government, in which we record with great care and accuracy what goes on in our legal system, and then make what we find public, so that an informed citizenry can see and judge what is done in their name. In the area of crime and punishment, there is often little disagreement about the many facts and statistics easily available in the public domain, and much disagreement about which facts are important or immutable. Sometimes there is open disagreement about what facts are relevant, or should be relevant. There is strong public disagreement about whether the current system of capital punishment in America is just, and about whether it exemplifies the rule of law, or its absence. Does the capital punishment system in America exemplify the best or the worst about our society in the twenty-first century?

To be respected, to be counted as worthy of a society governed under the rule of law, a government must identify those who kill without authority and punish them justly. No society will ever get rid of murder or wrongdoing. If understanding what justice is were simple, then there would be little for philosophers or the rest of us to argue about, outside of and inside the law. How simple it sounds: an eye for an eye, death for the person who kills. If indeed the death penalty were imposed for all murders there would be some sixteen thousand executions a year, for that is the approximate number of murders in the United States every year.[8]

Any society worthy of the name outlaws random killing among its members and does not allow killing absent state authority, absent justification. The purpose of having a police force is to preempt and prevent violence. If a police force, or an individual police officer, is corrupt or dishonest, it harms all of us. It is the job of the police to arrest, charge, and take to jail the murderer. And under our system the accused murderer is entitled to have his rights read to him and to be represented by counsel. The job of the state legislature—or the U.S. Congress—is to enact laws prohibiting murder or other offenses and to say how they will be punished. The job of judges and courts is to uphold and interpret the law.

The laws and rules governing when and how capital punishment shall be prosecuted and imposed have become extremely convoluted, and they vary enormously in substance and procedure, and from jurisdiction to jurisdiction. There are some federal capital statutes, but they pale in importance next to the vast and encrusted apparatus of thirty-eight very different state capital punishment systems.[9] In one state it is a capital crime to rape a child. In another state every felony murder, even for the person who did not commit the homicidal act, is a capital crime. In another state the only capital offense is the killing of a police officer or the killing of a guard in a prison. In all capital punishment states only a subset of all murders are capital cases—although the size of that subset varies—and if you take all the cases which are actually prosecuted as capital cases, it is an even tinier percentage of all murders. There is doctrine from the U.S. Supreme Court, repeatedly affirmed by other courts, which says that the death penalty should be reserved for the "worst of the worst." It turns out that the principle of an eye for an eye, a killing for a killing, is not the principle which governs the American capital punishment system.

Murder as a crime is one of the simpler ones: simply the unauthorized killing of another human being. Or, as the first chapter in this book argues, perhaps all murders are not alike. Some murders are "good" murders. One would think that counting the number of murders, and then counting the number of capital cases prosecuted, would be relatively easy: count the people who are dead from non-accidental or unnatural causes and eliminate the justified killings and then the suicides, which are always higher than the number of murders. But even counting the murders and sorting out which ones might be eligible for capital prosecution under the capital statute in the jurisdiction, and then counting the number of capital prosecutions which go forward, is not straightforward. We pride ourselves on having statistics on every aspect of crime and incarceration, and on executions, but data from different sources are contradictory and incomplete. Large omissions are immediately apparent.[10]

Counting the death-eligible cases has never been done in Illinois since the reimposition of the death penalty in the 1970s.[11] The Illinois Capital Punishment Reform Study Committee[12] will attempt to make such a count and publish it, but whether this committee, with the authority of the state behind it, will succeed remains to be seen.[13]

A capital punishment system in America has many parts. It is not immediate justice, in theory or practice. The system of instant justice is the stoning in the street of the woman accused of adultery, the hanging of the horse thief in the corral, or the summary shot in the head to the wayward gang member. For a bureaucratic society such as ours, there are many separate and linked institutions which play a role in imposing the death sentence. Who is going to catch the murderers when they run away, and who is going to decide upon where to put the murderers while they await trial or their appeal? Then, who will judge them and decide upon their punishment? Who will carry out the punishment? And who will take responsibility for the gross disparities and injustices in the American capital punishment system, as it now stands?

This is a new version of "The Tale of the Little Red Hen": who will take responsibility for the current situation regarding capital punishment in any one of the thirty-eight states?[14] No one. Not I, says the state legislature, all I do is define the capital crime, it is the murderer who commits the crime. It is my job to declare that for certain murders the penalty shall be death. Not I, say the state's attorneys, it is my job to prosecute and convict the accused under the capital statute. Not I, say the defense attorneys, it is my job to represent the defendant as well as I can under the circumstances, following the law. Not I, say the police officers, my job is to arrest the accused and keep him in custody until conviction, acquittal, or execution. Not I, say the trial court judges, I just administer the capital trial and sentence the defendant to death based upon the law and the facts of the case before me. Not I, say the jurors, we just decide whether to sentence the defendant to death following the instructions given to us. Not I, says the appellate court, we just decide the narrow issue presented in the case in front of us based on our precedent and the statutes. Not I, says the state high court, the legislature enacted the statute and the trial court imposed the sentence, and this court is not going to disturb a jury verdict or declare a system which has always been in place unconstitutional. Not I, says the U.S. Supreme Court, capital punishment is a matter for the states, and we are sick of wasting time on these cases. Who will stop the lethal injection? Not I, say the execution technicians, all I do is follow the training and the regulations set out in the Department of Corrections manual. And so it goes, with matters continuing and going forward, in fact with the situation having become more arbitrary and capricious since the U.S. Supreme Court first suspended all capital prosecutions and executions in 1972, only allowing them to go forward again in 1976. How does the system roll on, year after year, decade after decade when the way it operates is no secret? No one is willing to take responsibility for, or change, a dysfunctional system. Yet when it is time to eat the bread, all come forward.

Who will bring the next capital case? I will, say the state's attorneys. Who will arrest the murderer and then get a confession out of him? I will, say the police, I will bring that shaky confession or identification evidence to the state prosecutors and then to the court. I will defend the capital defendant, say the defense attorneys, although I am not paid enough and do not have the resources to mount a serious legal defense. I will conduct the capital trial, say the trial court judges, and I will hurry through it as fast as I can. How can I not try the case in front of me when all the rules seem to have been followed to get it here? I will sentence the criminal to death, say the jurors, everyone has gone to so much trouble to bring us here and give us all of those detailed instructions, isn't it our duty to sentence the murderer to death? And if we have any doubt about the fairness of executing this person, the case will be on appeal for years, and he won't ever be executed anyway. I will, I will affirm the death sentence, say the appellate judges, how can I not affirm this death sentence when the tiny legal issue which is brought on appeal under our rules is harmless error, all other issues having been excluded from our consideration? Besides, we have affirmed all those other death sentences, why not one more? I will, I will affirm the death sentence or refuse to decide it, says the present majority of the U.S. Supreme Court, who can make sense of this jurisprudence. Let the states figure it out, as it suits them. I will, I will go through the ritual of lethal injection, say the execution technicians and the corrections officials and doctors, I don't want to lose my job, and what is the point of having all of that training and following all of those rules if we aren't going to execute a man for that terrible crime committed so many years ago? And so, more murderers are prosecuted in capital cases, more men are sentenced to death, or not. Some few are executed. Proportionality review is not conducted by state high courts. Enormous amounts of money, energy, and time are wasted on keeping going a system which has long since lost any rational basis. Yet no one is willing to dismantle the system, to rock the boat. This is the system which is described in this book.

Vast differences between jurisdictions, and between different parts of the same state, persist and have become more exaggerated as more time passes and the same old practices remain in place. Ironically, the murder rate and the number of murders have gone down dramatically in the past decade, but no one argues that this is because a rational system of punishment deters a rational murderer. The statistical proof of deterrence put forward has long been discredited. The skill of individual attorneys and judges continues to make an enormous difference, in both directions: skilled prosecutors and defense attorneys will effect the outcome; inept, inattentive, or incompetent ones will be more likely to lose.

Who is responsible for spending a huge amount of state money to keep capital punishment going in America, when proportionately few cases are prosecuted as death cases, few people are sentenced to death, there are gross disproportions between states and regions, and the impact of the death penalty upon the poor and ethnic and racial minorities is undeniable? The financial cost of continuing with this system is huge, at a time when states don't have the money: the extra financial and economic cost of prosecuting a murderer in a capital case and then keeping him in a special prison is an add-on to the already enormous cost of keeping more than two million people in custody.[15] The large number of men sentenced to life without parole is partially a result of the imposition of that sentence as an alternative to the death penalty. Some argue that capital punishment saves the taxpayer money because if a man is executed the state is not required to keep him in jail for his natural life. This is not true. It is cheaper to keep a defendant in jail for life than to try him capitally. Is it really like the proliferation and storage of hundreds of thousands of nuclear weapons, where no one is willing to take responsibility for the present situation and say: this makes no sense?

Every time there is another brutal murder which puts the citizens in fear for their own lives and the safety of themselves and their family, the call comes up again: kill the killer; put him to death; never mind the irrationality; *this* crime, *this* heartless, brutal murderer deserves death as a sentence. And in some sense, he does. One would like to think that the blind rage, the fear and irrationality of the moment, and the sympathy for the victim and her family would drive these decisions to prosecute a case capitally. But it doesn't. In every state, even in Texas, there are all those heinous murders where the death penalty is not sought or imposed. If the sentiments of vengeance and revenge were the justification, then every murder would be prosecuted as a capital case. Every one of those sixteen thousand murders is an unasked-for death, a lost life.

There are some very unphilosophical, undramatic reasons why the capital punishment system remains. There are jobs, and people running for office. There are public positions to be stated, and affirmed in a campaign for public office. There is the deep-seated and justified fear among legislators, judges, and prosecutors that if they say they are against capital punishment, that they think it is an irrational system, then they will be targeted as soft on crime and defeated in the next election. And that does happen. The relationship between the law-and-order lobby and the gun lobby is strong, and both play an important role in elections, especially in the small-bore local elections where judges, prosecutors, sheriffs, and county officials are known in the community.[16] A prosecutor in a small town who does not prosecute a newsworthy murder as a capital case will answer to the community; the state's attorney in the more anonymous city may not be in the same position. He may answer to other complaints about how the death penalty is handled, but in a large number of murders, no one will object to the pleas and the summary dispositions. As many states as have capital punishment (but not the exact same states) elect judges, elect prosecutors, elect law enforcement officers, and everyone is afraid to say they are against the death penalty. Who is going to say they are not in favor of following the law, since it is the law in thirty-eight jurisdictions? Who is not in favor of punishing the wicked and the guilty as severely as the law allows?

The death penalty is certainly encrusted in law, at every level, with every discretionary decision, with every rule and decision of a court upholding it. The death penalty is so deeply embedded in every kind of law—the murder statutes, the capital punishment provisions and regulations, the rules of criminal procedure, the rules of the state supreme court, the opinions of the U.S. Supreme Court, the Department of Corrections regulations—that it is hard to know where to start to get rid of it. It is worse than getting rid of asbestos. Combing through the state codes and rules and removing every reference to capital crimes or the death sentence would be a major undertaking, but it is not necessary to effectuate the abolition of the death penalty. More difficult is the high-wire political balancing act required to abolish capital punishment, as was evident in the recent abolition in New Jersey.[17]

Who benefits from the present system of capital punishment staying in place just like it is? I might, say the judges and prosecutors who show scary pictures of capital defendants in their election campaigns. I might, say the employees of the prisons swollen with men who pled guilty to long mandatory terms to avoid capital prosecution, or were sentenced to life without parole as the only alternative to the death penalty. I might, say the employees of a court system clogged with criminal cases. I might, say the various towns, communities, and businesses that sell food, uniforms, computers, light bulbs, and television monitors to prisons, jails, and courts. I might, say the judges whose retention might hinge on whether or not they make sure the news covers them upholding or imposing a death sentence. I might, say the trial attorneys on both sides as they plead for more funds to prosecute and defend capital cases. I might, say the pro bono lawyers and academics whose area of expertise is capital litigation. I might, say the employees at the federal and state level who collect the statistics. Capital punishment is so dramatic that it can be counted on to get the attention of funders, legislators, voters, grant-givers, and those who make and watch the news.

Let's consider how the prosecution of a capital case proceeds, from the commission of the murder to the decision by the state's attorney to prosecute the case as a capital case and the imposition and carrying out of the death sentence. Let's look at how intricately entwined these institutions are. Assume that the police arrest the accused at the scene, and practices such as isolating a much later identified defendant for thirty-six hours and questioning him without interruption until he confesses, when there is no evidence, do not happen and are not tolerated by courts. And let's assume that it is not the law that the police can lie to the suspect and say that others have implicated him or identified him, telling him falsely that physical evidence linking him to the crime has been discovered. Let's further assume that the accused is not only over eighteen, but over twenty-one, and not perhaps mentally retarded, or impaired, or under the influence of a mind-altering substance, but of normal intelligence and capable of judgment, capable of resisting the pressure to confuse.

Let's further assume that the case goes to the jury of twelve, and that all twelve are without bias or prejudice and that they have been selected in accordance with the complicated rules set out by the U.S. Supreme Court decades ago and elaborated on since then. Let's assume this is a completely fair and open-minded jury, that anyone who has admitted to having any questions about capital punishment has not been removed. And let's assume that the case is being brought by a completely uninterested prosecutor, not someone who is running for office who knows that capital case prosecutions are regarded favorably by the public, and that the voters would like to see a capital conviction in this one. And let's assume the state court judge is fair, honest, and educated, that he reads the law and understands it, and that he is not worried about losing his job and his pension. Let's further assume that he also is not running for office, and that he is not influenced by the fact that capital case prosecutions are regarded favorably by voters, and that not imposing the death penalty is not something which might start a movement for his recall. After all, if the voters, the people, the citizens want capital punishment, want the death penalty, want convicted criminals to die, why isn't that enough? Why isn't that reason enough to execute convicted murderers, one by one, the way they killed their victims? Why isn't that fair? What is all of this about a "system" of capital punishment railroading defendants?

And let's assume that the jail is run by good jailers, not by people who put decoys and snitches in the jail to elicit a confession, or that these prisoners who testify against cellmates are not granted favors and early release for saying that the person in the cell with them confessed to the murder although the jury is not told that. And let's assume that there is no unreliable eyewitness testimony, no lineups at all, and that the evidence of guilt is overwhelming. Let's assume that all those defendants prosecuted for capital murder are arrested immediately at the scene covered in the victim's blood and there is not one shred of doubt about guilt or about the wrong person being arrested or prosecuted. Let's assume the system does not even allow confessions, or the admission of evidence from eyewitnesses. Let's assume that the prison system is just and fair, and the appellate courts are deliberative and honest, and that those judges too are uninfluenced by any fear that if they don't uphold a death sentence they will be regarded as soft on crime and removed from office, either by not being reelected or by being recalled.

Let's assume that all the defense attorneys are paid a reasonable wage, and that they have enough time to prepare a legitimate defense for a capital defendant, and that they are competent, educated, and that they too read the law, understand the subtleties—and the time constraints for filing and appeals—and that they understand all the hundreds of procedural rules which have grown up around capital case prosecutions in the various jurisdictions. Let's assume that defense attorneys are all publicly paid and adequately paid, from a single centralized source, not from the local source, and that they are people who take that job because they believe that defendants, even guilty defendants, deserve the best representation, and not that they have alcohol or substance abuse problems and cannot get another legal job which pays them more, and not that they are there because they have been in that job too long and are not qualified to do anything else. And let's assume that state's attorneys also are all principled prosecutors and they are doing what they do out of a commitment to the highest values and principles of the profession. And let's assume everyone, the prosecutors, the defense attorneys, and all the judges have read and understood all the U.S. Supreme Court opinions and all of the capital punishment opinions handed down by the state high court.

And let's assume that the state legislators who enact capital punishment legislation, adding a new capital offense every few years, adding a new capital crime which fits the latest murder which has the public in a state of panic and fear, are not influenced by the imminence of reelection. Let's assume that they are not worried that if they vote against a new capital offense—no matter how symbolic or meaningless it is—or even if they say they have questions about the capital punishment system in their state, they will be targeted as soft on crime or guns, and be threatened with defeat in their next election.

Let's assume all of that doesn't happen, that it isn't part of the reality of the capital punishment system in America today.

If all of that were true, would the American capital punishment system be a just system? In all honesty, I don't know. It's one thing to say that the U.S. Constitution does not guarantee a perfect trial, and another to say the U.S. Constitution tolerates the perpetuation of this capital punishment system.

Our present system is so far from the preceding description that we never get past the first hurdle of discussion. We are stuck on the debate over just how bad the American capital punishment system is in practice. But to get beyond that, what if a state capital punishment system didn't have these obvious injustices, what if it *really* was reformed? Would it make a difference? That would not get rid of the fact that the same murder would get the death penalty in Indiana, but not in Michigan. It would not get rid of the fact that the poor and racial minorities make up a disproportionate share of those executed and sentenced to death because they are disproportionately represented in the criminal justice system as a whole. It would not make it less likely that the inept, the incompetent, and those with a record who were innocently somewhere near the crime would be likely to be targeted for prosecution. It is so easy to charge them, convict them, and execute them. If there were a law which said that rich white men—no matter how heinous the murder—would basically never be executed or subject to capital prosecution, that law would be unconstitutional. If there was a law which said that the poor who commit murders in the cities—with the same common-law requirement of an evil and maligned heart—would be less likely to be prosecuted and sentenced to death than their brethren who commit the same murders in rural or suburban counties, that would be unconstitutional. Yet both propositions describe the way the present system operates in America. Those who criticize the present system aren't suggesting that murderers go free, or that prisons be abolished. Or, that there aren't people who have committed crimes so terrible that they should spend the remainder of their natural lives in prison.

The capital punishment system is a system like the financial and banking system, the health care system, and the military industrial complex. All are held in place by large institutions, and by social and economic interactions, many of which have little to do with the principles surrounding the stated justification for the system's existence. Who is against providing doctors and medicine to sick people? Who is against bringing murderers to justice? Who will say the United States should not have a well-equipped, well-staffed army, navy, and air force to defend itself and protect its democratic government?

Who will say that people who work hard and save shouldn't be able to invest their money, earn money from it, and even create financial instruments? So who benefits from the present capital punishment system? What does keep it in place, decade after decade? None of these allegations of malfunction are new. The situation has just become worse.

If the cost of prosecuting a murder as a capital case is ten or twenty times the cost of prosecuting a murder as non-capital, does that play a role in the decision-making? Somebody is getting the money spent. What if the cost of a capital prosecution can be off-loaded from out of the local prosecutor's budget and charged to a central state fund, so that the local prosecutor does not have to have the added cost, or even any cost, of a capital prosecution come out of his operating budget? Does that make it more likely the case will be prosecuted as a capital case? That has been alleged in Illinois. And is there anything wrong with that? Why should the local prosecutor, or the state public defender, spend all of his resources on one capital prosecution? Or what if the case against a murderer were not prosecuted capitally because the local prosecutor had run out of funds for the year, there was no central fund, and the county could not afford a capital prosecution? That was admitted to be the case by the prosecutor in Essex County, New Jersey a few years after reenactment. Recently, public defenders in several states have refused to represent defendants charged with capital crimes on the grounds that their offices have no more funds for capital defense. What happens when that happens?

At this time, the system described in this book is what we have, in the richest society, the most technologically advanced society, the society which prides itself on having done more to protect the civil and human rights of all its citizens than any other society in our known, recorded history. Who wants this? Why does this system persist? Who is benefiting from keeping those capital cases coming? That discussion is for another day.

Murder and Its Consequences

CHAPTER 1

"A Good Murder"

A good murder, a genuine murder, a fine murder, as fine as you could hope to see, we haven't had one like it for a long time.

—Georg Büchner, *Woyzeck* (1836)

I.

A sense of fairness and an outrage over injustice are emotions expressed strongly and clearly by young children in all cultures. People are profoundly interested in crimes because the law and legal punishments are supposed to address that fundamental human craving for justice. A legal system is set up to define prohibited behavior and punish criminals because we want to live in a society which is ruled by law and not by a mob, or so we say.

Courts, which hand down decisions in individual cases, are embedded in this system of law because we do not trust individuals alone or groups to judge fairly. As individuals we do not want to take that responsibility. We ask that far-reaching judgments of others and the imposition of consequences be made according to universal principles which are objective, if not quantifiable. The criminal justice system is supposed to be unclouded by personal idiosyncrasies, class bias, and racial prejudice. And it is supposed to work with reasonable efficiency and economy.

In short, because it is a system of law it is supposed to be just, for all of us. That is why we have created it, to judge us impersonally. And consequently we should all be willing to submit to its judgments. Of course we know it is imperfect, any institution managed by human beings is imperfect, but fairness is the standard. Behind all of the documents, the billions of words retrievable at a keystroke, is the idea that justice is the bedrock of our constitutional system: due process of law means among other things fundamental fairness.

Yet at the present time in America few would argue that the criminal justice system is effective. In our society, capital murder cases have become the most visible and dramatic example of the failure of the criminal justice system. Some would say segments of the criminal justice system are corrupt. Others would maintain the criminal justice system is dominated by the political and economic interests of the ruling class, as well as being racist, inefficient, and the opposite of cost-effective. According to this view, some individual civil servants are overworked and underpaid, but they are outnumbered by the incompetent and the cynical, and overwhelmed by the bureaucratic morass. If there is any truth to these allegations, why do we tolerate this situation? If our society can send a spaceship to Mars and snake a missile through a doorway from hundreds of miles away, why can't we institutionalize a criminal justice system which is efficient and fair?

Or perhaps the problem is one of image. If the public's impression of a criminal justice system in a state of collapse is a distortion put forward by demagogues or the media, why do we allow this false characterization to persist? This leads to another question: can we assess the operation of the criminal justice system on the basis of what we read in the newspapers and see on the television?

The live broadcast of urban violence in Los Angeles, coming after the Hill-Thomas hearings, blurred any remnants of the bright line which existed between the news and dramatizations of public events for a television audience. Both were cultural watersheds, bringing home a truth which is not entirely new: there is little distinction between reenactments or dramatizations and the reporting of actual events. Both appear on the same screen. Both are subject to immediate replay, commentary, and speculation. And, as can also be seen in the reporting of sports events, a striking disjunction exists between the highly sophisticated technology of visual presentation and expression and the relatively archaic and simple-minded conceptual framework for commentary and reporting.

Those who complain the theater is dead have not been to an urban criminal trial recently. The criminal courts are the popular theater of our day. The public is strongly attached to the stock characters who are regularly featured on the stage of our criminal courts. Lawyers, judges, and defendants on their way to jail all play to the crowd and expect to be watched by an audience far larger than the jurors selected to find the facts of the case, although the mood is rarely one of merriment.

Every culture has its own way of portraying death, of ritualizing murder. In America, representations of violent and ghoulish murders are pervasive in our entertainment and news. The reports of murders, especially capital murders, do not only tell us what is out there and what happened; they tell us what to think and how to feel. Portrayals of murder cases communicate important messages about who is in charge and who is a threat.

Sometimes the message is that the people who are convicted of capital murder are beneath contempt, unworthy of anything more than summary justice. They are so threatening to our lives and property that they can be kept in prisons, which are brutal and inhumane, or, better, executed. Sometimes the message is that society needs to continue to spend large amounts of money on law enforcement and the establishment and maintenance of prisons. Another frequently heard theme is that it is unfair for police and prosecutors to be forced to go into battle using laws which give an unfair advantage to the accused, that the courts have been sentimental and foolish in restricting the police in the area of search and seizure and in the use of evidence from confessions.

If the news presented its message in terms of those kinds of abstractions, no copies of newspapers would be sold, and no one would watch dramatizations of the day's events on television. So the news carries its cultural burden the way societies have always transmitted their most important messages, through stories and drama. Some dramatizations may airbrush out those facts of the case which do not fit within the stock script. Yet the dramatization will retain enough details from the actual crime so that the viewer's pleasure is heightened by the illusion of verisimilitude. It is no longer even necessary to change the names of the principals of the crime, which catches the fancy of the public before it becomes the subject of a television movie.

Murder, in other words, sells soap and beer and cars and newspapers. A good murder, that is, one the public wants to read about, will generate dozens of stories. The formerly prim "Metropolitan" section of the *New York Times* has become a daily reading of our cultural attitudes toward violence in general and murder in particular. New York City reports over a thousand homicides a year, the vast majority of which do not occur in Manhattan. Almost every day in the Manhattan daily newspapers, there is a story about murder. There are also many stories about capital murder prosecutions and detailed reports of executions in other states, since New York State has no capital punishment statute.

This fascination with murder and executions is not new or unique to us. Thousands of Londoners in Dickens's time attended public hangings. In the last decade of the twentieth century, thousands in China, Iran, Nigeria, and elsewhere attended public executions. It was not until 1906 that all executions in New Jersey were required to be conducted at the state prison, rather than in the courtyards of county jails.

In America today, the television news is the mechanism for making executions public and for sanitizing the execution process. Prior to an execution, the news is flooded with stories of the lawyers' last-minute pleas and the defendant's final words and actions. The execution of Robert Harris in California was actually videotaped as part of a challenge to the method for the imposition of capital punishment. Since it exists, the film may be shown in the future to the public.

The prosecution of murder cases, especially the prosecution of capital cases, has much to do with cultural stereotypes and dreams of revenge. Capital prosecutions are supposed to be reserved for the worst people, people who have committed crimes so terrible that society does not think they deserve to live. The need for vengeance and cultural expiation are central to justifications for the death penalty. Dramatizations of murders and capital trials are very effective in feeding people's desire for revenge. The prospect of an impending execution, as was recently seen in the *Wesley Dodd* case in Washington State, gives the media an opportunity to focus again and again upon the repellent and horrifying details of a murder. The public response is one of outrage and frustration, and this sense of rage is fueled by the daily repetition of details of brutality as the execution draws closer. The murder occurred once, but the public is presented with it again and again to justify the execution.

Choices about how and what to report in a crime story anticipate and play against assumptions concerning the expectations of an audience conditioned by heavily stereotyped dramatizations of violence. One scenario of urban murder which is seen frequently includes a black male defendant, or perhaps an illegal immigrant, possibly high on drugs or mentally unbalanced, or mentally deficient, or previously institutionalized, someone who is without a job, has a criminal record, possibly on parole or probation for another offense, who kills a middle-class victim, male or female, but often white. In these murders, which may briefly become obsessions for a community, the victim not only works but also symbolizes the values of the meritocracy. Often the victim is an incarnation of the myth of self-made success, a model which is a cruel rebuke to many of our citizens. The message of such stories is clear: someone who is worthless killed someone who was of value.

Reports of murders in the tabloids tend to be the comic book version, complete with bubble quotes and illustrations. And the level of tolerance for details of brutality and violence in the news continues to rise. The accepted level of brutality in entertainment has escalated to the point where two or three murders in a movie are considered trivial. The target audience of teenage boys pays to see graphic dismembering or explicit slashing of what is called in rape reform legislation the intimate parts. In a quiet evening at home the viewer can vicariously participate in a dozen homicides, identifying in turn with the victim, slayer, investigator, police, or prosecutor. The young men who are the target audience for action movies are especially death-obsessed, and they account for an increasingly large proportion of all murders committed.

Granting that the criminal justice system may be misrepresented in high-profile and high-action news stories, what do these dramatizations of murders have to do with actual homicides, with what murder in the cities really looks like? A single sensational murder has been known to be the impetus for changing the penalty for murder, but aside from that kind of isolated impact, can it be said that whether stereotyped or not, media representations of murder have any effect upon the criminal justice system?

Aside from despairing over the degraded character of our entertainment industry, why should anyone—lawyers, academics, or citizens—care that reports of murder cases are often distorted, or glamorized, in the media and on the news, or are just described in a sensational manner which misleads the public both as to the nature of the crime and the response of the criminal justice system? We pay a high-tech, multibillion-dollar international industry to scare us—how can this have only a negligible influence upon the criminal justice policies of legislators, members of the executive, or judges and jurors? The people who administer criminal justice institutions are part of the same society as the rest of us. If characterizations of violence and capital murder in the news are consistent with, or even tailored to mimic, the portrayal of murder in our mass-market entertainment industry, so what?

II.

This essay will describe a pattern which emerged when researchers examined all homicide cases in the state of New Jersey during the years immediately after the reimposition of capital punishment in 1982.[1] Particularly relevant is the pattern of capital prosecution for urban and suburban murders, and how those cases were regarded by law enforcement, the media, and the public.

In 1982 the New Jersey legislature reinstated capital punishment with a statute which identified eight aggravating factors that could be used to elevate the crime of ordinary murder to a capital offense. The capital statute in New Jersey is similar to capital statutes in effect in a number of other jurisdictions; indeed, it is similar to the statute which was proposed to reenact the death penalty in New York in 1991.

Several aspects of the New Jersey situation, however, are unusual. First, the New Jersey Supreme Court has had a history of being a leader in the development of state constitutional doctrine. Second, the Office of the Public Defender in New Jersey is unusual in that it is administered by a single administrative agency at both the trial and appellate level. Immediately after reenactment, the Office of the Public Defender was able to commit itself to a coordinated statewide challenge to the reimposition of capital punishment at both the trial and appellate level. This challenge included a data collection and analysis project dedicated to tracking all homicide cases and capital prosecutions in the state after reenactment.[2] The atypical institutional structure of the Public Defender's Office at the time made such a comprehensive, statewide data collection effort possible. The Public Defender database was eventually taken over by the Administrative Office of the New Jersey Supreme Court, and subsumed within the research of the New Jersey Supreme Court's Proportionality Review Project.[3]

Data were collected on all final dispositions of homicide indictments at the trial court stage,[4] a process which takes about two years for most murders and longer for cases which are declared capital. The Proportionality Review Project presented an analysis of dispositions in over 1,350 homicide cases[5] to the New Jersey Supreme Court in the capital appeal of *State v. Marshall.*[6] This case involved the first person in New Jersey to have a death sentence upheld by the state supreme court. The report presented to the *Marshall* court included a detailed analysis and description of over 260 death-eligible murder cases which had resulted in thirty-five death sentences actually being imposed, during the period from 1982 to 1989.

In New Jersey and most other capital jurisdictions, capital murders are a small proportion of all murders and only a fractional proportion of all homicides. The proponents of reenactment in New Jersey repeatedly stated that they intended the capital punishment statute to apply to few cases, that is, to the exceptional case. Only a few defendants have been sentenced to death in New Jersey since reenactment in 1982, a total of thirty-nine; and of these thirty-nine who were sentenced to death, only one person, Robert Marshall, has had his death sentence upheld through all stages of the state appeals process. The New Jersey Supreme Court reversed twenty-six death sentences in a row, an unprecedented series of reversals by any state supreme court, before upholding Robert Marshall's death sentence on direct appeal. The court then ordered a special and separate set of arguments to address the question of whether imposing the death sentence in this case was fair in comparison to the sentences imposed upon similar defendants for similar crimes.[7]

Although there were more than 250 cases where the death penalty could have been sought, and over 120 cases which went to a capital penalty trial after a verdict of guilty of capital murder, less than a quarter of all aggravated murders and less than a third of the cases which reached the second stage of a penalty trial resulted in the jury imposing a death sentence. In spite of the high level of support for capital punishment in the opinion polls, and in spite of the fact that the cases that reached penalty phase were typically very aggravated murders, actual jurors were reluctant to impose the death sentence when faced with that option in sentencing a real defendant who had murdered a real victim. National opinion polls reported that about 80 percent of the people in the state were in favor of capital punishment during this period, yet the death sentence, in New Jersey at least, has been imposed in a very small number of actual cases.[8] Some take that as a sign that the law is being applied justly.

The reason why there are few capital prosecutions in New Jersey and elsewhere is not because there are few killings that meet the legal criteria for capital prosecution. In New Jersey and elsewhere, the definition of death-eligible murder is broad enough to encompass many more cases than will ever be prosecuted as capital murders. Local prosecutors have a great deal of discretion in the cases they select for capital prosecution. The decision to prosecute for capital murder is usually not determined by limitations on the statutory definition of death-eligible murder. One statutory factor alone, the felony factor, which declares capital all murders associated with the commission of another felony, regularly presents a large number of death-eligible homicides.

When capital murder prosecutions in New Jersey were examined over a seven-year period immediately after reenactment, it became apparent that the number of potentially capital murders in urban areas is far larger than the number of such murders in rural and non-urban jurisdictions. Yet in New Jersey, prosecutions for capital murder are far less likely to occur in some urban jurisdictions.

Historically, in both the South and the North, racial disparities in the application of the death penalty have resulted in a disproportionate number of blacks being sentenced to death and executed. Recently there has been a widespread and well-documented pattern of defendants being more likely to be sentenced to death if their victims are white, irrespective of the race of the defendant.[9] In addition to race, many believe that factors of class and social status are influential in determining who is prosecuted for capital murder and sentenced to death.

Those who argue for capital murder as a way of championing the victims of homicide overlook the fact that there are so many victims. During the period of the New Jersey Proportionality Review Project, there were 35 death sentences imposed. During that same period, from over 1,300 homicides, 264 cases almost certainly could have been declared death-eligible by the prosecutor, and 119 cases actually resulted in a conviction at trial for capital murder. What was distinctive about the small number of cases where the death sentence was actually imposed? What characteristics did the capital cases have in common?

In New Jersey and most other states, the important unit is the county. The county defines the limits of trial court jurisdiction: prosecutors are county, not city, officials who may or may not be elected; and jurors are selected according to county vicinage. New Jersey is unusual in that a very large proportion of the state is classified by the U.S. Census Bureau as being within a metropolitan area, but New Jersey also has suburban and rural counties.

There are significant county-by-county disparities in income and economic vitality in New Jersey. Six counties have been identified by state urban planners as having large urban centers that are economically distressed: Essex, Camden, Hudson, Passaic, Mercer, and Union. Not surprisingly, these counties also have a high proportion of blacks and Hispanics, a high unemployment rate, and a relatively low per capita income. Together these six counties accounted for over 68 percent of all homicides and over 60 percent of all aggravated, potentially capital murders in the state. Some rural counties are also relatively poor, however, and not all suburban counties are wealthy.

Murder is overwhelmingly a crime which involves people of the same race. As a result, more often than not, the greater proportions of murders in the cities consist of blacks and Hispanics killing one another. Specifically, murders in the cities typically consist of black and Hispanic men between the ages of eighteen and twenty-six killing one another.

Essex County, which reported the largest number of homicides in the state, had a large proportion, seven out of thirty-five, of all death sentences in the study period. But those seven cases in Essex County in which the death sentence was imposed represented less than 2 percent of all homicides in the county and only 13 percent of all of the homicides in the county where there was a clear factual basis for the imposition of the death penalty under the statute.

Essex County had over 20 percent of all of the death-eligible cases in the state, yet the death sentence was imposed in only 13 percent of those cases. Over a fifth of all potentially capital homicides were disposed of in Essex County courts, yet capital prosecutions in Essex County accounted for less than 14 percent of all homicide dispositions. In other words, many serious, highly aggravated murders occurred in Essex County, but a very small proportion of them were prosecuted as capital cases.

In contrast, the Ocean County courts, which adjudicated a total of twenty-seven homicides in the entire study period of over seven years, imposed three death sentences from a pool of seven death-eligible cases. Ocean County, which accounted for 3 percent of all death-eligible homicides, imposed the death penalty in 38 percent of those cases, in comparison to Essex County's 13 percent. Hudson County had the same number of penalty trials as Ocean County, seven, and no death sentences were imposed in Hudson County during the period. Yet Hudson County, which includes Jersey City, had 159 homicides during the period, of which nineteen were eligible for capital prosecution on their facts.

There is some evidence that this pattern of widely varying rates of prosecution from one prosecutorial jurisdiction to another is not atypical. A recent report on capital case prosecutions in adjoining rural and urban jurisdictions in Georgia found striking differences between the Chattahoochee and Atlanta judicial districts.[10] The rural district of Chattahoochee imposed 75 percent more death sentences than Atlanta, a city with nearly three times its population and many more homicides. In potentially capital cases in Chattahoochee, the prosecutor sought the death penalty in 34 percent of the cases when the victim was white, but only 6 percent of the cases when the victim was black. Although black victim cases constituted 65 percent of all murder cases in the district, they accounted for only 15 percent of all cases which were prosecuted capitally in Chattahoochee.

Pennsylvania now has one of the larger death row populations. As elsewhere, race seems to be relevant to sentencing patterns. One Philadelphia judge has sentenced twenty-six men to death, twenty-four of them African American. The sentences of this Philadelphia judge alone account for about a fifth of the death row population in the state. Nevertheless, another type of pattern has been observed in Pennsylvania—one that suggests that race may be only one factor in creating large county-by-county disparities in patterns of capital sentencing.

Philadelphia, which does not allow public defenders to represent capital defendants, accounts for 14 percent of the state population and over 50 percent of all death sentences.[11] Allegheny County, which includes Pittsburgh and 12 percent of the state population, accounts for less than 5 percent of all the death sentences. Allegheny County does provide public defender representation in capital cases. In Philadelphia, capital cases are assigned at very low fees to the private bar.

The first case in which the New Jersey Supreme Court upheld a death sentence after reversing twenty-six in a row was a case in which a white male insurance executive from Monmouth County, a high-income suburban county, murdered his wife after taking out a million-dollar insurance policy on her life. Marshall paid two accomplices to commit the murder, and there is little doubt either that he planned the murder, that he paid his accomplices to commit the murder, or that his motive was to kill his wife for the insurance. Marshall is now the only person in New Jersey who has a death sentence which has been upheld through all stages of the state appellate review process, including proportionality review, and his appeal is now pending in the federal and state systems.

III.

The capital prosecution of Robert Marshall was portrayed in a series of widely popular retellings. A book about the case, Joe McGinniss's *Blind Faith,*[12] remained high on the best seller list, and it then became the basis for a television miniseries watched by an audience which numbered in the millions. The television miniseries left the audience with the impression that justice was done because a bad man who killed an innocent person was sentenced to death and will be executed. And at some simple level that is true. On the other hand, if that were the standard for justifiable legal executions, there would have been at least a hundred executions in the state of New Jersey alone since reenactment in 1982.

The verdict appeared fair to many because Robert Marshall was clearly guilty; and ambiguities, contradictions, and complexities in the case were either lied about or omitted from the book and other versions retelling this story. A general audience would have no sense of how Robert Marshall's culpability compared with that of others who may or may not have been sentenced to death. The popular audience was left with two misleading impressions: that every murder case is treated like Robert Marshall's case, and that his case was especially and uniquely aggravated. The dramatizations and news reports led the public to believe that a white middle-class person is as likely to be sentenced to death as a black person, or a poor person, because this particular capital trial did not fit the former stereotype of a poor black illiterate man being railroaded to the death sentence.

Partly because of the enormous media attention given to the *Marshall* case, the challenge to his death sentence became more than usually politically charged, especially since the New Jersey Supreme Court had already inspired the wrath of the legislature and some of the public by overturning twenty-six death sentences in a row before upholding the first one in the case of Robert Marshall.

Robert Marshall's murder was atypical of murders in New Jersey, and it would have been an unusual case in any jurisdiction. But the *Marshall* case did bear some resemblance to other capital murders. It was a made-for-media murder, and those who had the wit to recognize its commercial potential made substantial profits. It was not by chance that the case became the subject of a best-selling book and a television miniseries. The circumstances of Robert Marshall's case contained many standard features of Hollywood melodramas involving murder, and that made this murder especially appealing to the entertainment industry.

To imply that a murder must be Hollywood-worthy before it will be prosecuted capitally is only partially facetious. Cases will be selected for capital prosecution according to factors which demonstrate patterns of bias related to class and race and which reflect the unchecked discretion of local prosecutors.

The *Marshall* case is an extreme example: the reasons why the circumstances of this case became the plot for a best-selling book and a miniseries were not irrelevant to why and how Robert Marshall was prosecuted for capital murder. The *Marshall* case had a recognizable villain who could have been a character in a melodrama from the 1950s. He had a clearly discernible motive, which identified him as a bad guy, deserving of punishment. His victim could not have been more heroic or blameless, always a relevant factor for audience identification. Mrs. Marshall was a model mother and wife, and she devoted herself selflessly to her sons and her foolish and errant husband, who showed his gratitude by murdering her. There were circumstances in this case which made for a saga of injustice.

Not only did Robert Marshall have a comprehensible motive for killing his wife, but he was killing her for an insurance policy he took out on her life, without her knowledge, because he had gambling debts and wanted to run away with his mistress, who became, after some prosecutorial maneuvering, the state's star witness. Robert Marshall had a motive everyone could understand, and he articulated that motive to people who testified about it at trial. Ineptly he tried again and again to persuade marginal and incompetent petty criminals to kill his wife for him. Finally, they did it, by shooting her at a turnpike rest stop where Robert Marshall had pulled off the road and delivered her to be murdered, as prearranged.

The story aspects of the case were compelling. Interesting and colorful types were tangled up in the action, and this was capitalized upon in the various dramatizations and retellings of the murder. There were many ironic twists to the plot, and a dramatic ending, the imposition of the death sentence. The hit man, the person who allegedly fired the gun which killed the victim, was acquitted of murder at trial, and his partner at the killing was released pursuant to a plea bargain shortly after testifying for the prosecution at trial. By contrast, a marginal participant who had never set foot in New Jersey at the time of the murder, whose role was allegedly no more than passing on phone messages in Louisiana, was sentenced to thirty calendar years without parole. The mistress took the stand for the prosecution and testified at length about her clandestine love affair and that Robert Marshall told her he wanted to get rid of his wife. Her own role in the case could have been the subject of a whole other movie. Robert Marshall himself, the audience agreed, was villainous, cowardly, despicable, and stupid. He was sentenced to death by the jury after a very short penalty trial.

Is this an unjust result? Robert Marshall certainly committed murder, and there was little in his character or actions to excuse him. But he is no worse than several dozen others who committed equally cold-blooded murders, but who will not be executed for reasons that have nothing to do with the seriousness of their murders or the harm they caused to innocent victims or their threat to the public peace. Not only were there several cases which were very similar to the *Marshall* case in their circumstances, but there were other spousal murders in New Jersey which were at least as aggravated, where the death penalty was not imposed or even considered.

As reprehensible as Robert Marshall's motives were, and as blameless as his victim was, his case probably would not have been prosecuted capitally if it had occurred in Newark, Jersey City, or Camden. Wicked, foolish men kill their wives and get caught in those jurisdictions too, but rarely are they prosecuted for capital murder.

Consider a murder case that arose in Essex County, one which was also not typical but was somewhat akin to the *Marshall* case. Some of the circumstances of this case also might have been found in a dramatization. The murderer seems to have been a serial killer, although he lacked the glamour of the villain in *The Silence of the Lambs* or the newsworthiness of Richard Biegenwald, New Jersey's "thrill killer" who was the first person in the jurisdiction to be sentenced to death.

Like Robert Marshall, the defendant in this Essex County case was charged with murdering a woman with whom he was having a sexual relationship. As in *Marshall,* the man charged had other female sex partners, the body of one of them was found in a car, and several other women who had been seen in his company before disappearing also were later found dead. In fact, the defendant in this case was suspected of committing eight murders. He was charged for four of them and sentenced for two. He pled guilty to one count of murder and received a life term. He never was indicted for capital murder, although a conviction for any one prior murder would have served as an aggravating factor to make him eligible for capital prosecution on any of the subsequent murders.

Perhaps the difference was that all of these victims were marginal black women, women he picked up in bars, women that society does not much care about, women who might have been prostitutes, women who might have been using drugs. No one was likely to write a best-selling book or a television movie about those victims, or about this defendant who never articulated any motive for his crimes. Nor did anyone, for example, a news reporter or a television commentator, fill in the background story. In fact, everyone involved in prosecuting these cases kept very quiet about the number of victims. This defendant did not resemble an easily recognized character in a melodrama, such as the traitorous, philandering country club husband. There was no one with whom the cable audience could identify. Perhaps this defendant was not scary enough to the people who decide which case merits the hundreds of thousands of dollars required for capital prosecution. Still, to be suspected of killing eight and actually convicted of two murders, and no capital prosecution?

The pattern in New Jersey is an inversion of an earlier stereotype. This pattern may or may not persist, although there is some evidence that parts of this pattern are repeated in other jurisdictions. The former stereotype was that if you were poor and black and male, and represented by a public defender or assigned counsel, you were likely to be railroaded into a death sentence by an all-white prosecutorial system. And that may still be the case in some jurisdictions or in places where courts and legislatures refuse to allocate resources to the defense of capital cases, in spite of the constitutional requirement to provide indigents with adequate representation.

However, in New Jersey during the period studied, it was an advantage to be represented by the Public Defender's Office, counter to the earlier popular stereotype. In some jurisdictions it may still be the case that black defendants are significantly more likely to be sentenced to death than whites, other things being equal, although this effect is not seen in recent national studies. It is difficult to comprehend discrepancies such as those cited for Philadelphia and Chattahoochee outside of a racial context. The racial effect that recently has been documented independently in a number of states is a white victim effect: a person who kills a white victim is more likely to be prosecuted capitally and sentenced to death, other things being equal.

Since the reenactment of the death penalty in New Jersey, the following pattern emerged: if you were poor and black and committed a murder, and if your victim was poor and black and your case was processed in an urban jurisdiction, and if you were represented by the Public Defender's Office, you were less likely to be prosecuted and convicted for capital murder or to be sentenced to death, than if your crime was committed in a rural or suburban jurisdiction and your victim was white, and especially if your victim was white and middle class. Having a private attorney was no advantage, and the presence of a white victim was statistically significant. In part, this pattern in New Jersey reflects the same "white victim effect" which has been independently documented and verified in many other states in the North and South. Partly it is the result of other factors, such as the differential economic resources available to the prosecutor's office in urban and suburban counties.

Certainly the resources available to the prosecutors are one explanation for county disparities in capital case processing. Even though Essex County regularly reported over 140 homicides a year, it had no new capital prosecutions for over a year during the middle of the period studied. Part of the reason for the lack of such prosecutions was that the financial resources of the prosecutor's office were strained due to a county budgetary crisis. And a backlog in the county courts existed to the point where several judges in the Essex County courthouse only heard cases which had been indicted prior to

1982. Neither political nor institutional forces in Essex County at that time were pressing for expensive and lengthy capital trials.

Essex County juries are also different from the juries in Ocean County and Monmouth County: Essex County juries have more black people on them, more Hispanics, and the jurors are younger. We know that younger people, blacks, women, and Hispanics are less likely to be in favor of capital punishment than older white men, the group most likely to support capital punishment and to see it as in their interest. We also know that blacks have more skepticism about the fairness of the criminal justice system generally, and the system for imposing capital punishment in particular. The polls consistently indicate that black men and women are significantly more likely than whites to believe that the imposition of the death penalty is racially biased.

These may be some of the reasons why relatively few death sentences come from Essex County, even though many of the aggravated murders come from Essex County. So when the prosecutors are not charging capital murder in Essex County, it may not only be that the county's prosecutors are overburdened and underfunded, although that is certainly not irrelevant in spite of the county prosecutor's official protestations to the contrary. The Essex County prosecutors may know that an Essex County jury is unlikely to return a death verdict against some defendants, even though the circumstances of the murder theoretically meet the objective, legal criteria for death eligibility. There is another intangible factor that should not be discounted. Murders in Newark do not even make the front pages of the major newspapers any more. There are so many of them.

What about Hudson County, a county which includes Jersey City and accounts for quite a few murders? During the entire first decade that capital punishment has been in effect in New Jersey, there has not been a single death sentence imposed in Hudson County. Yet Hudson County had fifteen death-eligible cases and seven penalty trials during the period studied, twice as many as Ocean County, and Hudson County accounted for a total of 159 homicide cases in the database of over 1,300 cases. There were rumors that the county prosecutor in that county did not much like the death penalty, and that he did not believe the death penalty should be imposed upon minorities.

Is it credible to suggest that there was no case as aggravated or as serious as the murder of Mrs. Marshall among those 159 Hudson County cases? In the state as a whole there were over a hundred cases that involved a man killing his wife or sex partner during the period. There must have been at least one other wife as blameless as Mrs. Marshall. Some of the cases documented involved dismembering, over fifty stab wounds, and torturous homicidal incidents in which the victim suffered over a considerable period of time. Yet these cases did not result in the death sentence being imposed, or even sought.

The lesson here is that murder is ultimately a personal crime, in addition to being a crime against the person. A very particular person is the victim of murder. Of course the individual circumstances of the crime are important. A jury is going to be more likely to find an unsympathetic defendant guilty of capital murder if the victim is virtuous, blameless, educated, good-looking, and a parent, and everyone involved in prosecutorial decision-making along the way knows this and plays upon it.[13]

IV.

The way crime is reported, where some stories are selected over others, some tales told and some not, and the way murders are prosecuted, reveals who and what society values. Characterizations of killers and how they are brought to justice are an important part of our national identity, the reflection we get back from the cultural mirror. As Americans, one of our most dearly held self-images is that in the United States there is equality before the law, that the poor, racial minorities, the mentally retarded, and the illiterate receive as fair a trial as the rich. Whether or not this is true in each individual case, it comforts us as a people to believe our criminal justice system treats everyone alike. There is certainly no other society where both the state and federal government devote so many resources to providing poor people with lawyers.

What is frequently expressed now both in news stories and their dramatizations is a portrait of the criminal justice system as an ineffective and overwhelmed parent, sometimes a parent who is corrupt, sometimes just a bumbling parent who is well-intentioned but cannot cope. Sometimes the message is that the system is so badly broken that no one should even care about fixing it. The criminal justice system in this portrayal begins to resemble the nuclear arms industry: it costs too much, it does not do what we want, but we cannot do anything about it.

This orchestrated view absolves the rest of us from responsibility, and lets us believe that justice has nothing to do with us. Law-abiding citizens should stay away from the criminal courts and let the police and the prosecutors do the nasty job of protecting the hard-working, taxpaying people who bear little resemblance to those who end up in jail. It is us against the monsters out there. If the police have to be nasty, if prison conditions are inhumane, it is to protect the lives and property of the law-abiding.

In this scenario, defense attorneys and civil libertarians are naive do-gooders, troublemakers, or cynics who take advantage of a system in disrepair or dishonestly manipulate the law to try to bring about an unjust result, the acquittal of a guilty person. And since jobs are involved, we had better just leave the system as it is. The threat from criminals on the loose is too large and important for the ordinary citizen to understand: better let the men in uniforms and dark suits make all the decisions. It is probably good if middle-class people do not know too much about what goes on in our criminal courts and prisons. It is certainly better not to object when we suspect things are not as they ought to be, especially if we can tell ourselves that the experts are in charge.

If capital murder cases are no more than the good guys chasing down the bad guys, and homicidal maniacs are threatening my job, my house, and my kids, and it's all a mess anyway, why not call in Clint Eastwood or Charles Bronson? The death penalty, after all, just catches and stops one of those bad guys; there are so many of them and so few of us. Sentencing a person to death acts as a catharsis for everyone's general sense of overwhelming frustration.

This is not to suggest that the dramatized representations of crime in the news do not respond to real public concerns about crime and violence. News reports of murder are real, and important. The question is, how do emotionally heightened representations of murder cases influence how actual murder cases, and especially capital murders, are handled in the real criminal justice system? How do reports of murders justify the maintenance of the criminal justice system in its present form? Dramatizations, and the way in which murders are reported, have a powerful effect upon the selection of actual cases for capital prosecution and upon public perception. The portrayal of murders in the media shapes what the society believes to be important.

The pattern which emerges from an analysis of homicides over a decade in New Jersey suggests that urban homicides, especially those in which young blacks kill other blacks, mostly men but women too, or Hispanics kill Hispanics, are likely to be plea-bargained to relatively light sentences. Perhaps the likelihood of plea bargaining reflects the fact that the society does not care about these victims, or perhaps it is because these cases are not newsworthy. Or perhaps it is the other way around, and the cases are not newsworthy because they are plea-bargained. Or the cases are downgraded, both literally and procedurally, because we have no framework for the stories of the defendant or victim. Or is it because the urban counties have fewer resources, or more forgiving juries, or just because there are so many murders there?

Whatever the reason, this does not seem to be a random or isolated pattern. Rarely do urban homicides involving minorities result in a capital prosecution, even though their circumstances may be highly aggravated, and in spite of the fact that minorities in the cities are legitimately worried about the threat of crime and are disturbed by the reality that entire groups of young men are being removed from the community by homicide and the imprisonment for it. The public-minded citizens of the city do not think these murders among young men are trivial.

The media, both the commercialized entertainment industry and its cousin, the news industry, continue to dramatize capital murder either as an old-fashioned detective melodrama, as in the *Marshall* case, or as the hunting and banishment of monsters, because that is what a conditioned audience expects. The *Marshall* case was an atypical spouse murder. Most men who kill their wives do so in a fit of drunken rage, after a pattern of repeated, serious beatings. Audiences are pleasurably terrified by portrayals of murderers as Hollywood villains or lurking strangers. These scare tactics do not even serve a useful educational purpose. For self-protection women should receive the message that the man to fear is their abusive husband, or a familiar acquaintance, not the stranger in the alley.

By making monsters out of marginal or mentally ill murderers, by insisting that they are the threat, emotionally charged dramatizations of crime justify depriving many other people of their rights; they make brutal and inhumane conditions of imprisonment seem legitimate. Focusing on the high-profile, talismanic urban or suburban murders in which a minority person kills a middle-class white also justifies incarcerating large numbers of minorities for other types of offenses that are often relatively minor. The United States has more people absolutely, and more people per capita, in prison than any other country in the world, including Pakistan and South Africa. The Hollywood version of capital murder cases—which implies that the good guy cops are catching bad guy murderers, and that it ends up all right when a bad person is executed—is reassuring, but inaccurate.

The media also often imply that murderers are routinely let out on the streets after serving only minimal sentences, and this justifies the imposition of the death sentence. In New Jersey, people convicted of murder with no mention of a capital prosecution serve a mandatory minimum term of thirty calendar years without parole. It is also the fact in New Jersey, as it is in New

York, that there are thousands of people sitting in prison for relatively minor crimes such as stealing television sets or cars, forging checks, or possessing and selling relatively small amounts of drugs.

The threat to property caused by the savings and loan debacle and the Wall Street scandals of the 1980s involved billions of dollars and have now resulted in a serious threat to our national economic security, yet few of those defendants spent any time in prison. As defendants, those white men were not perceived as personally threatening by the other white men who plea-bargained them to non-custodial sentences, once a few high-profile prosecutions had set out the parameters of such bargains. The older white men who are overwhelmingly in charge of decision-making in the criminal justice system see young minority men as very threatening and want to put them in jail, even for relatively minor offenses, although ironically if they only kill one another they will bypass the capital case processing system.

The entertainment industry does not want to market stories about motiveless murders involving inarticulate blacks, or dramatize stories about black victims whose incomprehensible murders are not vindicated. Yet, in order to retain target black audiences, dramatizations of murders in the city instead will switch around the expected racial stereotypes identifying police and murderers, so that there are some good guy black cops and some bad guy white murderers who are punished.

Dramatizations like those of the *Marshall* case portray a criminal justice system which is comprehensible and fair, even if harsh. This conforms to what many white suburbanites and some middle-class blacks would like to believe. The death penalty is put in a context which both of these audiences find acceptable, and even desirable. Stories about murders that are not prosecuted, or murders where guilty defendants get off lightly, or where a retarded person, or a person who might not be guilty, is executed, imply that the system is unjust, is not working effectively. That does not make anyone feel good. So capital murders continue to be presented as revenge dramas, as westerns, good guys versus bad guys shooting it out at the OK Corral. This characterization of capital prosecutions tells us the criminal justice system is fine. It is effective. Justice is being done.

The death penalty is not about deterring murder. If lawmakers really wanted to prevent the deaths of innocent, helpless victims, lowering the speed limit to fifty-five miles per hour and vigorously prosecuting drunk drivers would result in a predictable reduction of highway fatalities. There is no reliable empirical evidence that reinstating capital punishment has any effect upon the homicide rate, or that it removes the worst murderers, although it is certain that reintroducing the death penalty will push up the costs of prosecuting murders.

There is something fundamentally wrong with a capital punishment system that selects people for execution on a random basis, or on the basis of whether the circumstances of their murders tell a story that will sell newspapers or television advertising. There is something very wrong with a society which allows its criminal justice system to seek vengeance for only a few who are murdered, especially if those few also happen to be the privileged in the society.

Our system for prosecuting murders is not working. We do not do ourselves a favor by lying to ourselves about this. The death penalty solves nothing, is nothing but a ghoulish entertainment, a distraction which keeps us from addressing the more serious structural problems of the entire criminal justice system. As law students, lawyers, judges, and most importantly citizens, we have been taken in, and we know better.

CHAPTER 2

Not Wiser After Thirty-Five Years of Contemplating the Death Penalty

This is an autobiographical essay provoked by the question: is the death penalty dying? Four illustrative case studies from my experience as a researcher on homicide and capital punishment over the past thirty-five years are an occasion to reflect upon my experience with capital punishment in very different circumstances over what seems like a long period of time. One theme is common to all these examples: how inextricable the law, both decisional law and statutory law, is from the larger, surrounding politics of time and place. If the death penalty is dying in the United States, individuals will play a decisive and pivotal role, but there must be a political moment, an opportunity, a confluence of forces, which may be fleeting, for that to happen.

In the description of the death penalty case studies that follows, the pattern which emerges, if there is one, is a pattern of particularity and individuality. New Jersey and Illinois have never had similar legal institutions. It would be hard to imagine a New Jersey governor acting as George Ryan did when he emptied death row in Illinois, and equally impossible to imagine the Supreme Court of Illinois taking the course chosen by the Supreme Court of New Jersey in the 1980s. Nigeria is offered as an example of a regime using capital punishment as a tool for different objectives. The lethal injection cases, popping up all over the United States after 2002, are an example of the unpredictability of legal outcomes in a system with thousands of actors and adjudicators when the political climate changes every moment and then momentum is established.

Illustrative Case No. 1: Nigeria and the Armed Robbery Tribunal in 1972–73

My first experience with capital punishment was in the Western State of Nigeria in 1971 when I was looking for a research project to earn six academic credits while on leave of absence after my first year of law school. The truth was that I had found the first year of legal education so devoid of intellectual and personal rewards that I had no commitment to continue. I had always loved research, and I was looking for a project to while away the time. This research on capital punishment in Nigeria, now so distant in time and place, and its methodology, so simple, continues to resonate with my present work on capital punishment thirty-five years later. Perhaps the commonality is the interplay between the law's overarching, studied formality, its seeming objectivity, and the deep human irrationality of its application in the particular. This juxtaposition, so striking in the many manifestations of capital punishment, makes the study of the death penalty endlessly seductive. Just when understanding seems imminent, a new conundrum, a fresh contradiction presents itself.

While reading through all of the books in English on African law in the University of Ibadan Library in 1970, I came across Paul Bohannan's *African Homicide and Suicide* (1960), a series of commissioned essays from the 1950s, mostly by British colonial officers who later became anthropologists, about patterns in homicide and suicide in their colonial districts. These anthropologists were careful observers, and this was the beginning of the academic study of homicide, coming into its own with the publication of Marvin Wolfgang's *Patterns in Criminal Homicide* (1958), just as quantitative sociology was transforming the discipline. One droll aspect of doing research on homicide in Nigeria in the 1970s was the repeated, solemn observation by British and American academics that the expected rates and patterns of homicide in Nigeria would resemble those of blacks in Philadelphia, because Wolfgang's study differentiated between blacks and whites. While this suggestion was absurd, the association of the study of homicide with issues of race, as well as class and gender, is long-standing and persistent (Bienen et al., 1988, 27).[1]

I designed a research project replicating the simple model suggested in *African Homicide and Suicide* (Bohannan, 1960). After many inquiries, and many people telling me no records existed, I came upon all the handwritten opinions of the Western State Supreme Court since they had started keeping written records of their opinions. These opinions were similar to records from the eighteenth or nineteenth century in Britain or America. The court first summarized the facts and the evidence presented, and then issued a brief legal ruling. There was an appellate avenue to the federal Supreme Court, but few cases were taken there. These case files, a few pages for each case, carefully written in dipped ink on slick British copying paper, included 114 homicides; this was a new and fresh set of data on Nigerian homicide cases from the late 1960s, which I addressed following the guidelines given by Paul Bohannan to his anthropologists in the 1950s. What little I knew of criminal law was based upon one semester of a textbook and lecture course in the first year of law school.

This seemed like a worthwhile and manageable project: a straightforward account of homicides in Western Nigeria, a state which then had a population about the size of my home state, New Jersey. The law was simple enough. Homicide was a crime, defined in the same way as it was defined in New Jersey: as the unlawful killing of another without justification. The penalty was life imprisonment, or death. The source of the law, including the law supporting the imposition of the death penalty, was British common law and some statutory law, just like in New Jersey. I counted the homicides, identified patterns, such as in the kind of weapon used, the relationship between victim and defendant, and the circumstances of the homicide, such as whether it occurred in the home or on the road, or during the commission of another felony such as robbery.[2] There was a new wrinkle, however. The military government had come to power in January 1966, and there had been a second military coup in July 1966 when Yakubu Gowon assumed power on August 1, 1966.[3] In 1970 the regime in power was the military government with Gowon as chair of the Supreme Military Council. The military government had suspended certain provisions of the federal constitution regarding the rights of criminal defendants. The criminal courts and the rules governing trials and procedures in the Western State of Nigeria, however, were basically unaffected by the fact of a military government with one important exception.

A legal body called the Armed Robbery Tribunal was created after the Nigerian Civil War under the authority of the military tribunal by a decree (Laws of the Federation of Nigeria, 1984).[4] The Nigerian Civil War (1967–70) had resulted in civilian and military deaths totaling between two and three million and had involved the secession of the Republic of Biafra in the southeastern region, which was primarily Ibo, and the subsequent blockade and siege of the region by the federal army, with many hundreds of thousands of deaths of soldiers, civilians, and children.

At the end of the war there was vast civil and economic disruption, with large numbers of weapons and arms in the hands of people who had no prospect of integration into the society or economy. Civilians in places such as Ibadan, where I was living and which had not been part of the former Republic of Biafra, were fearful of going out in cars at night, and there were daily reports of armed holdups, burglaries, and murders. Whether this was a crime wave, or hysteria promoted by the press or the government, was unknown. Evidence of the destruction of the civil war was everywhere, as was the sense of disorder and the lack of governmental control. Everyone had weapons: the government officers, the police, and the criminals.[5] Meanwhile, in this time before the Internet, when international telephone calls and telegrams were expensive, sporadic, and unreliable, I had three sources of information about homicide in Western Nigeria: some very dated books in the library, my collection of handwritten cases from the Western State Supreme Court Library, and the Nigerian newspapers and tabloids, which sold copies by reporting murders, the sexual escapades of prominent people, acts of violence, and the corruption and hypocrisy of politicians.[6] These same tabloids periodically featured gruesome reports, complete with photographs, of public executions on the Bar Beach in the national capital, Lagos, under the authority of the Armed Robbery Tribunal. Ten to twenty at a time would be executed by firing squad, their bodies then thrown to the sharks swimming in the bay while crowds numbering in the thousands watched.

So in the heat and dust and confusion of Western Nigeria in 1971–72—there was little or no air conditioning—I pursued two parallel tracks of inquiry, a pattern I have continued to this day: the first, an academic, formal, quantitative, seemingly objective annotation of patterns in homicide; and the second, a narrative description of the unstructured chaos that I observed around me. This is not to imply that one form of inquiry is superior to the other, but rather that the two approaches complement one another; indeed, each is deficient without the other. The seemingly objective approach of measuring the attributes of killers and victims and the circumstances of murder is also deeply irrational, in spite of its being couched in scientific rhetoric. And the observation of the irrational turns to the law, or science, to impose order.

There was the formal law, the cases and statutes, the rules of evidence—impeccable and impenetrable, and not very different from what I had read in my casebook in New Jersey—and there was the circus surrounding the public executions reported in the tabloids. The stories included pictures of those about to be executed, and, after execution, reports of last rites and the last words of penitence, or curses, by those being executed, as well as stern admonishments by judges from the tribunal and law enforcement officials.

Western Nigerians were at that time justifiably proud of their completely Africanized criminal justice system. True, there were cracks in the formal system—such as the rule that the standard for insanity for the law in Western Nigeria was what would be considered acceptable to the average man on the street in an English provincial city, such as Leeds or Manchester—but the consensus on the part of both professionals and the public was that this was a functioning legal system. The trial court judges assigned counsel to indigents in every murder case, protected the due process rights of defendants, and followed the British rules of evidence even when such legal protections were no longer required under the federal constitution.

While the formal criminal law was the British common law, including a provision for the death penalty, in fact, under the ordinary criminal system in the Western State of Nigeria, the death sentence was rarely imposed and only upheld after lengthy appeals. When executions under the ordinary criminal law did take place—perhaps three or four in a decade—there was no publicity or notoriety or sensationalism surrounding them. The next of kin were simply informed that the convicted murderer who had languished without publicity in prison during a series of British-type appeals based upon legal precedent had been executed.

Then there was this other legal system, the one which was tying the condemned to posts, shooting them, and throwing their bodies to the sharks in the bay. That legal system took its authority from the 1970 decree of the military government, not from a statute passed by a legislature, not from the common-law traditions of the British legal system, and not from traditional African legal norms.

The decree of 1970 had created a new quasi-judicial body called the Armed Robbery Tribunal, consisting of a trial court judge, a military officer, and a police officer. This tribunal had one function, to decide whether a defendant was guilty under the provisions of the decree (Development Policy Centre Nigeria, 2000).[7] Those eligible to be convicted were not just murderers and armed robbers, but also those "in the company of" those committing an armed robbery. If a person was found guilty, the sentence was an automatic death sentence.[8] There were no appeals to the ordinary state criminal justice system or to the federal courts from decisions of this tribunal, although the military governor did have the authority to grant clemency.[9] And the executions were public.

As my research proceeded, I decided to observe every level of adjudication in the criminal justice system.[10] I discovered when I went to my first murder trial—my journalistic instincts told me I should see what was actually happening in trials before writing anything—that the proceedings were conducted in a language the accused did not understand, English. The scholarly tomes in the library had not mentioned this fact, perhaps because it was so taken for granted that none of the commentators thought it remarkable, or even requiring explanation or justification.[11]

When I interviewed the members of the Armed Robbery Tribunal, one judge, who was a police officer, assured me that the purpose of the public executions was to deter crime, to stop the post-civil war violence by showing criminals what happened to those who were caught. Certainly there was widespread civil mayhem. No one with a car drove at night or on unknown roads, and there were many guns in the hands of people with grievances and no jobs or money.

The judge looked sternly at me and said that it was all very well to be against capital punishment in America—he had been to Atlanta for training at the Federal Bureau of Investigation headquarters—where there was a well-established tradition of respect for law and order (perhaps I demurred on the subject of the public executions, although I do not remember doing so), but the present chaos in Nigeria called for capital punishment, and public executions.

Neither the judges of the Armed Robbery Tribunal, nor the military officers who created the tribunal, nor the general population of Nigeria's millions, most of whom were law-abiding, nor I, can say with authority whether the public executions deterred any armed robberies or murders (Ilo, 2004),[12] beyond the possible future robberies and murders not committed by those thrown to the sharks at Bar Beach on a particular day.[13] The judge, however, firmly believed that these executions were a deterrent to further civil disorder and to future armed robberies and murders. It is certain that the violence did not stop.

My recollection is that the public executions usually took place on a weekend, so that more people would come. Probably they didn't take place on a Sunday. This was then a Christian part of the country. The carnival atmosphere of these occasions was striking. The crowds at the Bar Beach were market women and babies, pickpockets, boys with sticks and girls in colorful wrappers, according to the photographs and published reports—I never attended an execution—and what seemed to be a random, ordinary collection of men and women who had nothing better to do that day. People seemed to become exhilarated at the prospect of a killing, and some of the condemned commanded attention from their brief position on center stage.

Whether or not public executions deterred murder and armed robbery, at the end of the academic year, I was completely seduced by this research. The death penalty has remained an abiding preoccupation since then. Every time I plan on moving away from it, some new development will bring me back. In the 1970s I collected all of my data points on 114 homicides in Western Nigeria, observed every level of adjudication, including several murder trials, and interviewed every level of judge in the court system, as well as defense attorneys and prosecutors and legislators. I came to Nigeria prepared to leave law school when I returned to America. I returned as a homicide researcher. My first job after law school, on the recommendation of Marvin Wolfgang, was working as a research attorney for a fully funded National Institutes of Mental Health study of sexual assault in Philadelphia. I spent fifteen years as a public defender working on homicide and capital punishment in New Jersey and conduct similar research now in Illinois, all because I was mesmerized by the contradictions of capital punishment in Nigeria thirty-five years ago.

Illustrative Case No. 2: New Jersey, 1980–92

A few years after graduating from law school I went to work for the New Jersey Office of the Public Advocate, which then included the statewide Office of the Public Defender. When I brought up my research background, working on capital punishment and homicide in Nigeria, to the lawyer who would basically be my supervisor for the next fifteen years, he crisply informed me that New Jersey had no death penalty. The last execution had occurred more than twenty years ago.[14] And, he continued, it was unlikely there would be a death penalty in New Jersey in the future. The then governor had promised to veto any capital punishment bill out of the legislature, and the votes were not there to override his veto. Besides, he added, we do not do social science-type research at the Office of the Public Defender. This is a law office. By this time I had spent several years working on a scientific study of all reporting rape victims in Philadelphia and was familiar with the quantitative analysis of legal issues in the context of sexual assault. Statistics and the abstraction of legal analysis were a rudder and a distancer in the area of rape, as well as homicide, for me, for the courts, and for the legal system.

The year was 1976, when state legislatures had received the green light from the U.S. Supreme Court in *Gregg v. Georgia* (1976) to go ahead with capital prosecutions. New Jersey had reluctantly declared its system of capital punishment unconstitutional in *State v. Funicello* (1972).[15] After monitoring the passage of a new criminal code, which eventually included a death penalty, I ended up spending ten of my next fifteen years as a public defender constructing an empirical study of homicide in New Jersey. It was another attempt to impose objectivity, the science of quantitative analysis, on the chaos and confusion brought on with the reimplementation of capital punishment. It was the rationalist's hope that if only we could get enough information, and analyze it with sufficient scientific objectivity, we could control and understand what was happening. The application of the death penalty would be principled, under the law. That impulse, to make the application of capital punishment consistent and predictable, would come again in Illinois, and is seen in the lethal injection cases as well.

My colleague had been correct in predicting that the reenactment of capital punishment in New Jersey was not a foregone conclusion, even after *Gregg v. Georgia* (Bienen et al., 1988).[16] When constitutional provisions prevented Governor Brendan Byrne from running again in 1982, the newly elected Republican governor, Thomas Kean, did sign the bill reinstating the death penalty. The effective date of reenactment was August 6, 1982, the date that Governor Byrne's successor signed the bill. The first capital prosecution in New Jersey occurred soon after, and the New Jersey Supreme Court immediately began to hear a series of procedural and systemwide challenges to the reimposition (Bienen et al., 1988, 70–100).

The state legislators were unequivocally in favor of the death penalty, although it was never entirely clear why they were so keen to reenact.[17] The "father of the death penalty," Senator John Russo, was formerly a prosecutor, but it was not the county prosecutors who were pushing for the reenactment. New Jersey is one of the few states not to elect county prosecutors, or to elect judges. A majority of the twenty-one appointed county prosecutors in New Jersey did not favor reenactment of capital punishment, according to an informal poll taken at a county prosecutors' meeting just before the effective date of reenactment. Nonetheless, they all pledged to follow the law and prosecute death-eligible homicides as capital cases after reenactment.

The New Jersey legislature, which was so keen to reenact, never turned down a request for funds for capital defense from the Office of the Public Defender during the first decade after reenactment. That department regularly spent more than a million dollars on a single capital case, especially in the early years of the statute when no one, including the judges, the prosecutors, and the defense attorneys, knew how to interpret or apply the new death penalty law, with its two-tiered trial and its statutory aggravating and mitigating factors. When New Jersey reenacted, Illinois was well on the way to filling up its death row, although the first execution in Illinois was not until 1990. The first death sentence in Illinois was upheld in 1981 (Bienen, 1996). New Jersey in 1982 was already well behind Illinois in reestablishing a capital punishment system which regularly turned out death sentences and executed defendants.

This is where I became a homicide researcher again. With the expert assistance of colleagues from the Criminology Center at the University of Pennsylvania, the Supreme Court of New Jersey and skeptical defense attorneys and prosecutors were persuaded that the entire system of prosecuting and trying homicide cases in New Jersey should be examined in detail, using the methodology of social science. The basic tenet of proportionality review is to inquire whether a particular death penalty imposed upon a particular defendant is "just" or "proportionate" when compared to other cases in which the death penalty has and has not been imposed.

Whether or not all death-eligible cases as capital cases were prosecuted was one of the most important factual determinations of the long investigation into homicide and capital case processing which came to be known as proportionality review (Bienen, 1996).[18] It was surprising to the public defenders and others in New Jersey that jurors in the first capital trials in the state overwhelmingly rejected the imposition of the death sentence, even after finding the defendant guilty of a clearly death-eligible murder, in spite of the high level of public support for capital punishment reported in the polls. Out of more than 130 initial capital prosecutions, only 25 defendants were sentenced to death (Bienen et al., 1988, 170, table 2). The public defenders could congratulate themselves that the legal defense was effective, but perhaps it was that jurors, when faced with an actual defendant, even one who had been proved to have committed a horrific murder, did not want to vote to kill another human being. And these were jurors who had been death-qualified and were thus more likely than the general public to be in favor of capital punishment.

When the death penalty was reenacted in New Jersey in 1982, it was not clear who wanted it, except a few highly vocal state legislators. State Senator John Russo claimed he had persisted for years in reintroducing legislation reenacting capital punishment when it had no chance of becoming law in order to avenge his father, who was a victim of murder. Senator Russo was a powerful state legislator, a member of the Senate Judiciary Committee during the time when the Criminal Code was being passed.[19] He also repeatedly said he wanted the death penalty to be fair and for defendants to have all due process rights. Ironically, Senator Russo was acquainted with several of the personages in the *Marshall* case, the case from his county, Ocean County, which became the vehicle for the principal statewide challenge to the reimposition of capital punishment in New Jersey.

The facts in the *Marshall* case were the perfect foil for the challenge to the reimposition of capital punishment in New Jersey (Bienen, 1996, 183–212),[20] as evidenced by the fact that it was the subject of a best-selling book and then a made-for-television movie (Bienen, 1993).[21] The case exhibited a motley cast of clowns and bumblers, including the private defense attorney who took what money Robert Marshall had, did not call his children to testify at the penalty trial, and then dumped the defendant and his death sentence on the Office of the Public Defender for what turned out to be more than twenty years of appeals. Not only was Robert Marshall the perfect hero-villain for the ensuing death penalty drama, but the attributes of his case made this the perfect case for the New Jersey Supreme Court to address the legal and ethical conundrums raised by the new death penalty.

Led by Robert N. Wilentz, the son of the attorney general who orchestrated the drama which led to the execution of Bruno Richard Hauptmann in 1936 for the kidnapping and murder of the Lindbergh baby, the Supreme Court of New Jersey was in the 1980s the most intellectual and thoughtful state supreme court in the country. It was particularly known for developing state constitutional law doctrine, relying upon state constitutional principles at a time when the U.S. Supreme Court was becoming unwilling to reexamine the procedures in state capital convictions, look at state capital punishment systems, or halt executions.[22] The *Marshall* case became the occasion for the New Jersey Supreme Court to examine systemwide aspects of the legal ramifications of reenactment in New Jersey, before upholding his death sentence as constitutional in 1992, ten years after reenactment.

Robert Marshall was white, a college graduate, a successful insurance executive who seemed to live an ordinary small-town American life until this aberrational murder. He was clearly guilty of planning to kill his wife. The outcome of the case at trial exemplified the quixotic aspect of capital trials: Robert Marshall was sentenced to death; one of the assassins, probably not the triggerman, was sentenced to time served; the other assassin was acquitted at trial; while the "go-between," a clerk in a country store whose role was to allow his phone to be used and relay messages to the assassins, was sentenced to thirty years without parole. Recently, an interim governor commuted the sentence of this co-conspirator (Vaughan, 2006).[23] After twenty years of federal and state appeals, Robert Marshall's death sentence was set aside on grounds of incompetence of his trial counsel by the Third Circuit Court of Appeals in 2005 (*Marshall v. Cathel,* 2005).[24] The attorney general of New Jersey asked for a writ of certiorari to the U.S. Supreme Court on the last day of eligibility.[25] Robert Marshall will not be retried with the possibility of being resentenced to death.

The New Jersey Supreme Court, under the strong leadership of Hauptmann's prosecutor's serious son, addressed the legal and ethical conundrums of the "new" death penalty. Objective, statistical, and legal analysis was applied to the irrationality of murder and the bizarre outcomes at trial. This juxtaposition presented many conundrums. The reenactment of capital punishment in a number of states had been tarnished by the continuing taint of racial and economic bias in prosecution and sentencing. The poor, and mostly minorities, were sentenced to death. While that was uncontested, the reasons for it were confounded and, for some, inextricable from inequities which plagued the criminal justice system as a whole. Robert Marshall himself was not poor, mentally retarded, or socially or culturally disadvantaged. Nor was he mentally ill, psychotic, sadistic, a mass murderer, or any other kind of madman whose fate at the hands of an executioner would raise different legal and ethical issues. Although there was widespread publicity at his trial, Robert Marshall's death sentence presented a relatively straightforward case for the court to use as an occasion to consider systemwide inequities and procedural problems with the reimposition of capital punishment. His appeal also arose at a fortuitous moment in the development of capital punishment jurisprudence in New Jersey.

The Supreme Court of New Jersey did not uphold the statute as constitutional until five years after reenactment, and only after reversing twenty-six consecutive death sentences. This, along with the court's controversial stand on other issues, caused Chief Justice Wilentz serious problems at his seven-year confirmation hearing.[26] Several state legislators expressed their unhappiness with the fact that four years had passed since reenactment and no one had been executed under the new statute (Bienen, 1996, 209, n. 283).[27] Nonetheless he was confirmed, and the court continued to develop extraordinary constitutional doctrine regarding capital punishment. The Supreme Court of New Jersey was unperturbed by the fact that the U.S. Supreme Court in 1984 had declared that proportionality review was not required by the federal constitution and had rejected a systemwide challenge to a state capital punishment system in 1987. The Supreme Court of New Jersey simply said that law did not apply in New Jersey; state constitutional principles controlled. The Supreme Court of New Jersey also simply ignored a legislative provision restricting proportionality review in New Jersey to a limited comparison of death-only cases (Bienen, 1996, 211, n. 295).[28]

Instead the Supreme Court of New Jersey took over the study of all homicides in New Jersey since the reimposition of capital punishment, a study which was started at the Office of the Public Defender, hiring as its own special master Professor David Baldus from the University of Iowa, the expert whose elaborate statistical study had not been persuasive to the U.S. Supreme Court. He had been the academic who was principally in charge of the Georgia studies brought before the U.S. Supreme Court over decades of litigation, culminating in 1987. In New Jersey Professor Baldus and others devised a new methodology for comparing the characteristics of the offense and offender to determine whether the imposition of the death sentence in a particular case was proportionate, or just (Bienen, 1996, 183–207, n. 193).[29] The defining of this procedure and its application to individual cases took years and resulted in an elaborate jurisprudence, culminating with the upholding of Robert Marshall's death sentence as proportionate (*State v. Marshall, II,* 1992).

No other state supreme court before or since has been willing to hold an entire criminal justice system up to the light. Then the times changed, and the court's personnel changed. Chief Justice Wilentz died, and Justice Handler, who had been one of the most thoughtful of the contributors to the inquiry, retired, and other justices of the Supreme Court of New Jersey retired or were replaced (Bienen, 1996, 209, n. 284).[30] After ten years of research on homicide and the death penalty in New Jersey, after, as Justice Handler of the supreme court noted, thousands of hours and thousands of pages of New Jersey Supreme Court opinions, the grinding of many computers, and miles of green bar printouts—that was where the technology was then—what was accomplished by proportionality review in New Jersey? Robert Marshall himself will not be executed, but for other reasons.

In the *Marshall* case, after all of the statistics, after all of the systemwide analysis, after all of the technicalities of proportionality review, the most difficult fact for the court to reconcile was that there was another case from another county in New Jersey which was almost a twin of the *Marshall* case on its facts (Bienen, 1996, 196, n. 234). In this other case a relatively well-off white man—I do not use the term "middle-class" because there were suggestions of an organized crime association—hired two assassins to kill his wife. In some respects the circumstances of this case were "worse" than those of *Marshall.* The wife was tortured before being killed by the two thugs hired to kill her. As in *Marshall,* there was no question of the guilt of the defendant, and it was a killing for hire. And yet the county prosecutor in that case chose not to prosecute the case as a capital case, in spite of the fact that there was a strong factual basis for more than one statutory aggravating factor: the cold-blooded hiring of two assassins to kill, and the torture of the victim. How could the principle of proportionality be maintained in the face of such a contradiction? More than the statistics, more than the regression analysis, more than the philosophical principles, this simple intuitive comparison between two cases, one where death was imposed and a similar case where it was not because of a prosecutor's choice, proved to be intractable.

Yet, at the end of all of these extraordinary legal proceedings, after all the complicated methodology, the Supreme Court of New Jersey was still stuck with the death penalty. The court had been successful in postponing executions, at least for some time. Now the New Jersey legislature has taken an unprecedented step in imposing a moratorium on executions and creating a Study Commission whose mission it was to come up with reasons for keeping the death penalty. Probably the legislature could not have taken this stance if the Supreme Court of New Jersey had not engaged in fifteen years of extensive dialogue about the reimposition of capital punishment in New Jersey. The methodology developed for the *Marshall* case has been and will continue to be applied to others sentenced to death whose sentences automatically come to the New Jersey Supreme Court for review, as long as there is a death penalty in New Jersey.

There was a great deal of expense and little entertainment value in proportionality review, although, as with every aspect of the death penalty, there were many ironies. As a homicide researcher, it was enormously satisfying to be able to collect the data on all homicides in New Jersey since the reimposition of capital punishment in 1982, to participate in the creation of a workable model for analyzing cases by category of offense and offender, and then to watch the results and the contradictions rise to the surface in this relatively straightforward and scientific process. Though proportionality review did not result in the supreme court declaring the system unconstitutional, it did result in a substantial body of jurisprudence.

As of January 2006 there is a legislatively imposed moratorium on executions in New Jersey, and that same bill passed in January 2006 created a Study Commission to submit its findings to the New Jersey legislature before November 15, 2006 (An Act Creating a Study Commission on the Death Penalty and Imposing a Moratorium on Executions, 2005).[31] The Study Commission has published a cost study, detailing the entire cost of the reimposition of capital punishment in the state and the cost of individual cases. The bill asks the legislature to repeal the death penalty unless there can be shown a reason to continue it. At the time it was the only legislatively imposed moratorium on executions in any state, and the legislative findings announced in the statute were extraordinary.[32]

To understand what happened in New Jersey, it is very important to remember that the twenty-one county prosecutors are not elected, and that the last execution was in 1963. The legal institutions are not dug in with regard to a commitment to the death penalty. This is probably the most significant difference between Illinois and New Jersey. In Illinois the supreme court could hardly wait to affirm the first death penalty. They never recognized that the old statute was unconstitutional. In Nigeria the constitutionality of capital punishment was not even discussed. New Jersey is a unique political and legal culture, one without much interest or commitment to the reimposition of capital punishment. That cultural context was critical, as was the long-standing tradition of judicial independence and the respect in the legal community for the Supreme Court of New Jersey.

As always, there were unpredictable elements in New Jersey as well. The former governor of New Jersey, who opposed the bill creating the Study Commission and the moratorium on executions, resigned for reasons unrelated to the death penalty. The interim governor, having nothing to lose politically, was willing to sign the legislation establishing the moratorium and the bill with the findings creating the Study Commission. The present governor, John Corzine, supports the moratorium and the bill. The former attorney general of the state, Zulima Farber, who has since resigned for reasons unrelated to capital punishment, also was not in favor of capital punishment, and it remains to be seen whether her successor will take the same position.[33]

In New Jersey the death penalty does seem to be dying, but the death penalty had not for decades been strongly entrenched in the political or legal culture. It is as if the entire state is still recovering from the Hauptmann execution. For a critical decade the state supreme court was willing to distinguish its death penalty rulings from the trend at the U.S. Supreme Court and rule on the basis of the state constitutional law. The leadership and tenacity shown by Chief Justice Wilentz in this area could not have been predicted and will not be replicated. It is also important that the executions never started after reenactment, and few death sentences have been imposed or upheld by the state supreme court (National Association for the Advancement of Colored People Legal Defense and Education Fund, 2006).[34]

The Change in the Political Climate in the 1990s

In the 1990s the legal arguments in capital cases were becoming increasingly technical and incomprehensible to the public, replacing the dramas of revenge in some of the first death penalty cases after *Furman,* cases such as those involving Ted Bundy or Gary Gilmore. Perhaps the most telling analysis of the changes in the 1990s will be made by a demographic study of criminal defendants and the changes in the prison population during this decade. Nuances of federal appellate procedure were cast as rule interpretations and refined to tell death row inmates that they had no more avenues of appeal, even if they brought a new claim of innocence. The composition of the U.S. Supreme Court had changed, and the court had become impatient with protracted appeals in death cases. Lawyers who made careless mistakes, such as filing papers a day late, were responsible for sending their clients to the execution chamber. The technicalities of the questioning of jurors, who were qualified to vote for or against death based upon what they said in voir dire, were weighed down by an increasingly arcane body of precedent. Each state had different rules, and cases in the federal system were being bounced back to the states. Somewhere along the way the moral high ground was lost by those who had championed capital punishment as the return to a more principled criminal justice system based on the harsh punishment of murderers.

At the same time stories of death row inmates who were drugged, mentally incompetent, who did not realize they were not coming back from the execution chamber to eat their dessert, and inmates who were abused and brutalized as children became common currency, offset by the increasingly vocal victims' rights advocates. The discourse was all about pain and suffering on both sides. The reports were of local prosecutors running for reelection based on the number of murderers they sent to the gallows, of drunken and incompetent defense attorneys who were assigned cases after contributing to a judge's reelection campaign, of courts and counties that would not pay more than a few hundred dollars to defense attorneys, as well as allegations of false confessions, torture at the police station, rigged or mistaken identifications by eyewitnesses, lost evidence, forged evidence, suppressed exonerating evidence, and on and on (Medwed, 2006).

As the new death penalty was bringing forward tales of less than clean-cut or wholesome death penalty prosecutions, the innocence movement was gaining momentum. Dozens of inmates on death row were proved to be entirely innocent of the crime for which they had been sentenced to death. In state after state defense attorneys, who were learning to coordinate and collaborate on what came to be recognized as common patterns, were able to show that some people on death row were there because their false confessions had been coerced, or because evidence of their guilt had been manufactured and evidence of their innocence suppressed or ignored. Or just too many sloppy mistakes had been ignored, and no one cared. In trial courts across the country there were reports of things going on which did not comport with what many observers thought was fair or just. And the issues of race, of race and economic status, of race and ethnicity never went away. Meanwhile, courts and administrators of the death penalty seemed to be increasingly impatient with rational argument and objective evidence and what they called legal technicalities. It was time to move on with the executions.

As those on death row came out from the shadows, and the stories of their wrongful convictions were told, they were seen to be human, often pathetic bumblers with a record, who were in the wrong place when the police arrived. When dozens of claims of innocence became credible, prosecutors were backed into a corner. To admit prior mistakes was disloyal to their colleagues and institutions. People on death row were found innocent and released, but the number of people sentenced to death continued to grow. With the exception of Texas, no state was executing enough people to bring the numbers down. In the meantime our commercial entertainments became increasingly violent, showing widespread carnage, murder, and the dead stacked up like jacks or poker chips. The demographic of young men most likely to kill or be killed was especially addicted to ritualized violence on small and large screens. While the impact of this may be difficult to measure, arguments about the inhumanity of capital punishment seemed dated, or irrelevant, as the public became increasingly inured to public representations of violence and killing, and as the number of people sentenced to death continued to increase.

Illustrative Case No. 3: Illinois, 1998–2003

When I left New Jersey in 1995 to come to Illinois I was convinced I would never again do research on homicide or the death penalty. After all, nothing was happening in Illinois in 1995. There was a very large death row population. The Illinois Public Defender's Office did not have the advantage of a strong statewide administrative structure or a budget similar to that which allowed the New Jersey Office of the Public Defender to spend millions of dollars on the defense of a single capital case. The Illinois Supreme Court had declared that it did not and would not conduct proportionality review. The court regularly affirmed death sentences. The then governor was in favor of capital punishment, and executions had begun. Public support for the death penalty was high, although not significantly higher than the national levels.

The Illinois Supreme Court had through the 1970s and 1980s repeatedly affirmed death sentences (Bienen, 1996, 166, table 1). There was a brief moment in 1979 and then again in 1984 when the constitutionality of capital punishment was a live issue before the state supreme court and federal courts in Illinois (*People ex rel. Carey v. Cousins,* 1979; *People v. Lewis,* 1984; *People v. Silagy,* 1984).[35] Since that time the Supreme Court of Illinois has indicated in numerous opinions that it was uninterested in systemwide challenges to the capital punishment system. There had never been the institutional will or the leadership within the Illinois criminal justice system for an enterprise such as the comprehensive analysis of the criminal justice system undertaken by the Supreme Court of New Jersey with the participation and cooperation of numerous other courts and state agencies, including the Office of the Public Defender, the county prosecutors, and the attorney general.

The Illinois prosecutors, the state's attorneys, are individually elected and answer to no higher legal authority than the voters in their individual jurisdiction. And there are 102 of them. They are elected as county officials, and there is no limitation on the number of terms they may serve. These are 102 very autonomous local officials, each with the independent and unreviewable authority to select a case for capital prosecution, or not.[36] Given the breadth of the Illinois statutory aggravating factors, when I arrived in 1995 and began reading the daily newspapers, it seemed as if a capital case was always on deck, on trial, being investigated, or one of the more than 160 inmates on death row was coming up for execution. The culture of capital prosecutions was and is well entrenched in Illinois.

The state's attorney of Cook County is the most visible state's attorney in Illinois, and one of the most powerful and autonomous political figures in the state. Prosecutions by the Cook County state's attorney, like those by equivalent offices in Los Angeles and New York, regularly make national news. The state's attorney of Cook County and the other Illinois state's attorneys have always been visible and vocal advocates for the death penalty in the state, both in theory and practice. Cook County regularly accounts for about three quarters of the state's murders and the largest number, and the most visible, if not the largest proportion, of capital prosecutions (Illinois State Police, 2003).[37] Cook County prosecutes as capital cases a fraction of its potentially death-eligible cases. Some Illinois counties, such as DuPage County, capitally prosecute a much higher proportion of death-eligible cases. The state's attorneys in Illinois have often been legendary political figures. There has long been a well-marked path from the State's Attorney's Office, especially the Cook County State's Attorney's Office, to the state legislature, to the judiciary, to the Illinois Supreme Court, and to other state and occasionally national political offices.[38] The elected state judiciary, and the state supreme court, have always traditionally included many former state's attorneys.

In 1995 the Republican governor of Illinois, James Edgar, did not seem to be particularly eager to carry out executions. The first execution after reenactment in 1990, when James Thompson was governor, was of Charles Walker, who decided not to pursue further appeals (Warden, 2005, 398). The next execution, in May 1994, was of John Wayne Gacy, the notorious murderer of young boys and men. Governor James Edgar included in his campaign for governor in fall 1994 extensive publicity of his opponent's opposition to the death penalty (Warden, 2005, 399). After his election, Governor Edgar signed five death warrants. One of those cases was based upon a problematic confession, and this case attracted some attention from columnists after Northwestern University students investigated the case and launched a campaign on the defendant's behalf. In 1996 Governor Edgar did commute one death sentence, that of Guinevere Garcia, fourteen hours before she was to be executed (Warden, 2005, 401, n. 85).

In 1995 I and many others could not have anticipated what happened in the next several years. The institutional system supporting capital punishment did not change; the state's attorneys remained enthusiastic prosecutors of capital cases. The Illinois Supreme Court did not abandon its bizarre electoral system for state supreme court judges that divided representation, ensuring factionalism and precluding establishing, at least in recent decades, a court known for intellectual leadership and political independence. The Office of the Public Defender in Illinois did not become institutionally stronger, richer, or more capable of addressing issues on a statewide basis. Factors outside of the institutionalized criminal justice system were critical.

In 1998 the innocence movement was gaining momentum. An extraordinary conference at the Northwestern University School of Law, organized by Professor Lawrence Marshall and others, brought together some 1,500 advocates, representatives of the national and international press, and, most importantly, twenty-nine men and women who were the living embodiment of the fact that the innocent could be wrongfully convicted of capital murder (Sarat, 2005, chap. 1).[39] When these men and women told their individual stories of how they ended up on death row, the world began to watch and listen.

The sympathy of the public for the innocents did not happen overnight or because of one event, and it did not happen without an enormous amount of expert effort and coordination between old and new advocates for capital defendants. Many of those who ended up on death row for crimes they did not commit had committed other crimes, or had problems with addictions, and few were articulate enough or in a position to tell their stories effectively to a skeptical American public. A group of articulate and highly skilled advocates, writers, and journalists brought these cases and the national discussion of capital punishment to a new level. This is where individuals and the advocacy movement as a whole, as well as the journalists and the larger legal community, made an enormous difference. The mention of the conviction of the innocent formerly could elicit the response that this was just one of the unintended costs of the criminal justice system, analogous to highway deaths. And one case could always be dismissed as an aberration, or the result of the particularity of its circumstances.

In 1998, after the Northwestern University School of Law's National Conference on Wrongful Convictions and the Death Penalty, there was a step-level change in public perceptions and public discussion. The political climate changed, and support for a statewide moratorium gained momentum (Roper Center for Public Opinion, 2003).[40] I use those vague and impalpable terms because the change was like a change in the seasons; if you had been working on the death penalty for decades you could sense it in the air. No one was more surprised in 1998 than the old hands who had been seeing the same fifty people at death penalty conferences since *Gregg.* In 1998 it felt like the coming-together of elements which had been waiting to happen for some time. This change in the political weather was not immediate, nor was it the work of one person or group, or one case or series of events, although there were people without whom it would not have happened. But once the political atmosphere changed, there was no going back to the old assumptions.

For several years the national Innocence Project, under the direction of Professor Barry Scheck at Cardozo Law School and others, had been pursuing evidence of the actual innocence of some capital defendants by reexamining identification evidence with newly sensitive DNA tests. The DNA analysis offered a whole new avenue for the uncovering of wrongful convictions. The seminar on capital punishment taught in the Medill School of Journalism at Northwestern University by Professor David Protess had for more than a decade been working with undergraduates and law students in researching the factual basis for questionable capital convictions. The founding of the Center on Wrongful Convictions at the Northwestern University School of Law was another milestone. These activities came together in an extraordinary way after 1998 (Warden, 2005, 399–410).[41]

Another critical factor in Illinois was the expertise and experience of the columnists and crime reporters for the *Chicago Tribune* and several other prominent Chicago papers and legal journals. Television commentators also played an important role. For years, staff reporters and editors at the *Chicago Tribune* had collected data on capital cases, and on homicides in Cook County, and had written extensively about individual capital trials and appeals, and the questionable tactics and practices of all participants in the Illinois capital case processing system. No newspaper in New Jersey played a similar role. Then the perfect storm occurred: the case of Anthony Porter. The legal community and the public were forced to acknowledge that something was drastically wrong with a criminal justice system which could sentence Anthony Porter to death for a crime he did not commit.

The highly dramatic unraveling of the Anthony Porter death sentence was told in real time by several groups simultaneously: his attorneys; newspaper columnists and reporters, who quickly realized something extraordinary was happening; and the newly galvanized coalition of lawyers and advocates against capital punishment.[42] These were the unpredictable and mutually reinforcing elements of the *Porter* case: his actual innocence; he came within hours of being executed; his case and the circumstances of his conviction matched systemwide defects in the national criminal justice system (the evidence against him included uncorroborated eyewitness testimony and what turned out to be a false confession shortly after his arrest); he was an African

American man with a prior record, possibly mentally retarded, with no job or social support system at the time of his conviction; he was arrested because he was near the crime scene at the time of the murder; and there was no physical evidence connecting him to the murder. Yet he was sentenced to death, and the sentence was upheld.

I was teaching a seminar on homicide and capital punishment at Northwestern University School of Law before the *Porter* case began to unravel, and the seminar read the Illinois Supreme Court opinion unanimously affirming Anthony Porter's conviction (*People v. Porter*, 1986, 1329–30).[43] It contained several quotes, allegedly his statements, presumably from the police reports. I recall saying at the time to the students that the quotations sounded "canned," the kind of obviously incriminating, aggressive, hostile statements which I had seen attributed to defendants time and time again in police reports in New Jersey. It was not that defendants did not sometimes incriminate themselves, or confess, or make hostile and insensitive comments, but they did not all use the same language, the same phraseology, the same syntax and diction, especially those defendants who barely spoke English or were incoherent, inarticulate, or struck dumb by their arrest. Indeed, there is now a phalanx of experts trained to compare questionable statements attributed to defendants with the defendant's actual ordinary speech patterns.

When I mentioned my suspicions to one of Anthony Porter's attorneys at the time, he replied, correctly, that the Illinois Supreme Court had unanimously affirmed the conviction twice, and the conviction was the result of a jury verdict. There was no live challenge to the conviction. At that point no one had ever suggested Anthony Porter had not committed the murder. This same attorney uncovered evidence suggesting Anthony Porter might be retarded, an issue which had never been raised at trial, and it was the possibility of this—the question of his competency to be executed being a valid legal issue—which temporarily postponed Anthony Porter's execution. When his actual innocence was revealed, the facts and circumstances of Anthony Porter's conviction and appeals raised questions about the entire capital punishment system in Illinois at a time when people were prepared to listen.

In Illinois there were other totally unpredictable circumstances in the *Porter* case: the Northwestern University team videotaped the recantation of the eyewitness who lied at trial, and then videotaped the incriminating statements of the actual killer (these statements were later retracted). Not only was this persuasive, but the drama of the revelations was bolstered by the luck that both the recanting witness and the "actual" killer were alive and found by students and investigators. The unraveling of the foundation of Anthony Porter's death sentence took place in daily installments in the media, masterfully and expertly chronicled by the *Chicago Tribune*'s prizewinning reporters, columnists, and editors, and others (Warden, 2005, 403–4).[44]

Of course the real wild card, the card that trumped all others, was the character and circumstances of George Ryan himself. Most importantly, his political career was not associated with any of the Illinois state's attorney's offices, and thus he was not politically beholden to the entrenched pro–death penalty legal establishment (Sarat, 2005, 1–33).[45] Like the majority of the public, Ryan was a naïf when it came to the politics and realities of capital punishment, and the criminal justice system generally.

George Ryan repeatedly announced that he had voted for the reinstatement of capital punishment in 1977 when he was a legislator. He could sincerely express shock and outrage, thus taking the moral high ground, when it developed that in Illinois more people on death row had been exonerated than executed since reenactment. And at the time when the possibility of a blanket commutation arose, he was leaving office and leaving political life. He had nothing to lose by taking an unpopular position, and much to gain. There were other unreproducible circumstances of George Ryan's personal life and political position. Ryan neither looked nor acted like a "liberal." Ryan was not a Catholic, and thus the support of the Catholic Church, the pope, and anti–death penalty advocates, such as Sister Helen Prejean, counted doubly on the credit side, as did his lifelong membership and allegiance to the Republican Party. And, equally important, after the appointment of the 2002 Governor's Commission on Capital Punishment there was time for public support to build, with the help of a well-organized group of lawyers, judges, and other anti-death penalty advocates who had been working for a national and state moratorium on executions for years. When the moratorium was announced, it seemed inevitable.

The tale of the massive, unprecedented Ryan commutations, the emptying of Illinois' death row, has been told often and elsewhere. As a highly interested observer at the scene, my strongest impression was of the fortuitousness of the political circumstances: the luck and the hard work of the students and faculty at the Northwestern University School of Law and the Medill School of Journalism, and many others in uncovering the actual innocence of so many people on death row; the 1998 National Conference on Wrongful Convictions and the Death Penalty at Northwestern University; the appointment of a credible and expert, bipartisan Governor's Commission on Capital

Punishment which published a scholarly, factual analysis of the Illinois capital punishment system (Turow, 2003);[46] the new public seriousness after 9/11; the guidance of Governor Ryan's professional staff, especially his close adviser, former Assistant United States Attorney Matthew Bettenhausen, in shaping the Governor's Commission on Capital Punishment and its thoughtful report; the twists and turns of the Rolando Cruz case as a precursor and warm-up for the *Porter* case; the consistent, steady involvement of Professor Lawrence Marshall, Rob Warden, the Center on Wrongful Convictions, the Innocence Project, and many other longtime advocates; the careful cultivation and then the snowballing participation of the national, international, and local legal community; and the role of the media and especially of the expert and experienced editors, feature writers, such as Eric Zorn, and reporters of the *Chicago Tribune.* So many pieces had to fall into place, to reflect off of one another, and reverberate and magnify one another for that unique, historic moment in the history of capital punishment in America to happen. And lest we forget, the commutations almost did not happen ("Halt the Anguish, Gov. Ryan," 2002).[47] A groundswell of opposition to any commutations built in fall 2002 and came close to preventing them. George Ryan always said that he did not make up his mind until just before the commutations were announced.

While there has been some backlash, some retrenching since the commutations, support for the moratorium remains high in Illinois. Politicians running for office in 2004 discovered that the popular political position was the contradiction: to be in favor of the moratorium and to simultaneously express support for capital punishment itself. After the commutations, and after George Ryan left the governor's office, the Illinois legislature created the Capital Punishment Reform Study Committee in 2003, and that committee, of which I am a member, is collecting information and preparing a report, to be filed in 2009 (Capital Punishment Reform Study Committee Act, 2003).[48] In the meantime the statewide moratorium on executions imposed by Governor Ryan remains in effect. The number of death sentences imposed had been falling from before the commutations and the moratorium. But that is true elsewhere. And the exoneration of the innocent continues (Center on Wrongful Convictions, 2006). The Illinois Supreme Court has held that the state could not seek the death penalty again for a person whose sentence of death was pending on appeal at the time of the Ryan commutations, removing from death row several people whose status was unclear (*People v. Morris,* 2006).

Is the death penalty dying in Illinois? That question is too broad. The death penalty in Illinois does not exist as an abstraction. The Ryan commutations were a spectacular event, without precedent in Illinois or in the history of capital punishment in America. In Illinois, however, the very strong forces which have always supported the death penalty are still in place: the elected state's attorneys; the elected judges; continued public support for capital punishment; and, perhaps most important of all, the institutional pull, the sheer inertia of the capital punishment system still being in place, still proceeding with capital prosecutions, still imposing death sentences, and still pushing for executions.

There is less of that pull with the present moratorium on executions continuing, but the momentum of capital prosecutions and convictions, the preparation, the going forward with the trials, the training of the lawyers and judges, the publicity accompanying a capital trial and conviction, all continue to make the legal system, and the public, invested in keeping capital punishment. In Illinois the commitment to the prosecution of capital cases is deeply ingrained in the legal system. Capital prosecutions have been going on without interruption since before reenactment in 1974, continuing a long tradition established well before *Furman*. The impetus may have slowed, but the death penalty is a long way from dying in Illinois. The situation in Illinois is very different from that in New Jersey, where there is a good chance for the repeal of the death penalty under pending legislation. In Illinois the political impetus is in the direction of keeping capital punishment, although the enactment of the reforms of 2003, the continuing of the moratorium, and the appointment of the Study Committee are signals to the contrary.

Is the Death Penalty Dying? The Unexpected Momentum of the Lethal Injection Cases

This brings us to the present moment when the liveliest challenge to capital punishment as a system is, ironically, in the cases challenging the constitutionality of lethal injection. The U.S. Supreme Court recently agreed to hear a case challenging the procedures for lethal injection, causing several states to suspend executions.[49] While the legal events in New Jersey and Illinois were challenging the operation of the death penalty as a system and as applied to individual cases, an entirely different legal challenge to capital punishment was being developed: the argument that the method of execution used by most jurisdictions, lethal injection, was itself the infliction of cruel and unusual punishment, and hence unconstitutional. There is a long history of challenges to methods of execution, with classic challenges based upon Eighth Amendment jurisprudence going back centuries. What is new in the lethal injection cases, what makes them "the ringer" in this long series of legal challenges, is the presentation to courts of scientific and medical evidence documenting exactly what happens during a lethal injection.

The character of the evidence brought forward in these cases is unprecedented. This is what makes the lethal injection cases new. In addition, these are legal challenges to the entire system of capital punishment which are not based upon race, or economic status, or the abuse of prosecutorial discretion, or any characteristic of the defendant, the victim, or the circumstances of the offense or the case. This challenge is not all about the lawyers and judges not doing what they are supposed to do. This challenge has been gaining momentum just as all the reenacting states have either chosen lethal injection initially or have switched to it as the preferred or only method of execution.

Evidence of the mutilation of the body in the cut-down procedures, the bleeding, the continued consciousness, all are being brought to the attention of the courts and the public. Procedures which are supposed to have been "medical" and humane, controlled, highly civilized, are shown to have been the opposite. The people in the white coats are not doctors. The drugs are not just sedatives, but also paralytics. The evidence brought forward is "objective," couched in medical terminology, difficult to dispute. Those offering the evidence are strangers to the criminal justice system. It is not a question of how one judge interprets a statute or constitutional phrase. It is something anyone who has been inside a hospital can understand. The success of this legal tactic, as seen in cases postponing or halting executions in a number of states, is one of the surprises of the past decade and may have systemwide effects (Weinstein, 2006a).[50]

Lethal injection, which the states adopted quickly when evidence of malfunction and mishaps came to light with the electric chair, seemed to be benign until academics and advocates began to pull back the curtain hiding the process (Denno, 2002).[51] There was the bizarre development of the equipment itself, the Rube Goldberg contraption invented by a self-promoting crank ("Dr. Death and His Wonderful Machine," 1990).[52] Then, the embarrassing fact that all state and national medical societies have come out against medical doctors, and others governed by medical ethics provisions, participating in executions, although a recent poll of doctors showed that close to half of the doctors asked had no personal objection to participating in executions.

The fact is that many doctors, nurses, and other medically trained personnel are involved in executions. They do participate and observe executions, in spite of the ethical prohibitions and problems (Denno, 2002, table 17).

There is no sanction imposed upon doctors and medical personnel who participate in executions. Only half of all doctors are members of the state or national medical societies. It is the state licensing agency which can take away a doctor's license, not the professional medical society. Knowledge of doctors' involvement in the execution process is new, however. Their continued participation may be more problematic. The irony is that all of the trappings of a medical procedure which are supposed to make the death penalty more humane and civilized actually do the opposite. Through Freedom of Information Act challenges, information is now coming out about what actually goes on in execution chambers.

The state legislatures flocked to lethal injection in 1977 because it was politically palatable. The legislatures specified lethal injection and left it to the various state departments of corrections to figure out how to do it.[53] The procedures for lethal injection have not changed for thirty years. How it would work included what drugs would be used—the lethal cocktail, as it came to be called—and how and in what combination and sequence the drugs would be administered. Someone else, usually someone without much education who was afraid of losing a job with the state, was left to figure out the details, such as dosages and the implements for the dirty work of killing someone. And the results were not pretty (Denno, 2002, 146–260).[54]

At the time of reenactment, state legislators feared that doctors would not or could not participate in executions. The writers of the regulations engaged in elaborate distancing rituals to ensure that doctors were not the ones who actually pulled the trigger, so to speak (Denno, 2002, 207–60).[55] Many states specify that doctors, usually the state or county coroner, would only certify death. A new breed of civil employee, the execution technician, was created.[56] I was not aware until coming to Illinois of research by psychologists at Stanford and elsewhere which undertook an inquiry into the effects of execution upon those doing or observing the executions (Osofsky, Bandura, and Zimbardo, 2005).[57] Once again, the truth is more bizarre than the imagined situation, as details began to come to light about the protocols, the cavalier attitudes expressed by some legislators and judges, the training of personnel or its absence, and the ghoulish specifics of the procedures themselves.

Lethal injection procedures were adopted by corrections officials who received little or no guidance from the state legislators, and they turned out to be slapdash and designed to mimic a medical act, the giving of a medically appropriate injection. The rest was window dressing: the use of the hospital gurney or stretcher, the white sheets on the gurney, the curtain behind which the witnesses sat, the white coats of the technicians, and the giving of a sedative to the person to be executed. With the exception of the giving of the sedative, the rest of the procedures were all an elaborate stage show to reassure those observing or participating that what was going on was controlled and humane, and medically appropriate.

Evidence of botched lethal injections started to accumulate immediately. And the medical, legal, and academic communities challenged the procedure itself.[58] Meanwhile, everyone associated with the procedure's establishment could blame some other institution for the conundrum: what was supposed to be a kind of "euthanasia" was turning out to be tortuous. The legislators could blame the public for demanding capital punishment. The prosecutors and the defense attorneys could blame the corrections officials and the legislature, and say they were just following the law. The corrections officials and prison administrators, who had to figure out how exactly to put the new method into effect, could blame the lawyers, the judges, and the legislatures. And everyone could blame the convicted murderers about to be executed. After all, if they had not committed those terrible crimes, they would not be causing more trouble by making everyone else worry about whether a method of execution was humane.

The moral disengagement and ambivalence described in the scientific literature by academic psychologists became the subject of narratives in photographic essays, first-person accounts from death row inmates and their advocates, newspaper stories and books (some of which became best sellers), television shows, and highly successful commercial films.[59] Lethal injection had appealed to state legislators as putting murderers to sleep—painlessly, mercifully, cleanly, on a stainless steel table, surrounded by people in white coats who looked like doctors but were not doctors. Some commented that this peaceful a death was too good for people who had themselves tortured and made their victims suffer. The truth was often to the contrary.

The procedure, with minor variations among the thirty-seven states specifying lethal injection, is a three-stage process: the first drug is a sedative, the second drug is to paralyze the inmate; and the third drug stops the heart. The only reason for including the paralytic drug is to sanitize the process and mask the infliction of pain, to paralyze the person being executed so that there is no twitching, screaming, vomiting, or perceptible expression of pain. The only reason for including the paralytic drug is because doctors do not know how long it would take for the other drugs to act. The veterinarians now use quicker and better drugs to euthanize animals. The veterinarians will not use the paralytic agent used in lethal injections in the killing of animals. The pain experienced, if the sedative is inadequate or has not yet reached the brain, is the pain of having a heart attack.

In 2001 only nine states mentioned in their protocols the amount of drugs they were using. Only with the Freedom of Information Act requests did information come out on how the procedures were actually being implemented. This information, available for the first time now, is what makes these cases powerful. In 1978 Texas was not even required to say what drugs were being used. The constitutional theory of the challenge to the method of execution is not new; it is "cruel and unusual punishment," the same as the challenges to hanging and the electric chair, under the principles of the Eighth Amendment. It is the detailed information about what actually happens in the execution chamber, the level of incompetence and indifference, which has caught the attention of the courts, the advocates, and the public.

A factual inquiry in Missouri in 2006 has brought to light that the physician preparing the injections—in violation of the state and national ethics provisions—unilaterally halved the dose of the sedative because of difficulty in dissolving the powder in the liquid because the supplier used a different package. This same doctor testified that he had not seen any written protocols for executions, and the only way in which they might have been written down was if someone observed what he was doing during an execution and wrote that down. This same doctor admitted that he was "still improvising" his technique for executing people, and that he himself was dyslexic and thus it was not unusual for him to make mistakes with numbers. These mistakes, he alleged, were not critical to the work he does as a surgeon. The head of the Missouri Department of Corrections, to whom the doctor reported, had no background in corrections and no background in medicine. He told the dyslexic doctor that he was completely reliant on the doctor to advise him whether changes in the procedures for lethal injection needed to be made (*Taylor v. Crawford,* 2006, 7–10).[60]

Once again raids and inroads are being staked out as to who will take the moral high ground as the lawsuits began to multiply. Recently and surprisingly, the U.S. Supreme Court halted a Florida lethal injection in the last hours in May 2006, on the procedural question of whether the inmate could use Section 1983 to challenge lethal injection. This gives a broader legal theory for inmates to make substantive challenges to lethal injection procedures in the future. The Florida inmate was executed after another procedural ruling at the state level; however, no attorney today can bring a death penalty case without challenging lethal injection itself on constitutional grounds. It would be ineffective assistance to neglect to bring that constitutional challenge now.

At some point the U.S. Supreme Court will have to take a case addressing lethal injection challenges substantively, not just procedurally. And that is why these cases are "the ringer." Just as the Supreme Court appeared to have put to rest the last of the systemwide challenges to capital punishment in the United States, the lethal injection cases have gained a surprising amount of traction. The issue will reach the Supreme Court and have implications for all capital punishment systems currently in place in the thirty-seven states. A federal judge in California has ordered a hearing to take place in September 2006 to review the constitutionality of California's procedures. The prospect of new, protracted proceedings on behalf of the more than 650 men and women on death row in California is a startling new development.

One of the interesting aspects of these lawsuits is that they halt an execution on medical grounds, yet they are nonetheless challenges to the legal system imposing the death penalty as a whole. There are no allegations about due process violations to defendants during arrest, incarceration, or trial, or of discrimination based upon the race of the victim or defendant, or the socioeconomic status of the defendant or victim, or allegations about the inequities generally in the "criminal justice system." These are civil suits, mostly heard in the federal civil courts at the district level, by judges who are not typically criminal judges. They can and are also brought in state courts. This may be an important factor in the character of the decisions. Perhaps these judges, like former Governor George Ryan, are not inured to the brutalities of the criminal justice system. Although the cases may be brought under habeas corpus, they are also being brought as declaratory judgment cases, or simply as civil rights complaints under state or federal law.

For example, U.S. District Court Judge Jeremy Fogel in the *Morales* case in San Jose, California, sent a questionnaire to both counsel, asking counsel what would comprise a constitutionally acceptable procedure for lethal injection (Weinstein, 2006c). The judge wanted to know how the drugs would act and what the qualifications were of the "execution team." This is highly unusual, and not the dismissive treatment which capital defendants may typically receive in the lower federal courts when everyone in the system has seen too many cases. In the *Morales* case the lawyers have objected that it is not their responsibility to come up with constitutional methods for killing their clients. New litigants are bringing these cases, new arguments are being made and being heard afresh. The faces in court are not only the public defenders and members of the anti–death penalty establishment from prior capital punishment battles. As an example of the reach of these cases, the most recent execution in Virginia was an electrocution. In Tennessee an inmate also chose electrocution. These inmates chose electrocution over lethal injection because they thought it was more humane (Death Penalty Information Center, 2006).

The lethal injection cases are straightforward and very democratic: a challenge to the system for implementing the death penalty itself, assuming the death penalty has been correctly applied to a person whose guilt is not in question. It isn't necessary to frame the legal arguments in subtle terms to meet the refinements of the most recent interpretation of the habeas corpus jurisprudence. The arguments are politicized along different lines, and different alliances are being drawn. Having new advocates making the case adds another dimension of unpredictability. And since the other methods of execution have been problematic—hanging because it is too crude, and arguably "cruel" (*Rupe v. Wood,* 1994),[61] the electric chair as demonstrably cruel—the system must figure out another way to execute, or find a way to make this method not cruel.

Perhaps it is because the arguments are more factual than legal that the American Society of Anesthesiologists, who say they are neither for nor against the death penalty itself, has advised its forty thousand members to "steer clear" of participating in executions, saying that the legal system has painted itself into a corner with lethal injection, and it is not the responsibility of the professional anesthesiologists to resolve the legal issues. On the contrary, the society advises, professional anesthesiologists should not be involved in lethal injections in any manner; it is not a medically appropriate sedation.[62]

The federal judges, the lawyers, the journalists, and the advocates have put the information out about the circumstances of botched executions ("Capital Punishment: Cruel and Unusual," 1993). The fiction that lethal injection is analogous to putting the family pet to sleep is no longer tenable. Veterinarians and advocates for animals have gone on record as saying that the procedures used in lethal injections of people would not be sufficiently humane to use in the killing of animals. It will be awkward for state legislators to argue that such executions should continue in the face of this evidence.

A federal judge can hold a hearing under Section 1983 for further factfinding. This is one of the few unobstructed powers of the federal judiciary. U.S. District Court Judge Fernando J. Gaitan Jr., in an evidentiary hearing on lethal injection wrote the following as a factual finding:

> There is no dispute that if an inmate is not sufficiently anesthetized when the potassium chloride [the drug which stops the electrical activity of the heart] is administered, it will cause excruciating pain, as it is administered through the inmate's veins. The inmate, however, would be unable to show he was experiencing discomfort due to the paralyzing effects of the pancuronium bromide [the paralytic agent]. (*Taylor v. Crawford,* 2006, 6)[63]

The inquiry in California is pending and may prove to be the mechanism for Governor Schwarzenegger to declare a statewide moratorium on executions, or to find that there is no constitutionally acceptable method for carrying out the death penalty.[64] As the legal challenges to lethal injection in other state and federal courts proceed, each ruling halting an execution, each factual finding of pain and suffering is reinforcing similar allegations in other cases. Now a case has reached the U.S. Supreme Court. That case when it is decided may result in an unpredictable or surprising alignment among the new judges of this Supreme Court.

Conclusion and Summary

Is the death penalty dying? The illustrative cases put forward here do not answer that question. With the exception of the clear national trend in the lethal injection cases, no predictions are offered in this essay. If these reflections upon three very different case studies have a common theme, it is the unexpected nature of the events which resulted in a very dramatic change in the jurisdiction's application of the death penalty. Decades from now these end results may appear to have been foreordained and inevitable, but to this observer close to the ground, individual decision makers and the particularities of circumstances created a wobbling, momentary coherence that was unpredicted and not likely to be repeated.

In Nigeria the government established an extralegal system for imposing the death penalty, the Armed Robbery Tribunal, and used the very public application of the death penalty to intimidate the public and convince the polity of its legal authority. In the 1980s and early 1990s the Supreme Court of New Jersey, which had a long tradition of independence, fashioned a constitutionally required system for proportionality review and other court-imposed procedural due process guarantees under the leadership of a powerful chief justice who is no longer there.

In Illinois the way was paved for Governor Ryan's blanket commutation by more than two years of serious work by the governor's Commission on Capital Punishment (2002), by the concerted efforts of the national and local legal community supporting a moratorium on executions, and by a set of unpredictable cases, some long in preparation, others not, which unfolded in a relatively compressed time period and revealed that thirteen men on death row in Illinois were either innocent, wrongly convicted, or both.

Of course, Nigeria in the 1970s is sui generis in time, distance, and in the difference of its legal system. There has been a moratorium movement in Nigeria, but executions, including the executions of political prisoners and executions under traditional Sharia law, continue. The Armed Robbery Tribunal is still in effect. There are so many other illegal and unconstitutional state and private killings in that country that capital punishment as an issue of legal principle receives attention only from a few activists and from international human rights groups.

In New Jersey, capital punishment may literally be dying. The support for the death penalty within the legal community seems minimal. There is a legislatively imposed moratorium on executions, and the legislative initiative to abolish the death penalty is pending. Importantly, executions in New Jersey never started again after reenactment in 1982. A legal culture supporting and institutionalizing capital punishment has not been firmly entrenched for decades. The former attorney general, the present governor, some justices of the Supreme Court of New Jersey, as well as many legal organizations, have gone on record as being against the death penalty, and also as saying that capital punishment is a waste of government resources. Illinois is very different from New Jersey, yet both jurisdictions at present have a moratorium on executions. Illinois continues to have a strong institutional commitment to capital punishment within the offices of the state's attorneys, the elected judiciary, and the private bar. That the dramatic commutation of more than 160 death sentences occurred in Illinois is testament to the coming together of an extraordinary set of people, institutions, and circumstances unlikely to be replicated elsewhere. The Illinois commutations have had national reverberations, however, and the innocence movement continues to be strong in Illinois with the presence of the Center on Wrongful Convictions and the other advocacy institutions involved in national and Illinois exonerations.

Finally, some observations on the serendipity of the crop of cases challenging the application of lethal injection as a method for imposing the death penalty. This challenge crosses state and federal jurisdictional lines and threatens to halt all executions in the United States without raising any legal challenge to the death penalty itself, with regard to the manner and constitutionality of its imposition in the state or federal criminal justice system. Lethal injection may well be the next vehicle for overturning a large number of death sentences. I do not think there is the national will at the present time to devote large amounts of energy or invention to "improving" the method of execution in the face of unrelenting stories of execution botches and administrative bungling.

There is one caveat, however. That is, if this country finds itself in an international war, with substantial loss of life at home, then that would transform the political climate regarding domestic capital punishment in unpredictable ways. It might mean that in states such as Texas, executions would continue or escalate with no one paying any attention. Alternatively, it might be that the amount of time, effort, and resources spent on capital cases would suddenly seem to be an extravagant waste. There could be a general lack of interest in continuing our present capital punishment system.

Throwing out the death penalty because of the cruelty of the method has the great rhetorical advantage of not being a "victory" for either the defense or the prosecution. It allows those committed to capital trials and prosecutions not to be blamed, to say that only the last step is unconstitutional. It allows defense attorneys and the general public to argue against executions without appearing unsympathetic to victims or sentimental about defendants on death row. Perhaps this can be the excuse, the face-saving, for the country to realize how tired we all are of capital punishment. The federal constitutional principle of an evolving standard of decency incorporates the idea of "progress" in a civilized society, and might encompass outlawing lethal injection.

As Americans, we like to think there are certain things we do not do, or at least certain things we do not officially sanction. We like to think of ourselves as a country of laws and strong, independent legal institutions. When the state kills, or is poised to kill, the public, those within legal institutions, and those who watch and monitor those systems pay attention and, it is hoped, hold accountable the institutions and their administrators—courts, judges, lawyers, police officers, and prison officials—who are responsible for actions taken in the name of the rule of law.

The rule of law requires judges to ask the hard questions, and it asks lawyers to put the information before judges so that they may ask and answer those questions on the basis of facts. Our entertainment-driven culture is addicted to dramas about murder and will always address issues of guilt, innocence, and punishment on multiple levels. At the end of the day, however, the legal institutions, the courts, must take the responsibility for finding the facts and deciding upon the constitutionality of the official criminal justice system and its methods for imposing the law.

References

Africa Watch. 1991. "Nigeria—On the Eve of 'Change'—Transition to What?" New York: *Human Rights Watch,* October.

American Society of Anesthesiologists. 2006. "Message from the President." http://www.asahq.org.

Amnesty International. 2005. "Appeal for the Abolition of the Death Penalty in Africa." http://www.amnesty.org/.

———. 2006. "Nigeria." http://www. amnesty.org/.

An Act Creating a Study Commission on the Death Penalty and Imposing a Moratorium on Executions and Amending P.L. 1983, ch. 245. 2005. NJ P.L. Ch. 321.

An Act to Make Comprehensive Provisions for Matters Relating to Armed Robbery. Robbery and Firearms (Special Provisions) Act, Cap. 1984.

Bailey, B. 2006. "Lethal Injection Facing Scrutiny, Attention Likely to Amend but Not End Death Penalty." *San Jose Mercury News,* February 26, p. 1A.

Bandura, Albert. 1999. "Moral Disengagement in the Perpetration of Inhumanities." *Personality and Social Psychology Review* 3: 193–209.

Bienen, Leigh B. 1974. "Criminal Homicide in Western Nigeria, 1966–1972." *Journal of African Law* 18: 57–78.

———. 1976. "The Determination of Criminal Insanity in Western Nigeria." *Journal of Modern African Studies* 14: 219–45.

———. 1993. "A Good Murder." *Fordham Urban Law Journal* 20: 585–607.

———. 1996. "The Proportionality Review of Capital Cases by State High Courts After *Gregg:* Only 'the Appearance of Justice.'" *Journal of Criminal Law and Criminology* 87: 130–314.

———. 1998a. "The Quality of Justice in Capital Cases: Illinois as a Case Study." *Law and Contemporary Problems* 61: 193–217.

———. 1998b. "Technician." *TriQuarterly* 104: 192–271.

Bienen, Leigh B., and B. Rottinghaus. 2002. "Learning from the Past, Living in the Present: Understanding Homicide in Chicago, 1870–1930: Newspapers and the Political and Intellectual Climate of the Times." *Journal of Criminal Law and Criminology* 92: 437–554.

Bienen, Leigh B., Neil Alan Weiner, Deborah W. Denno, Douglas Lane Mills, and Paul Allison, 1988. "The Reimposition of Capital Punishment in New Jersey: The Role of Prosecutorial Discretion." *Rutgers Law Review* 41: 27–372.

Bienen, Leigh B., Neil Alan Weiner, Deborah W. Denno, Douglas Lane Mills, and Paul Allison, 1990. "The Reimposition of Capital Punishment in New Jersey: Felony Murder Cases." *Albany Law Review* 54: 709–817.

Bohannan, Paul. 1960. *African Homicide and Suicide.* Princeton, N.J.: Princeton University Press.

"Capital Punishment: Cruel and Unusual." 1993. *The Economist,* January 23, p. 86. Capital Punishment Reform Study Committee Act. 2003. Ill. P.A. 93–605.

Center on Wrongful Convictions. "Illinois Exonerations." 2006. Northwestern University School of Law. http://www.law.northwestern.edu/wrongfulconvictions/.

Consultation with and Supervision over County Prosecutors; Uniform Enforcement of Criminal Laws New Jersey States Annual Section 52: 17B–103. 2006.

Criminal Code Act. 1990. In *The Laws of the Federation of Nigeria,* ed. Law Revision Committee. Portsmouth: Grosvenor.

Death Penalty Information Center. 2006. "Statistics." http:// www.deathpenaltyinfo.org/.

Denno, Deborah W. 1994. "Is Electrocution an Unconstitutional Method of Execution? The Engineering of Death over the Century." *William and Mary Law Review* 35: 551–692.

———. 1997. "Getting to Death: Are Executions Constitutional?" *Iowa Law Review* 82: 319–464.

———. 2002. "When Legislatures Delegate Death: The Troubling Paradox Behind State Uses of Electrocution and Lethal Injection and What It Says About Us." *Ohio State Law Journal* 63: 63–260.

Development Policy Centre Nigeria. 2000. In *Laws of the Federation of Nigeria: A Subject of Analysis,* ed. O. Dina, A. Ajibade, M. Atinmo, and I. Mabawaonku, 262–63. Ibadan, Nigeria.

"Dr. Death and His Wonderful Machine." 1990. *New York Times,* October 18, p. A24.

Forsberg, Mary E. 2005. "Money for Nothing? The Financial Cost of New Jersey's Death Penalty." New Jersey Policy Perspective, http:// www.njadp.org/forms/Cost/Money.

Gregg v. Georgia. 428 U.S. 153 (1976).

"Halt the Anguish, Gov. Ryan." 2002. *Chicago Tribune,* October 20, p. 8.

Hoffman, Jan. 1996. "His Court, His Legacy." *New York Times,* June 30, 13NJ section, p. 1.

Illinois State Police. 2003. "Uniform Crime Reporting Program, Crime in Illinois." www.isp.state.il.us/crime/cii2003.cfm.

Ilo, U. 2004. "The Rope: Country Report on Death Penalty Application in Nigeria." In *Report of the United Nations High Commissioner for Refugees.* Presented at the First African Conference on Death Penalty Application in Commonwealth Africa, Entebbe, Uganda, May 10.

Internet Movie Database. 1995. "Dead Man Walking." http://www.imdb.com/title/tt0112818/.

Laws of the Federation of Nigeria. 1984. Section 402(2)(a)(b) Criminal Code Act, cap. 77.

Marshall v. Cathel. 428 F.3d 452 (3rd Cir. 2005).

McGinniss, Joe. 1991. *Blind Faith.* New York: Random House.

Medwed, Daniel S. 2006. "Anatomy of a Wrongful Conviction: Theoretical Implications and Practical Solutions." *Villanova Law Review* 51: 337–77.

National Association for the Advancement of Colored People Legal Defense and Education Fund. 2006. "Death Row U.S.A., Spring." http://www.naacpldf.org/content/pdf/pubs/drusa/DRUSA_Spring_2006.pdf.

New Jersey Constitution. Article V, section 1, paragraph 5.

Osofsky, Michael J., Albert Bandura, and Philip G. Zimbardo. 2005. "The Role of Moral Disengagement in the Execution Process." *Law and Human Behavior* 29: 371–93.

People ex rel. Carey v. Cousins. 397 N.E.2d 809 (Ill. 1979).

People v. Lewis. 473 N.E.2d 901 (Ill. 1984).

People v. Morris. 848 N.E.2d 1000 (Ill. 2006).

People v. Porter. 489 N.E.2d 1329 (Ill. 1986).

People v. Porter. 647 N.E.2d 972 (Ill. 1995).

People v. Silagy. 461 N.E.2d 415 (Ill. 1984).
Pulley v. Harris. 465 U.S. 37 (1984).
Roper Center for Public Opinion. 2003. Survey. Retrieved on November 2006 from website.
Rosen, B. S. 1984. "A Bold Court Forges Ahead." *National Law Journal* 1 (November 5).
Rupe v. Wood. 863 F. Supp. 1307 (W.D. Wash, 1994), pp. 1, 38–40, 44.
Sarat, Austin. 2005. *Mercy on Trial: What It Means to Stop an Execution.* Princeton, N.J.: Princeton University Press.
Schwaneberg, Robert. 2006. "Marshall Gets Life in Prison." *Star-Ledger,* August 19, p. 1.
State v. Funicello. 286 A.2d 55 (NJ 1972).
State v. Marshall. 586 A.2d 85 (NJ 1991).
State v. Marshall II. 613 A.2d 1059 (NJ 1992).
State v. Ramseur. 524 A.2d 188 (NJ 1987).
Sullivan, John F. 1978. "Penal Code Revision Easing Curbs on Sex Passed in New Jersey." *New York Times,* July 28, p. 1.
Taylor v. Crawford. 2006. No. 05-4173-CV-C-FJG (W.D. Mo., June 26).
Turow, Scott. 2003. *Ultimate Punishment.* New York: Farrar Straus and Giroux.
Vaughan, B. 2006. "New Jersey Seeks Appeal of *Marshall* Ruling." *Press of Atlantic City,* February 2, p. A1.
Waldron, M. 1978. "Byrne Pocket Vetoes Death Penalty Bill." *New York Times,* March 4, p. 45.
Warden, Rob. 2005. "Illinois Death Penalty Reform: How It Happened, What It Promises." *Journal of Criminal Law and Criminology* 95: 381–426.
Weinstein, Henry. 2006a. "Federal Judge Orders Missouri to Stop All Executions." *Los Angeles Times,* June 28, p. A16.
———. 2006b. "Anesthesiologists Advised to Avoid Executions." *Los Angeles Times,* July 2, p. A32.
———. 2006c. "Judge Considering Constitutionality of Lethal Injection Posing Tough Questions." *Los Angeles Times,* October 6, p. B3.
Wolfgang, Marvin E. 1958. *Patterns in Criminal Homicide.* Philadelphia: University of Pennsylvania Press.
———. 2002. "The Report of the Governor's Commission on Capital Punishment."

CHAPTER 3

Anomalies: Ritual and Language in Lethal Injection Regulations

Culture, in the sense of the public, standardized values of a community, mediates the experience of individuals. It provides in advance some basic categories, a positive pattern in which ideas and values are tidily ordered. And above all, it has authority, since each is induced to assent because of the assent of others. But its public character makes its categories more rigid. . . . Any given system of classification must give rise to anomalies, and any given culture must confront events which seem to defy its assumptions. It [the culture] cannot ignore the anomalies which its scheme produces, except at risk of forfeiting confidence.

—Mary Douglas, *Purity and Danger*

I.

When a horse, a cow, a dog, or a grizzly bear is killed under the authority of the government, or by a private party in a planned euthanasia, the veterinarian performing the execution will follow euthanasia guidelines adopted by the American Veterinary Medical Association ("AVMA Guidelines") for the method of euthanasia to be used, including any drugs, restraints, and anesthetics required, so that the pain to the animal is minimized.[1] The "AVMA Guidelines" are directed to the humane death of animals:

> It is our responsibility as veterinarians and human beings to ensure that if an animal's life is to be taken, it is done with the highest degree of respect, and with an emphasis on making the death as painless and distress free as possible. Euthanasia techniques [for

> animals] should result in rapid loss of consciousness followed by a cardiac or respiratory arrest and ultimate loss of brain function. In addition, the technique should minimize distress and anxiety experienced by the animal prior to loss of consciousness.[2]

The "AVMA Guidelines" provide a technical description of stimuli, neural pathways, receptors, feedback, and other scientific topics and terminology before focusing on a description of the anticipated pain for the animal and its prevention. The guidelines explain that the sensation of pain "results from nerve impulses reaching the cerebral cortex via ascending neural pathways."[3] Therefore, the guidelines continue, to the best of our knowledge, pain is perceived only under certain circumstances:

> On the basis of neurosurgical experience in humans, it is possible to separate the sensory-discriminative components from the motivational-affective components of pain.
>
> For pain to be experienced, the cerebral cortex and subcortical structures must be functional. If the cerebral cortex is not functional because of hypoxia, depression by drugs, electric shock, or concussion, pain is not experienced. Therefore, the choice of the euthanasia agent or method is less critical if it is to be used on an animal that is anesthetized or unconscious, provided that the animal does not regain consciousness prior to death.[4]

"The AVMA is fully committed to the concept that, whenever it becomes necessary to kill any animal for any reason whatsoever, death should be induced as painlessly and quickly as possible."[5] The "AVMA Guidelines" "summarize contemporary scientific knowledge on euthanasia in animals and call attention to the lack of scientific reports assessing pain, discomfort, and distress in animals being euthanatized."[6] The AVMA only cites well-supported sources.[7] Therefore, "many reports on various methods of euthanasia [that] are either anecdotal, testimonial narratives, or unsubstantiated opinions" are not included in their list.[8]

Attached to the "AVMA Guidelines" are four appendices categorizing types of euthanasia for animals.[9] For example, appendix 1 lists barbiturates, potassium chloride in conjunction with general anesthesia, and penetrating captive bolt as agents and methods acceptable for large mammals, such as horses and swine.[10] The "AMVA Guidelines" state outright that euthanasia of animals by injection of a paralytic agent without anesthetic is prohibited because it causes too much pain to the animal.[11] Likewise electrocution is not recommended, because the animal may be conscious for a period of time before death.[12] The "AVMA Guidelines" discourage the use of contested and unapproved products for animal euthanasia. Only drugs and methods that have been studied under scientific protocols can be justified.[13] In fact, the AVMA recommends convening "a panel of scientists at least once every ten years to review all literature that scientifically evaluates methods and potential methods of euthanasia for the purpose of producing AVMA Guidelines on Euthanasia."[14]

II.

The protocols and regulations issued by states for lethal injection of humans who have been sentenced to death by a state trial court and are to be killed under the authority of the state are indirect, incomplete, replete with medical and scientific inaccuracies, and padded with irrelevant statements and descriptions of imagined events. When medical doctors are asked for their opinion on the present lethal injection methods, some doctors recommend the three-drug method be replaced with a single large injection of barbiturates.[15] Their advice has been in large part ignored.[16] Prior to abolishing the death penalty, New Jersey was the only state not to include a paralytic drug in its lethal injection protocols.[17] The state protocols for the lethal injection of humans put their emphasis on: the decoration of the rooms where the executions take place, when the curtain should be pulled, the existence and number of syringes, and other miscellaneous paraphernalia and random annotations about equipment.[18] In sharp contrast to the guidelines for animals, the preparation for lethal injections and the procedures afterward often take more space than the instructions for the act itself.[19]

Presumably, Department of Corrections personnel, aided perhaps by other officials, such as the attorney general of the state, write these protocols. The details are distasteful even to read. It is not surprising, then, that state officials have typically resisted their disclosure.[20] Only recently have these regulations been subject to public scrutiny.[21] Professor Deborah Denno of the Fordham University School of Law conducted the first and only comprehensive study in 2001 collecting written protocols of states with public protocols and obtaining information by telephone and e-mail from states with partially private or private protocols.[22]

The protocols are generally addressed not to doctors but to others who carry out or witness the execution. Every professional medical society has forbidden doctors to participate in executions performed by the state.[23] The

American Society of Anesthesiologists has put a statement on its website stating that anesthesiologists should not facilitate or participate in executions.[24] Despite these admonitions, doctors do participate openly in executions in a number of states, at least to pronounce death, and often in other ways as well.[25] The professional competence of those doctors who have been involved has been questioned.[26] Some states go to elaborate lengths to assure their citizens that doctors are not performing the executions.[27]

In spite of the fact that doctors are not usually the writers or readers of these protocols, the protocols often adopt a pseudo-scientific diction and format. For example, Professor Denno notes that the South Dakota regulations declare:

> Any pharmacist . . . is authorized to dispense the substances . . . without prescription [and that] . . . the chemicals will be kept in a secured location. The chemicals to be used are Sodium Thiopental ([a] lethal dose ([to] sedate [the] person), Pancuronium Bromide ([a] muscle relaxant ([to] collapse [the] diaphragm and lungs), and Potassium Chloride ([to] stop [the] heart beat). In between each dose of the prescribed chemical, a saline solution will be run through the I.V. line(s) to ensure that the lines are kept free from any blockage.[28]

The reference to "secured location" in South Dakota's protocols is just one example of how the regulations imply order and control, but in actuality, camouflage carelessness, a lack of attention to relevant detail, or, even worse, avoidance of the law.

New Mexico has over six pages of protocols, according to Professor Denno's study, including a pre-execution inventory and equipment check which requires the injection team to inspect the expiration and/or sterilization dates of all applicable items—replacing outdated items immediately—detailed setup procedures, and a requirement that death be pronounced by a physician after the completion of the injections.[29] One might ask why sterile instruments and materials are required since no postoperative infection is possible.[30] If the procedure undergone is successful, then the recipient of the injection will be dead.

Missouri initially had no written lethal injection protocol.[31] The state public information office informed Professor Denno that the chemicals Missouri used were sodium pentothal, pancuronium bromide, and potassium chloride.[32] Prior to calling a halt to its lethal injections in 2007, Missouri had one of the highest numbers of executions, along with Texas, Virginia, and Oklahoma.[33] Later in 2007, Missouri said that its protocols were confidential and could not be revealed.[34] It is a typical pattern that the states who have executed the most people have been least forthcoming with their written regulations.[35]

Montana's protocols filled an entire page in Denno's study for an "equipment and material checklist" of thirty-nine items for "execution by injection" including: "40 needle [*sic*], 18 Ga., 1 1/2; . . . 18 angiocath; . . . 4 boxes of alcohol preps; . . . 16 rolls of Kling; 4 adhesive tape; . . . 4 scissors, bandage; . . . 3 batteries, flashlight (spares)."[36]

In Montana's Policy No. DOC 3.6.1, the state describes its method of execution:

> The punishment of death must be inflicted by administration of a continuous intravenous injection of a lethal quantity of an ultra fast acting barbiturate in combination with a chemical paralytic agent, until a coroner pronounces that the offender is dead according to accepted standards of medical practice . . . The identity of the executioner and alternate executioner(s) shall remain confidential.[37]

The language of medical equipment, which includes many specific details about ports, tubes, and other technical equipment to ensure a sterile environment, is mixed with the listing of ordinary items such as scissors, "Kling" (the brand name of a commercial wrapping paper), and "bandages."[38] The contrast between the litany of technical terms and the language of everyday items emphasizes the internal contradictions in the protocols. The ordinary items are a reassuring add-on. The state's pseudo-scientific specification of drugs and technical equipment is often without indication of dosage, or with an incorrect dosage, and without assurance that the drug will be administered by appropriately trained persons.[39]

By reciting the technical terms and adopting a tone of certainty, the protocols create the illusion that a "scientifically validated," approved "medical" procedure is taking place, even if competent doctors or trained or competent nonmedical personnel are not present or performing medical procedures such as giving an injection.[40] The repeated history of botched executions and the facts that have emerged from court inquiries give away the lie.[41] A lack of order and control is the reality. The protocols are a mask on chaos.

The protocols governing the killing of humans mix together the mundane and the technical. There is a haphazard nature to what is included or excluded,[42] although the protocols may be pages long with many lists.[43] The purpose is to reassure their readers, including perhaps prospective participants or monitors, that all will be performed in an orderly manner, consistent with the rule of law of which the execution is an expression. And yet the only systematic examination of these protocols to date concluded: "the criteria set out in many of the protocols were far too vague to allow for adequate assessment. When the protocols did offer details, such as the amount and type of chemicals that executioners inject, they often revealed striking errors and a shocking level of ignorance about the procedure."[44] *Morales v. Tilton,*[45] the 2006 case in California, has brought to light the impropriety that has surrounded many lethal injection procedures.[46] Dr. Robert C. Singler, a state medical expert, examined the official logs and records of lethal injections in California and testified during the trial to the disappearance of some of the controlled addictive substances and other improprieties and malfeasance.[47] The lethal injection procedure depends in large part upon precision as to the type and amount of drugs used in the injections. The mismanagement of the drugs is another example of the lack of competent oversight and the absence of training. In short, as Judge Fogel stated in *Morales,* instead of order and control, there exists "a pervasive lack of professionalism."[48]

Texas has executed more people than any other state since *Gregg v. Georgia*[49] was decided in 1976.[50] Its protocol lists the drugs used and announces without documentation or evidence that "the offender is usually pronounced dead approximately [seven] minutes after the lethal injection begins."[51] This statement is neither a rule, a documented fact, the result of "research," a specification, nor a protocol. Presumably this statement is intended to reassure the reader of the protocols that the executions by lethal injection are swift and therefore lawful and "humane." In fact, Texas has had several botched executions by lethal injection in which death did not occur in seven minutes.[52]

The Texas regulations detail how the warden's office shall serve as a command post and that a "medically trained individual (not to be identified) shall insert the intravenous catheter."[53] The Texas regulations serve to reassure someone, perhaps the author of the protocols and those who are going to observe or participate, that all is being done according to plan and in accordance with imagined law.

The Texas protocols also state how the warden will handle the public and the announcement of death.[54] Such statements are not law, nor do they regulate or guide the behavior of state officials when performing an execution. They are public relations text to orchestrate an event for the media and other interested persons. Furthermore, the references to the warden and the centrality of his role in the process, as portrayed in the protocols, strongly suggest that the warden's office wrote the protocols for its own public relations purposes. The South Dakota protocols also contain a strong public relations focus in their concern with ancillary matters such as preparations of surroundings and dress.[55]

Georgia's more than four pages of regulations wear the mantle of extreme technicality. Again, like the protocols in Texas, the following "statements" in Georgia's protocols are descriptions of "what happens next," an orchestration, not an instruction or declaration of "law":

> 16.3.18 The execution is carried out.
>
> 16.3.18.1 Three (3) designated staff members inject lethal solution into intravenous tubing leading to ports in the condemned's arm.
>
> 16.3.18.2 After ten (10) minutes have elapsed, or the heart monitor shows a "flat line" display, the condemned will be checked by two (2) physicians to determine if death had supervened.
>
> 16.3.18 If condemned shows residual life signs, repeat 16.3.18.1 and 16.3.18.2.[56]

If formality and precision are what is being conveyed by the three-digit designations, note that the numbering system is illogical. The regulation instructing to repeat the procedure if there is a botch, or the "condemned" does not die, has the same number, 16.3.18, as the first regulation: "the execution is carried out."[57] If the precise sequencing and orderly progression is the purpose of the numbering system, then the next number should be either "16.3.18.3" or "16.3.19."[58] The numbered precision simulating order and control is nothing more than a sham. It makes no sense.

III.

The killing of people masked by the trappings of medical procedure is not new. In Auschwitz from 1941 onward, an injection of phenol was the preferred method of killing prisoners quickly by doctors, including the notorious Dr. Mengele.[59] "When patients became debilitated or a medical block was considered overcrowded, the SS doctor in charge selected a row of prisoners who were immediately . . . killed by phenol injections."[60] The "injection procedure" was very much like a medical ceremony.[61] "Initially, phenol was injected into a victim's vein, maximizing the medical aura of the entire procedure."[62] "A patient was brought to a treatment room and there was administered a drug by a physician or (in most cases) his assistant, who wore a white coat and used a syringe and needle for the injection."[63]

The technique was later changed to injecting the phenol directly into the heart. Some thought this was a response to the fact that prisoners' veins were often hard to locate, but the actual reason seems to have been greater efficiency.[64] Patients injected by vein might linger for minutes or even an hour.[65] Injections into the heart gave almost immediate results.[66]

> The executioners used to boast about their records. "Three in a minute . . ." And they did not wait until the doomed person really died. During his agony he was taken from both sides under the armpits and thrown into a pile of corpses in another room opposite. And the next took his place on the stool.
>
> There was also substantial mechanization . . . Approximately fifty people could be killed during one and a half to two hours. Thus, an average of two minutes and [twenty-two] seconds sufficed to murder one prisoner.[67]

This testimony describing the manner in which these executions were carried out was not revealed by the government ordering the executions, but only in the postwar trials of German officials and doctors for genocide and war crimes. As lethal injection procedures in the United States are challenged and are scrutinized by courts, many states have responded by providing less, not more, information.[68] State officials seem to be overwhelmingly concerned with protecting and providing reassurance to the state actors issuing the regulations and the state employees carrying out the executions by lethal injection. Their focus is on the appearance of the execution and carrying on when the execution goes badly. The records of the botched executions show confusion and panic at the scene.

The execution of Saddam Hussein illustrates the behavior of a state authority desperate to give the impression that the hanging of a feared and notorious former dictator was carried out in a calm, controlled environment appropriate to a killing undertaken in a principled manner by a legal authority.[69] President Bush remarked, "Saddam Hussein received a fair trial. This would not have been possible without the Iraqi people's determination to create a society governed by the rule of law."[70] In the end, however, the execution came with terrible political swiftness less than two months after his sentence.[71] Hussein's lawyers were not allowed to see their client, nor were they informed of the details of his execution.[72] The details, however, have been saved for posterity. The execution was filmed as a historical record and to provide proof for those who may have doubted it occurred.[73]

The attention to the rituals before a state execution, especially of a notorious criminal, is not new.[74] Historically, in the United States, the executions of high-profile defendants have been public occasions. When the four Haymarket defendants[75] were executed in Chicago on November 11, 1887, a special scaffold was built in the alley next to the Cook County Jail.[76] Before their hangings, the inmates heard the noise of the saw and hammer as the scaffolding was being built all night long.[77] Their movements and conversations that night were well documented.[78]

In a highly ritualized proceeding, the four men to be hanged had a thick leather belt placed around their chests with their arms pinioned just above the elbows and their hands handcuffed behind their backs. [79] Their bodies were then draped in a white muslin shroud, and they were marched through the jail to the gallows rising outside at the closed end of the alley and bordered by the bare whitewashed walls of the jail.[80] In front of the gallows, seated on rows of benches, were the 170 chosen witnesses, more than fifty of whom were reporters, as well as the governor's son, doctors, and jurors, but not all of the wives of those to be executed.[81]

Straps were placed around their ankles, the hangman's noose placed around their necks and tightened, and the shrouds open at the back fastened.[82] "Then white caps, gathered by a string at the neck, were put on, completely hiding the head and face."[83] Their last words were widely reported but interrupted when the signal for the drop was given, and the four fell downwards together.[84] One of the condemned, Spies, writhed, twitched, and repeatedly drew up his legs, with the convulsions continuing for some time.[85] Then the bodies of Parsons and Fischer began to move and jerk.[86]

Beside each body stood a physician who announced, as time elapsed, the pulse of the hanged man.[87] The audience was silent.[88] "At 12:15 P.M. the bodies were cut down from the gallows and placed in wooden coffins . . . The necks of none of the men had been broken by the fall. They had all died from slow strangulation."[89]

IV.

British and Continental rituals and traditions surrounding state executions illustrated by the Haymarket executions continue to be observed today in a sporadic and haphazard manner in the United States. These holdovers from European practices are reflected in many state protocols: statements regarding the prisoner's choice of his method of death, his choice of his final meal, the visit of the religious figure, the solicitation of repentance, the reporting of the prisoner's last words, and the donning of ceremonial clothes.[90] For example, the California protocols specify that the inmate is to be given a new pair of denim trousers and a blue work shirt to wear thirty minutes before the execution.[91]

The white shrouds at the Haymarket executions had dual purposes. Besides being ceremonial, the shrouds served to shield the audience from the sight of faces and bodies expressing agony, as well as to contain bodily fluids and excretions during the execution.[92] When death occurs all muscles relax, and the contents or fluids in the bowels, the bladder, and the mouth are let go. Absent the paralytic agent used today, the observers and the administrators would be confronted with the same uncontrolled biological mess. Of course, this issue could be addressed otherwise, but under the present procedures it is the paralytic agent which accomplishes an easy death for the viewer and the administrators. Unfortunately, it is the inept application of the paralytic agent in the three-drug method which is most likely to make the execution torturous for the condemned, especially when injected incompetently.[93]

The state protocols' concern with cleanliness, unexpired drugs, the insistence upon the color white (white sheets, white walls, and white coats for the technicians), and requirements regarding sterility are analogous to primitive rules governing purity at sites where spirits or evil forces are to be expunged.[94] This attention to sterility both promotes the medical illusion and affirms the primitive need for rituals to purify the place where a controlled death or sacrifice will occur.

The state protocols never use the word "kill." Instead, the language is: "the technician will start the flow of chemicals";[95] or "the injection team shall administer the chemical agents."[96] Lethal injection regulations often adopt the passive voice and maintain a narrow focus on a fractured series of minute actions. This introduces a false solemnity and masks the fact that lethal injection, if performed competently, is an act of euthanasia, the painless killing of a person by medical means, which is illegal in every state.[97] The slowing down of the action in its description in the protocols implies that great care will be taken.

The New Jersey protocol in place until the repeal of the death penalty in December 2007 carefully described how the drugs should be administered, but never mentioned to whom they were administered: "the condemned shall be covered from the waist down with a white sheet and provided with a pillow for the head . . . [then] the institution team physician shall administer the appropriate dosage."[98] The protocol continues in the same manner, referring to arms, veins, buttocks, deltoid muscle, heart rate, and pulse, without attaching any of these to a person.[99] The one exception is its reference to a television monitor which is positioned to permit the executioner to view the condemned's head, chest, and intravenous insertion site.[100]

Veterinarians, on the other hand, are explicit about what they are doing, for example when discussing methods:

> Barbiturate overdose is an acceptable procedure for euthanasia of many species of animals raised for fur. The drug is injected intraperitoneally and the animal slowly loses consciousness. It is important that the death of each animal be confirmed following barbiturate injection. Barbiturates will contaminate the carcass; therefore the skinned carcass cannot be used for food.[101]

State legislators could create an exception for lethal injection to the state's prohibition of euthanasia. If executions were done without inflicting pain or suffering of the condemned, then they would essentially be acts of euthanasia committed without the person's consent. The regulations accompanying the Oregon Death with Dignity Act, for example, explicitly exempt involved professionals from liability under other statutes such as the ones prohibiting euthanasia.[102] A similar provision could be created for lethal injection.

There is a distinction to be made between aspects of suffering by the executed person which are held to be unconstitutional[103] and the perception of pain and suffering of the person being executed which is distasteful or unpleasant to those watching or carrying out the executions. There is no constitutional violation of the rights of the person watching the execution or participating in the execution when a botch causing suffering occurs. Yet complaints by observers of the gore produced by death by firing squad, the smell of burning flesh during electrocutions, and the distastefulness of seeing parts of people's faces being burned, or the twitching of the hanged, seem to have influenced the legislature's choice of the method of execution as well as the structure of the state protocols.[104]

Another variation on the Continental tradition of the anonymous executioner is the avoidance of direct references to the three executioners, who are placed behind a screen or curtain and none of whom are to know who actually operated the syringe with the lethal drug. Not only does this conceal the identity of the executioner from the public, but it also removes the responsibility for the act from those performing the killing.[105] The traditional hooding or masking of the executioner in Europe was to conceal his identity from the community so that the executioner would not be an outcast, a pariah, or the object of fear or retaliation.[106] The current lethal injection method takes the historical practice of concealment one step further. Now, not even the execution technicians know which of the three of them is responsible for the actual killing.[107]

V.

The form and content of the protocols are a grim parody of "real" laws and regulations. They neither define penalties for prohibited behavior (as criminal statutes do) nor establish a relationship of duty and responsibility (as civil regulations do). Instead, state protocols are excruciatingly detailed descriptions of imagined events. The performance of minor tasks and the orchestrations of the "event" are set out in slow motion with ludicrous precision. See, for example, the Indiana protocols:

> (3.) Shortly after midnight, the inmate is escorted from the holding cell, and placed on a gurney, secured to the gurney and moved to execution room.
>
> (4.) Curtains are only closed when the offender is brought to the holding cell.
>
> (5.) After all preparatory work has been completed, the witnesses are moved into area, seated, and the blinds are opened. The process begins and ends. The blinds are closed and the physician then makes pronouncement of death.[108]

"The process begins and ends" in the above protocol is not a statement of law or a direction as to how to proceed. It is a description of an imagined event in the future. If the regulations were instructions, such as those for unlocking a door or setting a clock, they would simply set out what to do. They would look more like the guidelines for killing animals set out by the AVMA.

Even in the most extreme situation of a completely botched and torturous execution, the failure to follow the protocols would not result in liability for state actors, nor would there be any penalty imposed upon the executioners for the botch.[109] The liability and responsibility for state actors is created by the Eighth Amendment to the U.S. Constitution, which purports to protect an individual against the imposition of cruel and unusual punishment by the state.[110] The penalty for professional incompetence in a state job is generally to be fired. Yet in reality, some states have explicitly held that the protocols for lethal injection are exempt from review under administrative procedures acts.[111]

The bizarre attention to minute, irrelevant detail—the ceremonial opening and closing of the curtain, the tolling of midnight, the precise details of the imagined time frame—are pure pronouncements of ritual. Care is not directed to whether the person being executed will suffer unnecessarily. The protocols are stage directions to ensure the reader, whomever that may be, that the execution will proceed in a controlled and orderly manner, even if it does not.

Note that the Indiana protocol states: "The time frame between escorting the offender from the holding cell to the pronouncement of death is approximately one (1) hour, twenty (20 minutes) [*sic*]. The time frame from the time the IV is inserted to the time of pronouncement of death is approximately twenty-five (25) minutes."[112] Does this imply that a longer time frame, one that exceeds "twenty-five minutes" for the insertion of the IV until the pronouncement of death, would be too long, perhaps even suggesting an Eighth Amendment violation? If the entire procedure takes more than one hour and twenty minutes, is that a violation of procedures, leading to a claim? Is a writ of mandamus a possibility? Such questions highlight the actual nonfunctionality of the legal limbo of the protocols.

The measurement of how long it takes to die during an execution is a historic part of the ritual and the factual record.[113] It is also often a crucial detail in reports of alleged botched executions.[114] Twenty-five minutes is a long time for a drug that stops the heart to take effect. Death should occur within a few seconds or minutes, if a barbiturate is administered competently. It is the administration of the other drugs, including the controversial paralytic agent, which takes longer. If the drugs are administered incompetently, death will take longer or not occur.[115] Does the reference to timing in the protocols imply that the administrators of the lethal injections are waiting to see when the paralytic drug takes effect before injecting the heart-stopping drug?

Georgia's protocol is highly ritualistic and includes pages of instructions for setting up the place of execution, the designation of the witnesses, the "communications checks," and other incidental preparations which occur one hour before execution.[116] In contrast, the execution itself is accorded only a few lines.[117] The detailed instructions even continue after the execution is completed. The protocol states the "microphone is turned on—the fact of death is then announced to the witnesses by the warden . . .—the microphone is turned off. The curtains . . . are then closed."[118] What is the purpose of these specifications? Would the warden be reprimanded or sanctioned if the microphone is not turned off at the "correct" time, or not turned on at all? Or is the protocol's purpose to ensure that the death rattle, breathing, or thrashing of the person being executed will not be heard by the witnesses?

Another kind of anomaly is seen in the phenomenon of the "ghost" regulations: elaborate protocols for imposing lethal injections in states where executions are unlikely to occur, or will never occur.[119] For example, New Jersey abolished the death penalty in December 2007, yet it had one of the most elaborate sets of regulations.[120] Even before abolition it was not likely New Jersey would have executed anyone in the near future. Before repeal the trial courts had sentenced few to death, and the state high court had overturned twenty-six death sentences before upholding one.[121] The state had executed no one since 1963.[122] Nonetheless, New Jersey published a highly detailed series of lethal injection protocols: "to ensure proper dispatch of the intent of the legislature and to ensure the integrity of the Department [of Corrections], death by lethal injection must be executed in a manner befitting the solemnity of such an act."[123]

VI.

To point out the discrepancies or lack of logic in the protocols, however, is to fall into the trap of ceding that the regulations are logical or that they may perform the function of imposing the law. The fact that a protocol addresses when the curtain (or the blinds) are to be closed or opened gives the game away. The protocols are window dressing, stage directions, the establishment of ritual, designed to create an illusion of an orderly, humane, dignified procedure for a controlled euthanasia. This illusion is important to those managing the killing because the appearance of order presented to the public provides protection if the execution does not proceed as portrayed.

When regulations are created to govern the painless killing of an animal, they don't fill pages with instructions about curtains, or the last meal, or how the witnesses shall be seated or escorted and what they will see or not see. The first concern is limiting the pain to the animal.[124] The question of the stress or difficulty for the actors performing the killings is addressed, but only as incidental to concerns for the animal.[125]

The lethal injection protocols attempt to overlay the execution with a civilized veneer. If the condemned screams or struggles with the catheter, that may make the observers uncomfortable.[126] The portentousness of the moment, crafted by the clock, the white sheets, the false solemnity of the staging, the authority of the lab coats and uniforms, would be undermined or destroyed by signs of suffering.

Execution by lethal injection as practiced must be intended to be punishment. If the state legislators authorizing the method for lethal injection simply intended to be humane, to bring about an easy death, they would write regulations authorizing a large single dose of a fast-acting barbiturate. The present inclusion of the paralytic drug, so that the colon, the lungs, and face are frozen, so that the person being executed won't scream or thrash, vomit or defecate, undermines the legitimacy of the death penalty and the rule of law itself.

If states continue to insist upon these semi-public executions, if the American commitment to the death penalty is so entrenched that society cannot give up these killings and their rituals, at the least we should admit, for our own self-respect, as well as out of respect for those sentenced to death, that the gurney, the white sheets, the curtains, the lab coats, are cultural trappings, stagecraft, for the comfort and satisfaction of the observers and the peace of mind of the actors. The law owes to itself and its practitioners that honesty, that acknowledgment.

A murderer is executed because his acts defy moral, social, and cultural principles and have, in the judgment of the law, warranted the taking of his life. The person being executed has been deemed by the law to be unfit to live in a civilized society. It is the state who has made that judgment and who must carry out the killing under the authority of its laws.

The state must conduct itself—through its agents, institutions, and regulations—with respect for what it is doing, with dignity and respect for the person receiving the punishment, and with an acknowledgment of the manner in which it metes out death.[127] For the highest court in a nation of laws to ignore the current practice of lethal injections and to put a rubber stamp on these lethal injection protocols, which do not regulate or monitor state-authorized punishment, but set out an imagined repetitive reassuring ritual, is to condone state-authorized ineptitude, bungling, and deception. To turn a blind eye to such activities by state actors undermines the legitimacy of the state and all legal institutions, including the court itself.

CHAPTER 4

The Quality of Justice in Capital Cases: Illinois as a Case Study

My colleagues are decent and good people. Just as the execution of an innocent person is inevitable, it is inevitable that one day the majority will no longer be able to deny that the Illinois death penalty scheme, as presently administered, is profoundly unjust. When that day comes, as it must, my colleagues will see what they have allowed to happen, and they will feel ashamed.

—J. Harrison, *People v. Bull* (1998)

I. Introduction

The federal constitutionality and moral authority of state capital punishment schemes are predicated upon the assumption that the system of state court appeals is thorough, reliable, and honest.[1] The relatively recent restrictions on the availability of federal habeas corpus have removed the possibility of federal court review to "correct," or adjust for deficiencies in, the administration of justice at the state level. By 1998, the procedural restrictions in capital cases on federal habeas corpus, which were designed to restrict constitutional challenges to state-imposed death sentences, had had their intended effect: it is now very difficult to receive a hearing in federal court on a constitutional challenge to a state death sentence.[2] At the same time, the politics surrounding the election and retention of state judges has made it more difficult for judges to overturn or to refuse to impose death sentences without losing their judgeships.[3] Recent analyses of juror decision-making in capital cases, moreover, suggest that jurors may be more fallible than previously thought.[4]

Despite these difficulties, most Americans assume that when innocent persons are sentenced to death, or when death sentences are imposed in an unfair trial (for example, because of inadequate representation or prejudice and bias), the matter will be corrected when these facts come to the attention of appellate courts or the press. This article asks whether such assumptions about the quality of justice are warranted.[5] It will do so by examining, as an example, the quality of appellate review in a single state, Illinois, since its reenactment of the death penalty in 1974.

The Illinois cases show us the contemporary death penalty in a large northern industrial state. The Illinois capital statute[6] is typical—it provides for the imposition of the death penalty upon the request of the prosecution only for first-degree murder, only after the consideration of statutory aggravating and mitigating factors, and may be imposed by a jury or by a judge without a jury. In theory, all the procedural due process protections are in place. Yet a recent study by the *Chicago Tribune* documented over three hundred cases of prosecutorial misconduct in Illinois, including many in capital cases.[7] The constitutional issues concerning the application of the capital statute, furthermore, have been extremely divisive in the Illinois Supreme Court and in the federal Court of Appeals for the Seventh Circuit (which has jurisdiction over federal collateral challenges to Illinois capital cases). At different points, some aspects of the Illinois capital statute have been declared unconstitutional by both federal and state judges. Those rulings ultimately have always been overturned. Even when four of seven sitting justices on the Illinois Supreme Court simultaneously believed that the statute was unconstitutional, neither the statute nor its application was held to violate federal or state constitutional principles.[8]

Twenty years after the first constitutional challenge to the capital statute reached the Illinois Supreme Court in 1979, the state's capital sentencing structure remains intact. The infirmities challenged repeatedly have remained basically unchanged. Capital issues are still the source of bitter and divisive exchanges between the justices of the Illinois Supreme Court.[9] The opinions, for all of their "consideration" and "argument" over constitutional issues and for all of their rhetoric, have left in place a capital case processing system in which death sentences are rarely overturned.

II. The Illinois Experience

The history of capital punishment in Illinois is in many respects unexceptional. The state has a long practice with the death penalty and has not engaged in any innovative experiments in its jurisprudence. Illinois is a large midwestern state and includes Chicago, one of the nation's legal centers. Illinois is not a traditional death penalty stronghold like Texas, Florida, California, or New York, nor is it in the South. Like most states, it elects judges and prosecutors.[10] It also has a strong and active defense bar, an especially active ACLU, and a long tradition of pro bono representation in capital cases.

Illinois has sentenced innocent persons to death and has set aside death sentences when the convictions were found to be wrongfully imposed.[11] Illinois did not rush to execute one of the most notorious serial killers, John Wayne Gacy.[12] In January 1996 Governor Edgar commuted the death sentence of Guinevere Garcia, the first death sentence commuted by a governor elected in 1994 on a strong pro–death penalty platform.[13] The case received national attention, but not nearly so much as was paid to the case of Karla Faye Tucker in Texas, who was ultimately executed in 1998.[14] Most recently, on November 27, 1998, the Illinois Supreme Court stayed the execution of Willie Enoch to allow for additional DNA testing. Newly elected Governor George Ryan now faces the decision whether to order this next execution; Ryan also campaigned as a strong supporter of the death penalty.[15]

Background

Illinois reenacted the death penalty in 1974. The Illinois Supreme Court upheld the capital statute in 1979 and 1981.[16] The first post-reenactment execution in the state did not occur until 1990. As of February 1, 1999, the Illinois death row population was 161, and the state had executed eleven persons.[17]

The Illinois capital statute is broad in the scope and inclusiveness of its statutory aggravating factors.[18] The statutory aggravating factors include the relatively narrow (such as the killing of a police officer, corrections officer, or witness; a two-victim homicide; an incarcerated killer; a victim over sixty years old or under twelve years old) and the broad (a drug conspiracy; a cold, calculated, and premeditated manner of killing; a murder involving torture; a murder involving a drive-by shooting). The felony-murder aggravating factor includes, in addition to the common-law felonies, "streetgang criminal drug conspiracy"[19] and aggravated stalking, and also encompasses even an attempt to commit any of the enumerated felonies. As in other states, the trend in Illinois in the 1990s has been to expand the list and broaden the scope of statutory aggravating factors;[20] the number of statutory aggravating factors has risen from seven to seventeen since reenactment. On the other hand, only the persons who committed the homicidal act are eligible for the death penalty, which decreases the range of death eligibility. Nonetheless, the range of potentially death-eligible cases, and consequently the range of the prosecutor's discretion, is broad. In addition, the statute is not specific about the timing of the state's decision to seek the death penalty; it states only that "where requested by the [s]tate, the court shall conduct a separate sentencing proceeding."[21] The judge may conduct the penalty phase without a jury. If a jury is used, Illinois does not allow the judge to override the jury's decision not to sentence to death, but the judge may override the jury's sentence of death and sentence the defendant to life imprisonment only.

Arbitrariness introduced by prosecutorial discretion. Soon after reenactment, the question arose whether the Illinois Supreme Court had authority to review the discretionary decisions of prosecutors or the possibility of arbitrariness or bias caused by different patterns of charging capital cases at the local level.[22] Different policies of prosecutors and the county-by-county disparities in capital prosecution and sentencing have long been identified as a source of arbitrariness in patterns of capital sentencing.[23] On the national level, the question of a state high court's willingness or power to review such patterns and discrepancies has a long history.[24] The fight over whether the Illinois Supreme Court could or would review prosecutorial discretion in the selection of cases for capital prosecution was an important and persistent issue in the state high court's appellate review of the constitutionality of the state's capital punishment statute. The debate split the court.

The issue of prosecutorial discretion is confusing because the justices have different, but overlapping, perspectives on the bias and arbitrariness introduced by prosecutorial discretion. The broad view is that the exercise of prosecutorial discretion in the selection of cases for capital prosecution within a single local jurisdiction is unlimited, unchecked, and unreviewed and unreviewable. This necessarily introduces arbitrariness because the local districts differ. Some are urban, and some are suburban; some local jurisdictions have few death-eligible homicides, and some have over a hundred each year. A related but distinct analysis is that prosecutors have different attitudes toward the death penalty; some are more zealous than others. Some prosecutors may charge every death-eligible case as a capital case, while others will select only a subset of death-eligible cases for capital prosecution. The individuality of the prosecutors necessarily introduces caprice and disparities. Therefore, whether a case is prosecuted as a capital case is a matter of chance depending upon the characteristics of the legal jurisdiction where the crime was committed.[25]

In addition, the justices considered contrasting arguments based on the separation of powers. On the one hand, by choosing which death-eligible cases will be prosecuted as capital cases, prosecutors are, in effect, engaging in the sentencing decision reserved for judges exclusively. On the other hand, it may violate the doctrine of separation of powers for the judiciary to review the exercise of prosecutorial discretion in the selection of cases for capital prosecution, either in individual cases or for systemwide and systematic arbitrariness and disproportionality.

A series of early cases challenged the constitutionality of the Illinois statute and the operation of the state's capital punishment system.[26] Initially, the debate before the state high court focused on the narrow issue of the doctrine of separation of powers.[27] Then an unusual and increasingly bitter debate arose over the precedential status of previous opinions by individual justices on the state high court, some of whom had changed their minds.[28]

In 1979 a trial court held the Illinois capital punishment system unconstitutional on the ground that the statute granted prosecutors unlimited discretion in the selection of cases for capital prosecution, encroaching upon the exclusive authority of the judicial branch to impose criminal sentences.[29] Under the statute, only the county prosecutor could request a capital penalty-phase hearing after the guilt phase; thus, the prosecutor was effectively engaging in a sentencing decision and intruding into the judicial branch's prerogative.[30]

In *Carey v. Cousins,* the Illinois Supreme Court overturned this outcome and upheld the capital statute despite the prosecutor's unilateral discretion in deciding when to charge a case as a capital one.[31] A four-justice majority of the seven-member court held that this prosecutorial discretion did not differ significantly from the procedures upheld by the U.S. Supreme Court in *Gregg v. Georgia.*[32] The *Cousins* dissent (Justice Ryan, joined by Justices Goldenhersh and Clark) argued that the statute contained no guidelines to prevent the arbitrary exercise of discretion by the prosecutor. Consequently, the statute violated the separation of powers provision of the state constitution[33] because the imposition of a sentence within the limits prescribed by the legislature is purely a judicial function.[34] The language of the dissenting opinion was unequivocal.[35]

The majority focused on the timing of the prosecutor's decision to seek the death penalty. The dissent emphasized the arbitrariness and county-by-county disparities in the state system as a whole. The timing of the prosecutor's announcement of the decision to seek the death penalty is an unconvincing technicality;[36] it does not answer the general objections articulated by the dissent.

Because the prosecutor's decision to request a penalty phase hearing was unguided, the dissent argued that some prosecutors will consider the offense and the offender, while others will consider the statutory aggravating factors but not the mitigating factors. The same potential for arbitrariness exists in the prosecutor's decision to seek the death penalty at the charging stage or at any other time. Indeed, because the defense is under no duty to disclose mitigating evidence prior to the sentencing phase, the prosecutor may be unaware of mitigating factors when deciding whether to seek the death penalty. The dissent concluded "that the statute confers this discretion not upon one individual, but upon the State's Attorney in each of the 102 counties in this [s]tate. In view of the absence of statutory directive to the prosecutor, each State's Attorney is free to establish his own policy as to when sentencing hearings [that is, the imposition of the death penalty] will be requested."[37]

Five years later, the Illinois Supreme Court addressed a series of due process and constitutional issues in capital cases in *People v. Lewis* (*Lewis I*), including the standard for incompetence of counsel.[38] The court again upheld the statute against several challenges to capital case prosecutorial decision-making, including the prosecutor's authority to seek the death penalty after the defendant rejects a plea of guilty to a non-death sentence.[39]

In 1981, however, the character of the court's decision changed. The previous dissenters now voted to sustain the law. Chief Justice Goldenhersh, who had dissented in *Cousins,* now concurred in upholding the statute, stating that the statute as applied was constitutional and that the court had an obligation to follow the holding of *Cousins.*[40] The only justice new to the court since *Cousins,* Justice Simon, dissented in *Lewis I* on the grounds explained in the *Cousins* dissent.[41] Justice Simon singled out county-by-county disparities as the overriding constitutional infirmity.[42] Thus, four of the seven justices (the three *Cousins* dissenters and Justice Simon) believed that the statute was unconstitutional, but the court nevertheless upheld it.[43] The court was at a curious juncture.

The same defendant was subsequently resentenced to death. In 1984 the constitutionality of this second death sentence came before the Illinois Supreme Court in *Lewis II,* along with other challenges to the capital statute.[44] In this appeal, the court considered a compilation of statistics presented by the defense on the application of the death penalty in felony murder cases; the statistics again raised the question of the arbitrariness introduced by unguided and unreviewable prosecutorial discretion in the selection of capital cases, apparent from the county-by-county disparities.[45] Although the *Lewis*

II appeal primarily focused on the duty of the prosecutor to disclose information favorable to the defense and on the competence of counsel, the majority declared that the statistical evidence of discrimination presented was inconclusive and unreliable (on the basis of the one expert witness called to testify as to the evidence's validity), and ruled that any arbitrariness caused by the exercise of prosecutorial discretion was not unconstitutional.[46]

Lewis's case was then reviewed on a federal habeas corpus petition. The federal district court held for the petitioner on the issue of ineffective assistance of counsel at the sentencing phase, but it did not reach the issue of the constitutionality of the death sentence as applied.[47] Despite an extraordinary effort by a team of subsequent defense advocates who uncovered shocking evidence of prosecutorial suppression of exculpatory evidence and other serious constitutional violations, the U.S. Court of Appeals for the Seventh Circuit affirmed, upholding the conviction as to guilt, but overturning the death sentence on the grounds of ineffective assistance of counsel and prosecutorial misconduct at the penalty phase.[48]

The unusually divided character of the Illinois Supreme Court also was evident in another 1984 case, *People v. Silagy.*[49] The *Silagy* opinion is disturbing for a number of reasons. The extreme nature of the defendant's mental abnormalities, including past and present delusions, appears throughout the opinion, distracting from the court's focus upon the legal technicalities of waiver and other issues. The defendant dismissed his counsel and represented himself at the penalty phase, refusing to submit any mitigating evidence.[50] The defendant even asked to be executed. The prosecution's own psychiatrist referred to the defendant as a psychotic. Despite the defendant's argument that the psychiatric testimony on insanity would have been presented differently at trial had the defense known the prosecution would seek the death penalty, the court reiterated its earlier holding that the defendant did not need to know the state's intention to seek death before the penalty phase.[51]

The same year, in *People v. Albanese,*[52] two of the three justices who had dissented in *Cousins* concurred specially in again upholding the statute, stating that the majority opinion in *Cousins* was the law until overturned by the U.S. Supreme Court.[53] (Ultimately, the U.S. Supreme Court never reviewed the constitutionality of the Illinois capital statute as applied, or addressed the issues raised in these cases.)[54] The chief justice of the Illinois Supreme Court noted that he had authored several opinions upholding the death penalty statute on the authority of *Cousins.*[55] Justice Clark stated that he thought that when the court did not strike down the statute as unconstitutional in

Cousins, the court "permitted prosecutors, the General Assembly, the judiciary, and criminal defendants, as well as the citizens of Illinois, to rely on our pronouncement that the act was constitutional . . . A great disservice to the stability of the law would be perpetrated by this court [if it now declared the statute unconstitutional]."[56]

Justice Simon again rejected the majority's (the former *Cousins* dissenters') reliance upon the doctrine of stare decisis,[57] noting that the chief justice's specially concurring opinion was delivered to him only "moments before the opinions in this case were made public,"[58] perhaps indicating the extent of the division of the court on this issue. Justice Simon subsequently resigned from the court.

A considerable amount of prosecutorial discretion still exists in the Illinois death penalty system in 1998.[59] In Cook County, the county which includes Chicago, the prosecutor is still under no obligation to notify the defense of his intention to seek the death penalty until the first day of trial, when jury selection begins. As a matter of practice, the judge will ask the prosecutor in pretrial conference whether he is planning to death-qualify[60] the jury, which requires special jury calls. The state may indicate its intention at that point, but is not required to do so. The defense may file a motion requesting the state's intent to seek the death penalty, but the prosecution is under no obligation to reply. The state need not declare its intent at the outset, even if the facts of the case make clear that the defendant's crime is death-eligible.[61] (Other states have not followed this practice.)[62] The state may also accept a plea bargain for a sentence less than death until the beginning of the sentencing phase of a capital trial.

The federal practice[63] is in sharp contrast to the standard in Illinois. Under the two federal death penalty statutes, the drug kingpin statute[64] and the Clinton crime bill,[65] the decision to prosecute a case as capital in any federal jurisdiction must be approved personally by the attorney general of the United States in Washington, D.C. The U.S. attorney must also serve notice to the defense within "a reasonable time before trial" that the United States intends to seek the death penalty and which statutory and nonstatutory[66] aggravating factors will be introduced at trial.[67] After the filing of the notice, additional aggravating factors may not be added without a showing of cause. (The prosecutor may withdraw the notice of factors at any time, however, without the approval of the attorney general.) In practice, the Notice of Intention to Seek the Death Penalty, including the specific facts of the statutory and nonstatutory aggravating factors, is served soon after indictment because whether the case is capital triggers other important procedural features, including how many defense attorneys will be appointed, their qualifications, the rate at which the defense will be paid, whether the defense counsel will be Public Defender staff or private counsel from a panel of eligible attorneys, the length of the trial, the number of jurors, and the different character of jury selection in a capital case.

The aggregate data on capital sentences and executions in Illinois. The amount of time and money courts spend on capital appeals has been characterized as "staggering."[68] In 1984 the death row population in Illinois was 59; it increased by 178 percent between 1984 and 1996.[69] There had been 7 executions by 1996, and 164 persons were on death row. Executions as a percentage of the death row population were 4 percent in Illinois, compared to 42 percent in Delaware, 33 percent in Utah, and 21 percent in Texas.[70] By January 1, 1998, Illinois had executed 10 persons, 2.3 percent of all executions nationwide, ranking the state tenth in the number of executions.[71]

The first execution in Illinois after reenactment took place in 1990, nine years after the constitutionality of the death penalty statute was upheld.[72] Illinois' death row population ranks at the high end of the middle group of states (with, for example, Pennsylvania, Alabama, North Carolina, and Ohio).[73] Illinois has a larger death row population than its neighboring state, Indiana, and a larger death row population than some states considered the bedrock of the death belt: Louisiana, Mississippi, and Georgia.[74]

Illinois Supreme Court reversal and affirmance patterns.[75] According to the Department of Corrections, a total of 255 death sentences have been imposed in Illinois since 1977.[76] The Illinois Supreme Court has set aside 94.[77] The court reversed and remanded for a new trial 42 convictions; the sentence of death was reversed and remanded for a new penalty hearing in 36 cases. In 16 cases, the court vacated the death sentence and remanded for a sentence less than death.

The reasons for the reversals included a wide range of appellate issues: errors in judicial instructions and in the finding of statutory aggravating factors, errors in the admission of evidence, many cases of ineffective assistance of counsel, instances of improper and prejudicial conduct by prosecutors, errors in jury selection, and other familiar and commonplace trial errors.[78]

Death Sentences Imposed by Corrupt Judges

In 1996 the U.S. Court of Appeals for the Seventh Circuit held in *Bracy v. Gramley* that the habeas corpus petitioners, who had been sentenced to death, were not entitled to a new trial or to seek discovery to further examine the possibility that the trial judge had been biased, despite the fact that they had been sentenced to death by Judge Thomas Maloney, who had been convicted of taking bribes during the period when he considered their cases.[79] The court concluded that a habeas petitioner must show actual bias, not simply the appearance of bias. While refusing to allow the petitioners the opportunity to gather evidence of judicial bias, the majority offered its opinion that the defendants were guilty:

> The evidence that was admissible shows that they were guilty and this is important because, with a few exceptions, a person convicted in a state court may not obtain an order for a new trial from a federal court on the basis of constitutional errors committed at the trial unless the errors result in actual prejudice, or, equivalently, unless they substantially influenced the verdict.[80]

The Seventh Circuit rejected a large body of law holding that the appearance of justice is as important as the fact of justice, and stated that "for bias to be an automatic ground for the reversal of a criminal conviction the defendant must show either the actuality, rather than just the appearance, of judicial bias, or a possible temptation so severe that we might presume an actual, substantial incentive to be biased."[81] For the majority of the Seventh Circuit,

> The argument that a judge who accepts bribes in some cases is corrupt in all is not a sufficiently compelling empirical proposition to persuade us to treat this case as if Judge Maloney had taken a bribe from the government to convict. If the argument is rejected, ours is a case in which there is merely an appearance of impropriety in the judge's presiding, and an appearance of impropriety does not constitute a denial of due process. Appearance of impropriety there was. We know this because if a judge were under indictment for accepting bribes he would not be permitted to hear any cases.[82]

Yet Judge Maloney was not simply indicted for bribery—he was convicted of bribery. If he was unfit to be a judge, why was he not unfit in all the cases he had heard?[83]

Ironically, the fact that the judge took bribes probably would have met the standard for disqualification of the judge prior to trial under the standard for recusal for extrajudicial bias: "Parties seeking to recuse a judge for extrajudicial bias must show only that a reasonable person, aware of the relevant circumstances, might harbor doubts about the judge's impartiality."[84]

The Seventh Circuit claimed that it was not minimizing the problem of judicial corruption.[85] Its reliance on the "guilty anyway" principle, however, itself violates the norms of ethical and principled judicial decision-making. Even with the petitioners' additional proof that the prosecution had knowingly introduced perjured testimony from the principal identifying witness, the Seventh Circuit held that all of the evidence produced was insufficient to grant a new trial.[86]

The opinion of dissenting Judge Rovner is stinging:

> No right is more fundamental to the notion of a fair trial than the right to an impartial judge . . . The constitutions of our nation and of our states, the rules of evidence and of procedure, and 200 years of case law promise a full panoply of rights to the accused. But ultimately the guarantee of these rights is no stronger than the integrity and fairness of the judge to whom the trial is entrusted. The State of Illinois placed the fate of [the defendants] in the hands of a racketeer.[87]

Judge Rovner argued that all the petitioners needed to prove to establish a violation of due process was circumstances "which might lead him not to hold the balance nice, clear, and true between the state and the accused."[88]

A unanimous U.S. Supreme Court reversed the Seventh Circuit. The Supreme Court's opinion noted that the evidence the Seventh Circuit had not found "sufficiently compelling" to grant a motion for discovery included the following: testimony from Judge Maloney's accomplice that Judge Maloney's opinions in favor of the prosecution were not unbiased; evidence that the judge took bribes in three other murder cases; evidence that he regularly fixed felony cases when he was a practicing defense attorney; evidence that he assigned as counsel to Bracy's codefendant a former law associate who, it is not unreasonable to suspect, knew of the judge's proclivities and corrupt habits; and evidence that this former law associate "hurried the case along" at the request of the judge in a manner prejudicial to the defendants.[89] The Seventh Circuit had reasoned that "[a] judge could be biased and yet the bias not affect the outcome of the case."[90] The Supreme Court disagreed: "[U]nfortunately, the presumption [that public officials have properly discharged their official duties] has been soundly rebutted: Maloney was shown to be thoroughly steeped in corruption through his public trial and conviction."[91]

After *Bracy,* the Illinois courts reconsidered the case of several convictions for murder and death sentences imposed in 1986 because the judge—Judge Maloney—had accepted a $10,000 bribe to fix the case.[92] At the original trial, the defendants waived their right to a jury for the guilt phase and expected a (bribed) verdict of acquittal from Judge Maloney. The judge changed his mind, however, because he was worried his illegal conduct would be detected. He instead returned the bribe and convicted the defendants of capital murder at a bench trial. The judge then advised the defendants that he was planning to sentence them to death, and the defendants elected a jury sentencing. When the jury found no mitigating circumstances at the penalty phase, the judge sentenced the defendants to death.[93] The defendants' direct appeals and initial post-conviction proceedings did not mention the bribes. The Supreme Court of Illinois affirmed the death sentences, even though the petitioners argued that the judge "came down hard" in cases where he was not bribed in order to avoid the suspicion (which turned out to be well-founded!) that he was "on the take."

In 1996 a state trial court judge vacated the defendants' convictions and ordered a new trial because Judge Maloney had held a "direct, personal, substantial, pecuniary interest" in the outcome of the trial.[94] On appeal, the state argued that the defendants had waived their right to attack their convictions on due process grounds because they themselves had offered the bribe. The state also argued procedural default—because the defendants did not object to the bribery at the time of their conviction, they had waived the right to object—and the doctrine of laches, which bars recovery by a litigant who delays pursuing a remedy. Finally, the state argued that the "unclean hands" doctrine prohibited relief.

The Illinois Supreme Court rejected the state's arguments. The court argued that "[a] fair and impartial jury cannot be permitted to draw the conclusion that, because a defendant attempted to fix his trial, he is guilty of the offense for which he is being tried."[95] Attempting to bribe a judge is a separate and distinct offense, and prosecution for that crime is the proper means for addressing that conduct: "Allowing the [s]tate to execute defendants as 'punishment' for their 'unclean hands' is not an acceptable alternative."[96] The court rejected the state's argument on "injected error" for similar reasons. Although no bribe would have occurred without the defendants offering the bribe, no bribe would have occurred if the judge had not been willing to accept it. The court concluded that it is impossible to know whether the same verdict would have been rendered by an uncorrupted judge.

The cases involving the corrupt Judge Maloney raise fundamental questions about the integrity of the judicial process. In the period when he was taking bribes, Judge Maloney imposed eight death sentences.[97] Unfortunately, judicial corruption and questionable ethical behavior also are not unknown on the Illinois Supreme Court.[98]

Sentencing Innocent Persons to Death

It is not a rare or infrequent occurrence that innocent persons are convicted of murder.[99] Nor are reversals of such sentences easy to come by.[100] According to the U.S. Department of Justice, twenty-eight men convicted of rape recently have been released when DNA evidence proved their innocence.[101]

This situation is particularly troubling when the innocent person has "confessed" to the capital crime. The idea that an innocent person would confess to a crime, especially a crime such as capital murder, is counterintuitive and extremely difficult for jurors, judges, journalists, and others to understand. Surely, the commonsense view is, if someone confessed to a crime, they must be guilty. Yet persuasive scientific and factual evidence exists documenting instances of persons confessing to crimes they did not commit. At the Northwestern Conference on Wrongful Convictions,[102] more than one person who had been sentenced to death in spite of being innocent of the offense described how a person could "confess" to a crime he did not commit.[103] Such death sentences, however, may be just as hard to overturn as others.

In Illinois, ten persons have been freed since 1977—eight in the last four years—from Illinois' death row because of acquittals on retrial or prosecutorial decisions to drop further charges.[104] This constitutes a rate of error of more than 3 percent. In these cases, perjured testimony or corrupt practices by police and prosecutors were used to obtain the wrongful convictions. Such practices have been tolerated by the Illinois courts.[105]

The presumption of innocence vanishes upon conviction and is replaced by presumptions that the trial was fair and that the conviction and sentence were justly imposed. It was due to fortuitous circumstances that the death sentences of innocent defendants were set aside, not because of the diligence of the appellate courts in Illinois.[106] The cruelest irony is the argument that the system works because a person who served years or decades on death row is finally released when found to be totally innocent.

When death sentences are reversed, it is usually only after extraordinary efforts by persons outside of the criminal justice system, rather than through the operation of "ordinary" appellate procedures.[107] In the Illinois cases, volunteer lawyers, investigators, and university professors have been the ones who found the evidence of innocence. In Ohio, the heirs and supporters of Sam Sheppard, whose conviction was overturned after he spent ten years in jail for murdering his wife, have not yet been successful in persuading the state prosecutor to charge another person for the offense, even though the family claims to have DNA evidence linking another suspect to the offense.[108]

Conclusion

It is impossible for the appellate courts to scrutinize relentlessly every aspect of each capital case. At the very least, however, the appearance of justice requires principled decision-making by those courts. This must mean more than a routine affirmance of death sentences, when there are so many to review and the procedural and substantive issues are fundamental and complex.[109] Murders may have a certain similarity, but each case is different.

Unfortunately, corruption in government exists. While the corrupt judge, the prosecutor who suborns perjury or does not turn over to the defense exculpatory evidence, or the government official who uses his office for personal gain are but a tiny fraction of the hundreds of thousands of loyal and trustworthy public servants with the power to influence the decision to impose a capital sentence in Illinois, their number is not and never will be zero. The U.S. Supreme Court noted in *Bracy v. Gramley* that while Thomas Maloney might have been the first judge in Illinois to have fixed murder cases, he was not the first judge to be convicted of taking bribes in murder cases.[110] And unfortunately it is not rare to hear of government officials who have breached the public's trust.[111] A corrupt judge who has taken a bribe cannot be trusted with any judicial decision.[112] Appellate courts call into question their own integrity and credibility when they uphold the outcomes of corrupted capital trials.

The even more troublesome cases involve mentally disturbed and marginally competent defendants and the incompetent or nonexistent presentation of evidence on their mental capacity. Anthony Porter was granted an initial stay of execution, which eventually led to his being found innocent, because his IQ of fifty-one raised the question of his competency to be executed.[113] Yet the trial court that convicted and sentenced Anthony Porter never considered the issue of his fitness to stand trial, his ability to form the requisite criminal intent, or his mental retardation as a mitigating factor.[114]

What finally can be said about the system for imposing capital sentences in Illinois? Certainly, the courts have been busy with capital cases. Some death sentences unjustly imposed have been reversed. Some persons who were innocent have had their death sentences overturned. Yet the record does not inspire confidence. A system that does not even appear to protect the constitutional rights of defendants when they are sentenced to death, no matter how guilty those defendants may be, or how heinous their crimes, is not tolerable. Ironically, two national commentators have identified Illinois as a state that has followed the U.S. Supreme Court's injunction to select only the most heinous cases for the death sentence.[115]

The quality of justice in the trial and appeal of capital cases in Illinois is of a deplorably low standard. Whether this standard is typical of, better than, or worse than the quality of justice in capital cases in other states remains for another day's consideration.[116] In the meantime, perhaps the national attention brought to the recent cases of the release of the innocents whose death sentences had been upheld on appeal will result in institutional changes.[117] The present system is indeed, in the words of Justice Harrison, profoundly unjust.

CHAPTER 5

The Proportionality Review of Capital Cases by State High Courts After *Gregg*: Only "the Appearance of Justice"

> *Much of the discussion is designed to explain the process of record-gathering and the methods of analyses, both of science and law, that can be used to conduct proportionality review and to assess the relevance of the data to systemwide claims of unconstitutional infliction of the death penalty . . .*
>
> *Although we recognize that proportionality is not a scientific determination, we have attempted to make our determinations as precise in terms of their bases and reasoning and as objective as possible. We have used scientific and statistical measures, when helpful, although we recognize that a value judgment is built into practically every measurement. A life is at stake, and although some degree of subjective value judgment may be required, we have attempted to make those judgments explicit so that they can be analyzed and tested against whatever objective measurements are applicable.*
>
> —*State v. Marshall* (1992)

In the twenty years after the U.S. Supreme Court approved the parameters for the reimposition of capital punishment in *Gregg v. Georgia*[1] and its accompanying cases,[2] state and federal courts have been presented with constitutional challenges to capital punishment based upon statistical evidence of racial and geographic disparities in state capital case processing systems.[3] These challenges are supported by the Supreme Court decisions in *Furman v. Georgia*[4]

This article is dedicated to the memory of Robert N. Wilentz, the late chief justice of the New Jersey Supreme Court.

and *Coker v. Georgia*,[5] which both implied, without explicitly holding, that racially and geographically based disparities in the implementation of capital punishment were fundamental constitutional infirmities.

The majority of state legislatures and supreme courts took the U.S. Supreme Court at its word and believed that *Gregg* meant what it said: newly revised state capital punishment systems were going to be different from the old systems, and one important difference would be the requirement of proportionality review. *Gregg* in the context of *Furman* strongly implied that a state capital punishment scheme would be declared unconstitutional if it exhibited the patterns of disparity declared unconstitutional in *Furman*.

The post-*Gregg* statutes enacted by various states addressed the structure and substance of jury decision-making at trial.[6] As an additional safeguard, *Gregg* endorsed Georgia's statutory requirement of proportionality review,[7] a new appellate procedure designed to assure that the imposition of the death sentence under the revised statutes would not be characterized by the fundamental flaw of arbitrariness that made the former system unjust.[8] Proportionality review is the comparison of a death sentence with sentences imposed in similar cases, to determine whether the sentence is fair or proportionate. The principle is that the death sentence is disproportionate if other defendants in similar cases are not sentenced to death. This statutory mandate can implicate broad principles of federal and state constitutional law and trigger the implementation of an empirical examination of the state's entire capital case processing system, raising issues of racial and economic disparity and questioning the charging practices and autonomy of local prosecutors. Or it can result in no more than a conclusory sentence tacked on to the end of a state high court's affirmance of a death sentence.

The increasing use of proportionality review by state high courts in the period 1976–91 mirrored tremendous changes in the jurisprudence and politics of capital punishment nationally: the withdrawal of federal courts, especially the U.S. Supreme Court, from the death penalty arena; increased political pressure upon state judicial institutions from both state legislatures and the electorate;[9] and polarized debate within the courts themselves. How state high courts approach proportionality review expresses a great deal about how these courts see themselves and their role within their own states and in the national criminal justice system.[10]

But despite the mandate given them by the absence of the U.S. Supreme Court on these issues, many state high courts ignored or dismissed statistical evidence of systemic disparities in capital case processing. Some courts held that such evidence could not even be presented to a state appellate court, neither within the context of proportionality review, nor as part of the direct appeal of an individual death sentence. Some members of these state high courts expressed the view that the issue of racial and geographic disparities in capital case processing was not justiciable if these disparities were caused by prosecutorial discretion, since prosecutorial decision-making is not subject to judicial review. In several jurisdictions, the question provoked dissension among the justices and conflict between the state high court and the state legislature. Other state high court justices believed these considerations went to the heart of proportionality review.

Were state supreme courts only interested in maintaining the "appearance of justice"[11] on the issue of racial and geographic disparities in capital sentencing?[12] After the U.S. Supreme Court held in *Pulley v. Harris*[13] that proportionality review was not mandated by federal constitutional principles, the majority of state high courts reduced proportionality review to a perfunctory exercise.[14] Perhaps state high courts were simply responding to more generalized political pressures to uphold death sentences.[15] When the U.S. Supreme Court declared in *McCleskey v. Kemp*[16] that evidence of statistically significant racial disparities based on the race of the victim was not a sufficient ground for declaring the Georgia capital punishment system unconstitutional, many state high courts used the federal case as an excuse not to consider constitutional challenges to capital punishment based on statistical evidence of racial or geographical disparities in any context, undermining the entire foundation of proportionality review as defined in *Gregg*.

Is the "appearance of justice" the same as the doing of justice?[17] The just result in these cases may not be the reversal of death sentences, but rather the establishment and maintenance of systematic and meaningful proportionality review. The opinions show many state high courts to be troubled about their responsibilities, suspicious of statistical evidence, and uneasy about the reliability of the factual record documenting disparities. In such states, the opinions illustrate the tension created when a law-and-order appellate court, whose judges are often mindful of their own retention, is both presented with a clearly guilty defendant and evidence of systemwide disparities with a possibly significant relationship to the race of the victim or defendant.[18]

The Supreme Court of New Jersey is the exception.[19] It has taken considerable initiative to implement proportionality review: the court appointed a special master, ordered the preparation of a database to compile statistics for proportionality review, and allocated the time and resources necessary to develop the factual predicate, methodological tools, and constitutional principles for proportionality review.[20] Nonetheless, to date no death sentence in New Jersey has been held to be disproportionate, even after subjection to this scrutiny.

Are state courts only going through the motions on proportionality review? The buck should have stopped at the state supreme court; in most states it did not. Is proportionality review now continued only to maintain the "appearance of justice"? This examination of how state high courts have actually implemented proportionality review will, hopefully, offer a perspective on these questions.

This article analyzes how state courts have addressed issues of racial and geographical disparities in capital case processing in the context of proportionality review. The first part of this article, "The Foundation for Proportionality Review in Capital Cases," sets out the doctrinal foundation for proportionality review established by the U.S. Supreme Court in 1976. After *Gregg*, however, the Supreme Court shifted away from an analysis of state capital punishment systems, as systems. In a series of landmark rulings, the Supreme Court indicated it would not overturn state capital punishment systems on the basis of aggregate challenges. The first part of this article sets out the difference between an analysis of a capital case processing system and a challenge to an individual death sentence.

The second part of this article, "State High Court Decisions and Changing Attitudes Toward Crime and Race," examines how state high courts and legislatures redefined and interpreted the principles of proportionality when sharp doctrinal changes in the capital jurisprudence of the U.S. Supreme Court became apparent. Immediately after *Gregg* all capital punishment jurisdictions faced the same situation. The U.S. Supreme Court in 1976 had strongly endorsed the procedures and principle of proportionality review set out in Georgia, but no state actually had conducted a systematic proportionality review. Neither state high courts nor state legislatures wanted to risk the prospect of having their capital case processing system or newly reenacted statute declared unconstitutional by the U.S. Supreme Court. Most reenacting states included a provision for proportionality review in their capital statute. The state high court typically took charge of implementing proportionality review after the legislature enacted the skeletal language of proportionality from *Gregg*.

Each state developed its own capital punishment jurisprudence over the course of the next two decades, against the backdrop of changing attitudes toward crime and race in the country as whole. This jurisprudence frequently included the state high court's response to empirical evidence of racial and geographical disparities in capital case processing within the state. State high courts responded with a great deal of variety to the presentation of these data and to being presented with quantitative evidence of disparities and disproportionality in capital case processing. Yet some state high courts did take the responsibility for preparing and maintaining a reliable factual record of capital case processing in the jurisdiction.

Table 1 provides the details of dates of reenactment, of the state's first affirmance of the statute and the date of first execution, and the time differences between these events, for each capital punishment state. In several states it was ten years between reenactment and the state high court's first affirmance of a death sentence. And there were waves in the patterns of reenactment and executions.

Table 2 sets out the specifics on death row populations and executions, and some ratios between these levels as of 1984, 1987, and 1996, again for each capital punishment state. Some surprising relationships are seen when states are compared with regard to these data. Some states reenacted early but have relatively small death row populations. Other states have large death row populations, but relatively few executions. Still other states reenacted early and are at a high level on all measures and have been so since reenactment. The ratio between a state's death row population and the number of executions in the state is interesting and surprising.

The second part of this article continues the analysis of patterns observed in the jurisprudence of proportionality review in the individual states by setting out the principal ways in which states responded to the disappearing mandate of the U.S. Supreme Court by (1) repealing their statutory requirement or by (2) severely limiting the pool of cases or scope of review. In addition, some states simply let the process atrophy through disuse.

The third part of this article, "Proportionality Review in Practice: Three States, Three Approaches," describes proportionality review in practice in three very different states, illustrating the conflicts that arose between state legislatures and state high courts over proportionality review and the presentation of empirical evidence of racial and geographical disparities in capital case processing. The first section of this part details the scenario to date in Connecticut, where issues of proportionality are still pending although the legislature repealed the statutory requirement. The second section sets out the unusual dialogue between the state legislature and the state high court in Nebraska.

The third section outlines in greater detail the considerable capital jurisprudence of the Supreme Court of New Jersey, and the conflict between the Supreme Court of New Jersey, the state legislature, and the attorney general of New Jersey. During the decade between reenactment and the court's first affirmance and proportionality review, a body of state constitutional case law was developed under the leadership of the late Chief Justice Robert N. Wilentz.

The fourth part of this article, "The 1995 Reeenactment in New York: New Rules for the Reimposition of Capital Punishment in the 1990s," places the 1995 reenactment in New York within the context of the experience of other states, and especially New Jersey. The unique legislative history in New York and the timing of the New York reenactment resulted in proportionality review provisions unlike those in any other jurisdiction. These are the most specific provisions for proportionality review enacted by any state legislature. They include two provisions requiring the state high court to consider aggregate data on racial and geographic disparities. Even though no death sentence has yet been imposed in New York, the expectation is that racial and jurisdictional disparities will be a principal issue. The New York Court of Appeals has anticipated this development by calling for expert advice on issues of data collection and analysis for the purpose of proportionality review.

The fifth part of this article concludes by noting that state high courts have been the principal, if somewhat reluctant, interpreters of constitutional doctrine regarding proportionality review since *Gregg,* for better or for worse. Strong differences have emerged across states and within a single state's jurisprudence during the twenty-year period since *Gregg,* as the numbers on death row increased. Each state legislature and court has been its own conscience. As this decade comes to a close, it is clear that issues of proportionality in the application of capital statutes will remain salient into the next.

The Foundation for Proportionality Review in Capital Cases

Taking the Supreme Court at Its Word

When the U.S. Supreme Court upheld the new capital punishment statutes in *Gregg v. Georgia,*[21] it did so on the premise that the procedural safeguards introduced in capital statutes after 1972 addressed the fundamental inequities which led the Court to declare all state capital punishment schemes unconstitutional in *Furman v. Georgia.*[22] While there was no majority opinion in *Furman,* there was a consensus that the imposition of capital punishment under then-existing statutory schemes violated fundamental rights guaranteed by the U.S. Constitution.[23] The perceived infirmity of the then-existing capital statutes was that they provided capital sentencers with unbridled discretion, producing death sentencing patterns that could only be described as "wanton" or "freakish."[24]

A cornerstone of the *Furman* holding was that the death penalty is inflicted in a trivial number of the cases in which it is legally available.[25] There was, therefore, no meaningful basis for distinguishing the cases of those few who were executed from the many who were not.[26] This recognition became the bedrock of proportionality review, a new principle arising from the principles expressed in *Furman.* It was the number of cases that could have resulted in a death sentence but did not, in proportion to the number of death sentences actually imposed, which forced the Court to conclude that execution was arbitrary and fundamentally unjust.[27]

So that death sentences would no longer be "cruel and unusual in the same way that being struck by lightning is cruel and unusual,"[28] the revised capital punishment statutes which followed *Gregg* introduced a structure of aggravating and mitigating factors intended to guide the discretion of the sentencer. In *Gregg* the Court held that the infirmities of the former capital punishment schemes had been addressed by Georgia's revised statute.[29] The Georgia statute restructured the decision to impose the death sentence by requiring the jury to make specific factual findings as to the presence or absence of statutorily defined aggravating and mitigating factors.[30]

The caprice and arbitrariness of the former system would also be prevented by multilayered, expanded appellate review, including proportionality review. Proportionality review created the framework for a comprehensive analysis of the state capital punishment system. The Georgia statute required the state's highest court to conduct proportionality review by examining the operation of the capital punishment system as a whole, adding to the refashioned death penalty decision-making a new system for comparing the death sentence on appeal with similar cases throughout the state. Heightened judicial scrutiny at the appellate level, with the inclusion of proportionality review, has since been viewed by some justices as fundamental to the constitutionality of the death penalty itself.[31]

Gregg and its companion cases upholding the revised capital statutes sent a clear signal to the state legislatures: enact a capital punishment statute resembling the Georgia statute, including a provision for proportionality review, and that statue will be upheld by the Court. Eager to reenact death penalty provisions, state legislatures took the Supreme Court at what seemed to be its word, and read *Gregg* as a how-to manual for constructing a constitutional capital punishment statute.[32] Over thirty states almost immediately enacted proportionality review procedures similar to those upheld in *Gregg*.[33] Although the U.S. Supreme Court declared in 1984 that proportionality review was not mandated under the Constitution, twenty-two states continue to require some form of proportionality review as part of their appellate review of capital cases.[34]

Under the post-*Gregg* scheme, only some of the circumstances of the offense and a very limited set of defendant characteristics may be identified as statutory aggravating factors justifying a capital sentence. Nonstatutory or extralegal factors are, in principle, irrelevant. Disparities based upon the race of the defendant or victim, or county boundaries of prosecutorial jurisdiction, are prime examples of extralegal factors which are theoretically impermissible under *Gregg*.[35] If a statute is proven to place significant reliance upon an extralegal factor, then the constitutionality of the entire system is questionable.[36]

Different Approaches: The Analysis of a Capital Case System Versus the Review of a Single Death Sentence

It is now almost twenty-five years since *Furman* and over twenty years since *Gregg*. In addition to ideological changes at the U.S. Supreme Court, much has changed in the state and federal courts and in the state legislatures. Since *Furman,* two methods of analyzing capital case processing systems have become clear: one views the imposition of a death sentence as the outcome of a decision-making system, and the other regards the imposition of a death sentence as a single isolated sentencing event.[37] The distinction between these two approaches is not merely whether or not one agrees with the proposition that "death is different," and consequently capital cases require more rigorous or heightened appellate review.

A systems approach begins with the collection of information on all potential capital cases to analyze aggregate data on intake and exit from the capital case processing system as a whole, regardless of whether that system is viewed as fair. Systems analysis identifies discrete, decision-making stages within capital case processing, and analyzes the characteristics of cases and defendants and how they move through the system at each identified stage.[38]

The case-specific approach, on the other hand, sees the imposition of the death penalty upon a particular defendant simply as a sentence imposed for a specific crime; the decision of a particular jury at a unique time and place. Under this approach, each death sentence is an independent event, an idiosyncratic and essentially unpredictable individual result. This isolated decision-making event is seen as unrelated to any other decision-making event in that case or any other. According to this approach, no systems analysis can ever account for the individual characteristics of any case, and attempts to impose aggregate analysis or quantitative uniformity are irrelevant, distorting, futile, and, worse, dehumanizing.[39]

In *Furman* and *Coker,* the U.S. Supreme Court assessed an entire system for imposing capital punishment within a single state, although the opinions in *Furman* did not use the terminology of systems analysis. In *Furman* the Court declared the Georgia death penalty unconstitutional because of the way the Georgia capital case processing system, and by analogy the systems in all states, operated as a whole. The remedy to the constitutional infirmity identified in *Furman* was therefore the abandonment of the previous system for imposing capital punishment in all of the states.[40] The *Gregg* court, by contrast, focused upon specific statutory remedies addressed to jury decision-making during the penalty phase of a capital trial.[41] *Gregg*'s emphasis on jurors was a shift from *Furman*'s focus on the capital case processing system as an institution.[42] However, the Court's emphasis in *Gregg* upon restructuring the decisions of jurors at the penalty phase of a capital trial[43] implied not only that jury decisions were autonomous and separable, but also that jurors might be the only actors whose decisions could be directly addressed by federal judicial fiat without violating separation of powers doctrines.[44] For example, separating the guilt and penalty phases of the capital trial and insisting on the specification of statutory aggravating and mitigating factors were legislative reforms addressed to jury decision-making, although these changes also required prosecutors, defense attorneys, and judges to alter the way they structured a case for the jury. Because the focus was on jurors, however, these reforms could never be challenged on the basis of separation of powers doctrine.

Although one purpose of proportionality review was to correct aberrant decisions of jurors, proportionality review was not aimed at restructuring jury decision-making. The repeated references to jurors made in *Gregg* may have been rhetorical.[45] The Court's focus upon jury decision-making at the penalty stage, however, implied that the jury or judge's life/death vote at sentencing was the principal locus of arbitrariness.[46] Proportionality review was rather designed to institute a different kind of constitutional protection.

The systemic discrimination which proportionality review is designed to address occurs independently of the decision-making of possibly biased individual jurors. The racial imbalances occurring within and across capital punishment systems are strongly related to prosecutorial discretion, the political factors influencing the selection and retention of prosecutors and judges, and racial stereotyping. These systemwide effects have been found to be especially pronounced in the middle range of capital cases.[47] These are the cases which might be capital in one county or state and not capital in another county or state. These differences partly explain the large discrepancies in death row populations between states.[48] The theoretical or doctrinal foundations for protection from racial discrimination in the application of capital case processing systems are the same principles which find a constitutional infirmity in systemwide discrimination in employment, jury selection, or the entitlement to government benefits.[49] The protection from being punished by a racially discriminatory sentencing structure is grounded in the Eighth Amendment and in the requirements of due process.[50]

Although the jury's decision to impose the death sentence is a discrete, dichotomous event at the conclusion of the capital trial, the jury's decision to impose the death sentence is not isolated. Nor is the decision-making of jurors the end of a linear progression. After *Gregg,* the jury's decision to impose the death penalty is preceded by specific factual findings of statutory aggravating and mitigating factors that the jury must weigh or balance. A juror's decision to impose the death sentence is therefore the end result of a dynamic, interactive process embedded in strata of procedural and substantive law. Long before a juror addresses the evidence at the penalty phase, what the juror confronts has been structured by the rules, procedures, and discretionary decisions made by police, prosecutors, defense attorneys, administrators, and judges at every step of the way.

The process begins well before the jury is convened, long before the judge's instructions at jury selection. It encompasses the legal criteria for jury selection and the admissibility of evidence, and is inextricably bound up with the legal system's restraints and sequencing imposed upon the parade of testimony and evidence. Why, then, did the *Gregg* court choose to focus on this end result?

Perhaps the jurors' decision to impose the death sentence was the segment of the decision-making process which was perceived to be the most amenable to reform from above.[51] Or the U.S. Supreme Court may have concluded that it was politically more acceptable to frame its decision in terms of jury decision-making, rather than to attempt to regulate the behavior of prosecutors or judges.[52] There could be no objection from the other institutionalized decision makers to rules aimed at restructuring the decision-making of jurors. On the other hand, an opinion which attempted to influence the discretionary decision-making of thousands of local prosecutors or judges in over thirty autonomous and very different legal jurisdictions of states could be controversial, unacceptable, or simply ignored.

Pulley and McCleskey: The Supreme Court Stops Monitoring Capital Case Processing Systems

After *Gregg* the Court continued its retreat from *Furman*'s emphasis on examining state capital punishment systems. *Pulley v. Harris*[53] in 1984 and *McCleskey v. Kemp*[54] in 1987 both rejected challenges to death sentences based upon a systems approach to capital case processing.

Pulley challenged the capital case processing system in California because it did not have a statutory requirement of proportionality review. The question was whether proportionality review of the state's entire system for imposing capital punishment was required at all.[55] Thus, *Pulley* did not address the sufficiency or adequacy of an established proportionality review process or a statistical methodology.[56] The litigation had the potential of forcing states which did not conduct proportionality review to adopt it. Presumably the Court would have set out minimal proportionality review standards for the states if it had required such review. Instead, the Court held that proportionality review was not constitutionally required.[57]

Pulley was decided at a time when some state supreme courts were expanding their recognition of rights under state constitutional provisions.[58] When *Pulley* declared that the federal Constitution did not require proportionality review, the state supreme courts had the alternative of shifting the requirement for proportionality review to analogous provisions of the state constitution. To date only the New Jersey Supreme Court has taken an unequivocal position that proportionality review and the systematic analysis of capital case processing are mandated by the state constitution.[59]

Like *Pulley, McCleskey v. Kemp*[60] was a challenge to Georgia's entire system of imposing capital punishment, and by implication a challenge not only to the Georgia scheme but to every analogous state system developed after *Gregg*. The claim in *McCleskey* was that a pattern of racial discrimination based upon the race of the victim had been demonstrated in a statistical study of the state's capital punishment system.[61] If *McCleskey* had declared the Georgia capital punishment system unconstitutional on the basis of the statistical evidence presented, every state system would have been subject to question because of inherent discrepancies in capital case processing. Even in states with few minorities, group differences exist between rural and urban jurisdictions.[62]

But *McCleskey* did not involve an explicit challenge based upon Georgia's proportionality review procedures or upon Georgia's method for conducting proportionality review.[63] Rather, the challenge to Warren McCleskey's death sentence was based upon principles closely related to the doctrinal foundations of proportionality.[64] The argument was that McCleskey's death sentence was unconstitutional because similarly situated defendants did not receive the death sentence and there was statistical evidence that the imposition of the death sentence in Georgia was influenced by the extralegal factor of race, in this case the race of the victim.

The challenge to the defendant's death sentence in *McCleskey* was based upon a comprehensive, systemwide study of the imposition of the death penalty in Georgia over a period of years.[65] In *McCleskey* the defense presented statistical evidence that certain defendants who killed whites were significantly more likely to be sentenced to death than similar defendants whose victims were not white, and that these racial differences remained statistically significant when other possibly explanatory variables were controlled.[66] Even when confronted with this evidence, the Court did not reverse McCleskey's death sentence.

The immediately apparent implication of *McCleskey* was that the U.S. Supreme Court would not set aside a death sentence or overturn a state capital punishment system on the basis of an empirical analysis of a state system presented in the context of proportionality review. *McCleskey* held that such statistical evidence was irrelevant to the validity of the individual death sentence on appeal, unless it could be demonstrated that there had been a specific intent to discriminate against this particular defendant on the part of some identified individual decision maker.[67] Consequently, *McCleskey* was interpreted by most state high courts as negating the federal constitutional underpinnings for state proportionality review.[68]

Read together, *McCleskey*[69] and *Pulley*[70] sent a message to the states which was crystal clear: the Supreme Court was no longer willing to reverse individual death sentences or declare capital punishment statutes unconstitutional in response to evidence of arbitrariness or caprice, bias or systematic racial discrimination within a particular capital case processing system. *McCleskey* foreclosed further arguments to the Supreme Court based upon a statistical showing of a race-of-victim effect in the overall functioning of a capital case processing system, whether or not in the context of proportionality review. The execution of Warren McCleskey himself in 1991, as well as subsequent executions after the Supreme Court summarily denied relief, underscored the Court's new intransigence.

Given the green light to do so by the U.S. Supreme Court, many state high courts after *McCleskey* refused to use the independent authority of their state constitutions to consider evidence of systemwide racial disparities in their capital case processing schemes.[71] Systemwide arbitrariness in state capital punishment systems presented state supreme courts with the opportunity to use state constitutional guaranties to replace federal due process protections for capital defendants which were no longer recognized by the U.S. Supreme Court, but it was a challenge and an opportunity which the state high courts overwhelmingly chose to decline.[72]

The combined effect of *Pulley* and *McCleskey* is that state high courts no longer need to demonstrate to the U.S. Supreme Court that their capital punishment systems are free from systemic racial or jurisdictional bias. As far as the Supreme Court is concerned, the presumption is that these systems operate free from racial bias, or, if they don't, the court will accept the way they do operate.[73] The Supreme Court is no longer in the business of overturning state-imposed death sentences for any reason at all and especially not on the basis of seemingly abstract arguments based upon statistics describing capital case processing systems.[74]

The majority of states also took the U.S. Supreme Court at its word when *Pulley v. Harris* declared that probably proportionality review was not required by the federal Constitution. After *McCleskey v. Kemp,* state legislatures and state supreme courts understood that the U.S. Supreme Court was no longer interested in reviewing allegations of arbitrariness based upon racial disparities in state capital punishment systems.[75] State courts took the U.S. Supreme Court at its word as it became clear that the Court was unlikely to overturn a state-imposed death sentence on any grounds.[76] The way for state high courts to insulate themselves from changes at the U.S. Supreme Court was well mapped: avoid federal constitutional issues altogether or rely upon state constitutional doctrine.

Nonetheless, twenty-two states continue to require some form of proportionality review as part of the appellate review of death sentences.[77] For example, the 1995 statute reenacting capital punishment in New York includes a proportionality review provision directing the state high court to consider empirical evidence of systemwide bias, with a specific reference to race. However, empirical evidence in a number of jurisdictions indicates that the risk of arbitrariness and systematic bias in the application of capital punishment continues to exist and that this risk is greatest in the so-called middle range, or low-visibility cases.[78] While one purpose of proportionality review is to minimize or eliminate systematic and systemic bias in the application of capital punishment statutes, especially with regard to racial and geographic disparities, almost without exception state institutions have refused to address that issue.

Explaining the Variance in the Opinions of State High Courts

Every state with proportionality review has adopted its own methodology. However, the procedure necessarily involves the comparison of the death sentence under review with other cases which the appellate court considers to be equivalent or similar in terms of the culpability or blameworthiness of the defendant and the relative aggravation of the circumstances of the offense.

Once the Supreme Court sent the message that a multiplicity of state capital punishment systems is acceptable, state high courts shared no common constitutional doctrine.[79] For example, Texas and California are sui generis. Texas has a unique statutory structure, upheld by the Supreme Court at the time of *Gregg*. California had one jurisprudence when Rose Bird was chief justice and another when she and two other justices were replaced in a recall election in which the California Supreme Court's reversal of death sentences was critical.[80] With little risk of reversal by the U.S. Supreme Court, high courts in states with large death row populations tend to conduct minimal proportionality review, and some of these courts have become factories for affirmances. In states where reenactment was relatively late, or where there have been few capital cases—such as New Jersey and Connecticut—whether for reasons of local culture, or simply a small number of homicide cases, capital jurisprudence and its microcosm, proportionality review, are an entirely different enterprise. These state high courts have continued a careful and individualized appellate review of death sentences, including proportionality review, in the face of administrative and political pressures to abandon it.

The general sense one gets from these formidable state high court opinions, which during the period of 1976–91 were overwhelmingly pointed in a single direction, is that absent the threat of reversal by the Supreme Court, there is no motivation to address the issue of racial and geographic disparities in capital case processing. State legislatures enacted proportionality review procedures because they believed, on the basis of language in *Gregg*, that state capital punishment statutes lacking proportionality review provisions would be declared unconstitutional by the Supreme Court.[81] After *Pulley* and *McCleskey*, many state supreme courts found themselves in an awkward position: statutory proportionality review provisions remained intact,[82] and a number of state high courts had institutionalized proportionality review, either as part of their ordinary appellate review of individual death sentences or by creating a special internal administrative procedure.[83] Now they were stuck with it.

However, many state high courts did revise existing procedures for proportionality review and reduce proportionality review to a formality after *Pulley* and *McCleskey*. Some courts did this in a technical manner by changing the definition of cases which would be considered similar. Other state high courts changed the character of the review conducted by simply refusing to consider any systemwide challenges to their capital punishment system, thereby restricting proportionality review to a narrow comparison. Finally, some other state courts limited proportionality review to a very narrow comparison between the sentences of codefendants in the same case.[84]

State High Court Decisions and Changing Attitudes Toward Crime and Race

However complicated its implementation history, the principle behind proportionality review is simple and the same everywhere: it is unjust to impose a death sentence upon one defendant when a similarly situated defendant whose murder was equally aggravated is not sentenced to death or executed. Generalizing across jurisdictions and courts over a time period of fifteen years is hazardous; nonetheless, certain patterns in state supreme court opinions are observable during the period between *Gregg* in 1976 and the second and final rejection of the federal appeal of Warren McCleskey's death sentence and his execution in 1991.[85] Racial and jurisdictional disparities were not the sole component of McCleskey's appellate arguments. Racial and geographic disparities, however, were the only basis for challenging a state's entire capital case processing system before a federal court, and by implication in all of the states. Racial and geographic disparities are therefore at the heart of the concept of proportionality itself, both in capital sentencing and in other areas, as the factors which show the most disparate results.

Commentary on state high court opinions, even on issues of national dimensions, is typically sporadic or relegated to footnotes. Yet these institutions are now the principal interpreters of constitutional principles in capital jurisprudence and other areas of constitutional law formerly the province of federal courts. Even if, as many say, state high court opinions are less erudite or well-reasoned than the constitutional discourse of the higher federal courts or academic journals, these opinions nonetheless began to define constitutional doctrine on this question in the period 1976–91.[86]

Both state judicial institutions and legislatures faced similar circumstances in this period. Legislatures were apprehensive that the Supreme Court would declare their state capital case processing systems and statutes unconstitutional. At the same time, the political climate grew increasingly favorable to the implementation of the death penalty. People became impatient with reversals of capital sentences on what were perceived as "legal technicalities,"[87] as well as the disparity between the large number of people sentenced to death and the few who were executed.[88]

Furthermore, the issue of proportionality always had race lurking in the background. On the other hand, consensus on issues of race generally did not exist during this period. The trend in decision-making by the federal courts during the 1980s was in the direction of denying relief to claims based upon allegations of racial discrimination generally. Certainly, arguments alleging that capital sentencing systems had disparate impact upon different racial groups were not heard by state high courts in a jurisprudential or political vacuum.[89] Arguments based upon differential racial impact in the capital punishment context were being considered by state high court justices who had witnessed the checkered history of court-imposed orders regarding school and housing desegregation and redistricting—orders which were neither straightforward nor uncontroversial. The ineffective role of courts in many of these proceedings, and the political pressures placed upon them, may have made state high courts even more reluctant to intervene where these issues arose in the criminal justice arena.[90]

Where responsibility rested for defining the parameters of proportionality review was ambiguous. In some states neither the legislature nor the state high court firmly took charge of the process. In other states the legislature clearly ceded authority for defining proportionality review to the state high court. In other states institutional conflicts emerged between the state high court and the legislature. For example, if the legislature wanted to limit the scope of review by the court, the legislature limited the pool of comparison cases by statute. Most state legislatures had little conception of what proportionality review entailed at the time of enactment. State legislatures typically passed simply worded proportionality review statutes in response to *Gregg*,[91] and a few state high courts almost immediately reversed one or two death sentences on grounds of disproportionality.

In the early 1980s, then, implementation of proportionality review seemed relatively straightforward, but this seeming simplicity was short-lived. Ordinary delays met by the early capital cases as they made their way through state appellate systems were often further extended for proportionality review. Some state supreme courts did not conduct proportionality review until all other issues on appeal had already been decided. Some states waited until more than one death sentence had been affirmed so that there would be a pool of cases for comparison.[92]

Proportionality review was also thrust into legal limbo during the pendency of the appeal in *Pulley*.[93] State legislatures and high courts were both reluctant to take a stand on proportionality which might subject them to reversal. Then, as the Supreme Court reduced the grounds for the reversal of death sentences in the late 1980s, state high courts reconsidered the status of proportionality review. If it wasn't a federal constitutional remedy, what was it? It had been enacted in response to an endorsement from a very different Supreme Court, that of the 1970s.[94] Now it was wholly a matter of state law, based upon either state statute, state court rule, or state common law. Proportionality review could be transformed into a state constitutional requirement, or it could be institutionalized as a statutory interpretation. The overwhelming response to the withdrawal of the federal constitutional requirement of proportionality review established in *Gregg* was the concomitant withdrawal of the state requirement, either through legislative action, irrespective of its procedural underpinnings, or through the action or inaction of the state supreme court.[95]

In fact, the jurisprudence of proportionality review by state supreme courts between 1976 and 1991 became in large part the story of how state high courts responded to constitutional arguments based upon statistical evidence of racial and geographic disparities. State high courts are typically presented with variations upon several related arguments about proportionality. Some argue that the data show county-by-county disparities within the state, and that such disparities passively create racial and/or geographical differences with constitutional dimensions in capital sentencing. Others say that there are rural/urban differences in capital case processing, attributable to bureaucratic pressures, differing policies of individual prosecutors, or both. Finally, some argue that differences in capital case processing are introduced via the overtly different charging policies of autonomous local prosecutors within the same state.[96] The factual evidence for these arguments was strong, even if its presentation was sometimes unsystematic. Nonetheless, state high courts have been extremely reluctant to grant credence to statistical evidence of any of these disparities, or to regulate the effects of prosecutorial discretion on such grounds.[97]

In capital cases, where a life is in the balance, state high courts might be expected to be more likely to give the benefit of the doubt to statistical evidence of racial disparities, which may be at least partially attributable to prosecutorial charging practices. In fact, the opposite appears to be true.[98] As state high courts have become increasingly confident that the Supreme Court would not declare state capital systems unconstitutional, they have become increasingly unwilling to entertain arguments alleging racial and jurisdictional disparities in capital case processing. In some states which reenacted the death penalty early, there was a period in the mid-1980s during which proportionality review was a viable appellate issue since it was established in those states, and its federal fate was unclear. As the tide of popular opinion, however, continued to turn in the direction of increased support for executions, state high courts were content to let proportionality review wither on the vine. In many states not-so-benign neglect was as effective as the repeal of a statute or an explicit ruling overturning the requirement.

The Response of State High Courts to Quantitative Analysis

Perhaps state high courts are justifiably suspicious of empirical data and social science evidence, and especially of statistical analyses of racial disparities in the criminal justice system.[99] Appellate courts are particularly distrustful of statistics developed by the defense in criminal cases,[100] and the prosecution has no motivation to develop such evidence. A state high court is then left with two alternatives: (1) producing its own accurate data on the capital case processing system (not a trivial research task) and overseeing its analysis; or (2) accepting the analysis and data put forward by defense counsel. Very few courts have been willing to undertake research and data collection themselves, although many state high courts already maintain ongoing records of all capital appeals in their role as administrator of the court system. Transforming such records into a reliable database for systematic analysis of capital sentencing would be feasible, especially since state high courts administer their court systems by using computerized case-tracking systems.[101]

When presented with quantitative evidence of racial disparity, some courts did not understand how to interpret it or how to use it. Courts justifiably feared they would not be able to evaluate the objectivity of such evidence, especially when the findings were not unambiguous. Perhaps because many justices were unfamiliar with social science research and its norms, they expected more definitive results than an increased likelihood or statements regarding probability.

The impact of racial and geographical disparities on capital case processing is counterintuitive and inferential, in addition to being controversial and politically unpopular. This evidence supports arguments that the demonstrated racial differentials are caused by explicit or implicit racial discrimination, or by passive discrimination related to geographical differences among counties. Contributing to misunderstanding is the fact that the statistical results based upon county or jurisdictional disparities may demonstrate an unanticipated effect, namely that cases involving black or minority defendants and victims are treated less harshly because they are less likely to be declared capital. Jurisdictional disparities may then be articulated as the devaluing of minority or low-status victims, while murders involving white or higher-status victims are aggressively prosecuted as capital cases.[102] Furthermore, the data involving geographical disparities may be articulated as a rural/urban distinction, such that homicides are downgraded in urban jurisdictions with overburdened dockets and strained bureaucratic resources, while similar crimes in relatively affluent rural or suburban districts are prosecuted capitally.[103] In every jurisdiction the potential exists for discussions of proportionality to be mired in technicalities. The more ambitious and sophisticated the scope and analysis of data, the greater the likelihood of frustration, confusion, and misunderstanding.[104] A systematic, reliable study takes time and causes further appellate delay to executions, creating an additional source of unpopularity.

In the face of a judiciary unfamiliar with statistical arguments, persons convicted of capital murder and their court-appointed lawyers are not in the best position to persuade a state high court to set aside death sentences on the basis of subtle quantitative analyses of capital case processing.[105] But these problems are surmountable. For instance, the response of the Supreme Court of New Jersey was to appoint an expert to advise the court on technical issues of data interpretation.[106] How unusual it was for the Supreme Court of New Jersey to create a Proportionality Review Project under the direction of this special master can be appreciated against the backdrop of what other state high courts chose to do, or not to do.[107]

During this period the New Jersey Supreme Court was considered to be the leading state high court for the development of state constitutional doctrine.[108] In particular, the chief justice of the New Jersey Supreme Court played a critical role throughout the development of proportionality review in the state.[109] The commitment demonstrated by this court to proportionality review was in part due to several other factors: the independent character of the New Jersey Supreme Court itself, the experience and expertise of the special master hired by the court to compile and analyze the relevant data,[110] and institutional factors which made it possible for first the Office of the Public Defender and then the Administrative Office of the Courts to conduct a comprehensive research and analysis project.[111] The research conducted by the Proportionality Review Project, as it came to be called, refined and developed a broadly conceived methodology for measuring defendant culpability and the aggravation level of homicide. These measures are now available and applicable to studies of homicide and other analyses of criminal behavior and responsibility. The development of systematic, analytic categories for gradations of criminal culpability and aggravation levels in homicide is a path-breaking intellectual achievement. That such conceptual development should occur in a court-sponsored research project is all the more extraordinary.

The State High Court's Duty as Court Administrator to Prepare and Maintain a Reliable Factual Record on Capital Case Processing

In addition to New Jersey, a small number of state high courts have initiated comprehensive data collection and assumed responsibility for creating and maintaining a factual record on homicide cases within their jurisdiction. Without a reliable factual record documenting the movement of potentially capital cases through the system, however, there can be no meaningful proportionality review.

For example, an extensive data collection effort has been in place in Pennsylvania since that state reenacted the death penalty. Data have been collected and made available to the Pennsylvania Supreme Court since at least 1983, with some information on cases going back to 1978.[112] The data are now being updated and corrected by the Philadelphia office of the Public Defender.[113]

The Pennsylvania data set has the potential of providing a comprehensive factual basis for the systemwide analysis of a capital punishment system which seems to have wide disparities.[114] At the present time, however, defendants challenging the application of the statute are verifying basic case-processing data and collecting information on additional variables.[115] In sum, the Pennsylvania experience proves that collecting data without controls on accuracy and comprehensiveness cannot provide a reliable factual basis for proportionality analysis by a court or anyone else.

Indeed, state courts are disingenuous when they refuse to consider issues of racial and geographic disparity because of an absence of reliable data. The statutory mandate to conduct proportionality review necessarily implies creating and maintaining an adequate factual record. A critical distinction between the states is whether or not the state high court itself takes the initiative in institutionalizing data collection and certifies its accuracy; the data analysis which follows is relatively straightforward.[116]

Patterns Observed in the Jurisprudence of Proportionality Review in the Individual States

While each state has a unique statute and body of capital punishment jurisprudence, certain patterns are discernible. There are stark differences between states with large death row populations and states with a small number of capital cases.[117]

Table 1 summarizes the experience of the states since *Gregg.* In table 1 the date of death penalty reenactment (column 1), the date of the first affirmance of a death sentence (column 2), and the date of the first execution (column 3) are tracked for each reenacting state.[118] The next three columns show the period of time elapsing between reenactment and the first death sentence affirmed (column 4), the period of time from reenactment to the first execution in the state (column 5), and the number of years from the first death sentence affirmed to the first execution (column 6). The final two columns show the death row population as of 1996 (column 7) and the number of executions between 1976 and 1996 (column 8).

When the states are ranked by these different measures several patterns emerge.[119] Texas, with over one hundred executions since 1976, is grossly out of proportion in comparison to other states, even considering only other southern states. For example, Florida has executed 34, Virginia, 27, Louisiana, 22, and Georgia, 20. Eight states have had 6, 5, or 4 executions; four states have executed 3 or 2; and five states have executed 1 person. Twelve reenacting states have had no executions, including Connecticut, which reenacted in 1973, Tennessee, which reenacted in 1974, and Colorado and New Mexico, which both reenacted in 1975. While the rhetoric of the capital punishment jurisprudence in these states may be favorable to capital punishment, the state high court is not expediting executions.

Table 1

Date of Reenactment, Date of First Capital Affirmance, Date of First Execution, and Time Periods Between, by State

State	Date Death Penalty Reenacted Col. 1	Date First Death Sentence Affirmed Col. 2	Date of First Execution Col. 3	Years from Reenactment to First Death Sentence Affirmed (col. 2-col. 1) Col. 4	Years from Reenactment to First Execution (col. 3-col. 1) Col. 5	Years from First Death Sentence Affirmed to First Execution (col. 3-col. 2) Col. 6	Death Row Population as of 1996 Col. 7	Executions Since 1976 as of 1996 Col. 8
Alabama	3/ 5/76	9/ 9/77	4/22/83	1.5	7.2	5.7	144	13
Arizona	8/ 8/73	12/20/76	4/ 6/92	3.4	18.9	15.5	121	4
Arkansas	3/23/73	12/22/75	6/18/90	2.8	17.5	14.7	37	11
California	1/ 1/74	10/12/80	4/21/92	6.9	18.6	11.7	444	3
Colorado	1/ 1/75	5/14/90		15.6			4	
Connecticut	10/ 1/73						5	
Delaware	3/29/74	9/20/84	3/14/92	10.6	18.2	7.6	11	8
Florida	12/ 8/72	11/27/74	5/25/79	2.0	6.6	4.6	351	36
Georgia	3/28/73	4/ 4/74	12/15/83	1.0	10.9	9.8	108	20
Idaho	7/ 1/73	5/23/83	1/ 6/94	10.0	20.8	10.8	19	1
Illinois	7/ 1/74	11/13/81	9/12/90	7.5	16.4	9.0	164	7
Indiana	5/ 1/73	1/30/81	3/ 9/81	7.9	8.0	0.1	50	3
Kansas	4/22/94							
Kentucky	1/ 1/75	11/ 2/80		5.9			28	
Louisiana	7/ 2/73	10/11/74	12/14/83	1.3	10.6	9.3	53	23
Maryland	7/ 1/75	11/ 3/83	5/16/94	8.5	19.2	10.7	17	1
Mississippi	4/23/74	5/24/78	9/ 2/83	4.1	9.5	5.4	54	4
Missouri	9/28/75	5/11/81	1/ 6/89	5.7	13.5	7.8	92	19
Montana	3/11/74	11/12/76	5/10/95	2.7	21.5	18.8	6	1
Nebraska	4/20/73	2/ 2/77	9/ 2/94	3.8	21.7	17.8	10	1
Nevada	7/ 1/73	5/17/78	10/22/79	4.9	6.4	1.5	85	6
New Hampshire	1/ 1/91							
New Jersey	8/ 6/82	7/28/92		10.1			12	
New Mexico	7/ 1/79	1/20/83		3.6			3	
New York	9/ 1/95							
North Carolina	6/ 1/77	11/ 3/81	3/16/84	4.5	6.9	2.4	154	8
Ohio	1/ 1/74	11/24/76		2.9			150	
Oklahoma	5/17/73	3/21/80	9/10/90	6.9	17.6	10.6	119	7
Oregon	12/ 7/78	2/26/88		9.4			22	
Pennsylvania	3/26/74	12/30/82	5/ 2/95	8.9	21.4	12.5	200	2
South Carolina	7/ 2/74	2/11/76	1/11/85	1.6	10.7	9.0	71	5
South Dakota	1/ 1/79						2	
Tennessee	2/27/74	1/ 7/80		5.9			102	
Texas	1/ 1/74	4/16/75	12/ 7/82	1.3	9.1	7.8	394	106
Utah+	7/ 1/73	11/25/77	1/17/77	4.5	3.6	–0.9	10	5
Virginia	10/ 1/75	9/ 5/75	8/10/82	–0.1	7.0	7.0	54	31
Washington	11/ 4/75	11/ 6/84	1/ 5/93	9.1	17.4	8.3	13	2
Wyoming	2/28/77	5/27/83	1/22/92	6.3	15.1	8.8		1

Source: For date of reenactment, individual state statutes and session laws. Date of reenactment is the effective date of the statute. For date of affirmance, individual state high court opinions. Date of affirmance is the date the state high court upheld the first post-*Furman* death sentence on appeal, including proportionality review. Source for death row population and executions (as of April 30, 1996): NAACP Legal Defense and Educational Fund, "Death Row U.S.A., Spring 1996." Source for New Jersey death row population, Administrative Office of the Courts, New Jersey, as of Aug. 1, 1996.

+ Utah executed Gary Gilmore when he withdrew his appeals, before his conviction and death sentence were affirmed.

Ranking by date of reenactment, Florida was the first state to reenact, which it did on December 8, 1972, before *Gregg* was handed down. A total of eleven states then reenacted in 1973, and an additional ten reenacted in 1974. Another six reenacted in 1975. Before *Gregg* was handed down, then, twenty-eight states had already reenacted.[120] After *Gregg*, two states reenacted in 1977 and 1979, and in all other years only one state reenacted, with no states at all reenacting in twelve of the years between 1980 and 1995.[121] Generalizations about the rush to capital punishment in the 1980s do not hold. Reenactments occurred primarily in the 1970s.

When the dates for the first death sentence affirmed are ranked, a more even distribution is seen, with four states each having affirmances in the years 1976, 1980, 1981, and 1983. Georgia was the first state to affirm, with Louisiana, Florida, Texas, Virginia, and Arkansas all affirming the constitutionality of their statutes before 1976, and before *Gregg*. After *Gregg* it might have been expected that there would be a cluster of affirmances in 1977, but there were only three. Similarly, by 1984, when *Pulley* was decided, most states had already affirmed their first death sentence, although a surprising number, five, had not.[122]

The distribution of dates of first execution in column 3 shows Utah to have been first, in 1977. Following Utah were Florida, Nevada, Indiana, Virginia, and Texas, all before 1983. Then four states had their first execution in 1984. No additional states began executions until 1990, and then seven states executed their first person between 1990 and 1992. Three other states initiated executions in 1994. Eleven death penalty states had not yet executed anyone in 1996.

Column 4 shows that the time lapse between reenactment and the first death sentence affirmed was less than two years in six states, and less than five years in seventeen states. Four states took ten years or more to affirm their first death sentence after reenactment, and five states had not yet affirmed their first death sentence in 1996.

The distribution of years from reenactment to the first execution for those twenty-seven (including Ohio) states which have had executions shows Utah to be the outlier, with only 3.6 years elapsing between reenactment and execution. Eight other states executed their first capital defendant before 10 years; thirteen took between 10 and 20 years, and four took more than 20 years.

The ranking of years between the first affirmance and the first execution shows that twelve states are between 5 and 10 years, and nine states are between 10 and 20 years. Utah has a negative value, since Gary Gilmore was

Table 2
Death Row Population and Percentage Increases, Number of Executions, by State, and Years 1984, 1987, and 1996

State	Death Row Population as of 1984 Col. 1	Death Row Population as of 1987 Col. 2	Executions as of 1987 Col. 3	Death Row Population 1996 Col. 4	% Increase 1984-1996 Col. 5	Executions as of 1996 Col. 6	Executions as a % of Death Row Population 1996 Col. 7
Alabama	71	86	2	144	103%	13	8%
Arizona	50	64	0	121	142%	4	3%
Arkansas	23	33	0	37	61%	11	23%
California	153	196	0	444	190%	3	
Colorado	2	2	0	4	100%	0	
Connecticut	0	0	0	5		0	
Delaware	6	6	0	11	83%	8	42%
Florida	203	267	16	351	73%	36	9%
Georgia	114	107	7	108	–5%	20	16%
Idaho	9	14	0	19	111%	1	5%
Illinois	59	105	0	164	178%	7	4%
Indiana	25	42	2	50	100%	3	6%
Kansas	0	0	0			0	
Kentucky	19	31	0	28	47%	0	
Louisiana	36	52	7	53	47%	23	30%
Maryland	13	19	0	17	31%	1	6%
Mississippi	38	48	1	54	42%	4	7%
Missouri	23	50	0	92	300%	19	17%
Montana	4	6	0	6	50%	1	14%
Nebraska	11	14	0	10	–9%	1	9%
Nevada	20	39	2	85	325%	6	7%
New Hampshire	0	0	0			0	
New Jersey	5	24	0	12	140%	0	
New Mexico	0	0	0	3		0	
New York	0	0	0			0	
North Carolina	34	65	3	154	353%	8	5%
Ohio	21	76	0	150	614%	0	
Oklahoma	40	69	0	119	198%	7	6%
Oregon	0	3	0	22		0	
Pennsylvania	56	86	0	200	257%	2	1%
South Carolina	33	50	2	71	115%	5	7%
South Dakota	0	0	0	2		0	
Tennessee	38	59	0	102	168%	0	
Texas	172	245	22	394	129%	106	21%
Utah	4	7	1	10	150%	5	33%
Virginia	21	36	5	54	157%	31	36%
Washington	4	7	0	13	225%	2	13%
Wyoming	3	3	0	0	–100%	1	100%

Source: NAACP Legal Defense and Educational Fund, "Death Row U.S.A., Spring 1996"; Mar. 1, 1984, and May 1, 1987 (the dates immediately after *Pulley v. Harris* and *McCleskey v. Kemp,* respectively). The New Jersey figure for 1996 from Administrative Office of the Courts, as of Sept. 1, 1996.

Percentage increases are calculated as follows: Col. 5 = (Col. 4 – Col. 1)/Col. 1; Col. 7 = (Col. 6/Col. 6 + Col. 4).

Note: As of Mar. 1, 1984, there were a total of thirteen post-1976 executions: one each in Alabama, Georgia, Indiana, Mississippi, Nevada, Texas, Utah, and Virginia; two in Louisiana; and three in Florida.

executed before his direct appeal was decided. This is followed by Indiana, which executed its first person less than a year after affirmance. At the other extreme, Montana and Nebraska had 18.8 years and 17.8 years elapse, respectively, between the first affirmance and the first execution. Other relationships in table 1 are noteworthy: Florida was the first state to reenact, one of the first states to affirm its statute, the second state to execute a defendant, and the state with the third-largest death row population, yet the state has executed less than 10 percent of that population.[123] By contrast, Texas, which reenacted early and affirmed early, did not execute its first defendant until 1982; but as of 1995 it had executed almost 25 percent of that population. Similarly, Virginia had executed almost one-third of its death row population as of 1996, although the state did not have an execution until 1982.

Table 2 lists death row population by state. In 1984, the year *Pulley* was decided, California already had 153 people on death row, placing it third. Only Florida, with 203, and Texas, with 172, had more people on death row.[124] Eleven states had between 20 and 40 prisoners on death row in 1984, while seven states had none. By 1987, when *McCleskey* was decided, Florida, with 267, still had more people on death row than any other state, followed by Texas with 245, and California with 196.[125] In 1987 only six states had no defendants on death row.

In 1996 the top three death row populations were in California, Texas, and Florida, with populations of 444, 394, and 351, respectively. The biggest change since 1987, however, is that twelve states have over 100. Seven other states had 50 or more people on death row, and nine states had less than 5 defendants on death row. Percentage changes in death row populations from 1984 to 1987 and from 1987 to 1995 show large and varied percentage changes, as well as negative percentages, but these large variations in percentages often occur when working with a small base.

The three states with the largest death row population in 1984, Florida, Texas, and California, showed increases of 32 percent, 42 percent, and 28 percent, respectively, between 1984 and 1987. By comparison, those same states show even greater percentage increases in their death row population from 1984 to 1996: Florida, 73 percent; Texas, 129 percent; and California, 190 percent. Overall, however, Texas has had the most persons sentenced to death. The current death row population in Texas only ranks below California because Texas has executed over a hundred defendants, and California less than half a dozen.

Finally, the percentage of the death row population executed shows both expected and surprising comparisons. Texas has the highest number of executions, but Delaware, Virginia, Utah, and Louisiana have executed the largest percentage of their death row populations, each with more than 30 percent on varying bases. In several indicators, Virginia emerges as a state almost as aggressive as Texas in its death penalty policies.[126] Florida again emerges as the surprising figure, having executed 9 percent of its death row population. This results in a large number of actual executions for Florida, but a small proportion of the total death row population. The same effect occurs in the numbers for some other southern states.

The high courts of Texas, Florida, and California spend a substantial amount of time on capital appeals, and have a highly developed capital jurisprudence.[127] However, goaded by political pressures, and staffed by judges who know they may be voted out of office if they reverse death sentences, these courts have almost become factories for affirmances.[128] The next tier of state high courts, those with death row populations above one hundred, are now being pushed in that direction.[129] Those state high courts with a small number of capital appeals engage in an entirely different enterprise when they review death sentences.

After *McCleskey* the majority of states no longer took proportionality review seriously. If the state high court remained under a statutory mandate to conduct proportionality review, the manner and method for conducting such review changed. However, it is not always easy to tell when a state high court is setting aside a death sentence as disproportionate, since courts may give multiple reasons for setting aside a capital conviction.[130] Sometimes this fact was explicitly acknowledged by the state high courts, sometimes it was not. *McCleskey* shocked the defense bar, but it was welcomed by members of the legal community who thought that defendants had been too successful in postponing executions.[131]

Systematic, statistical analysis of a capital punishment system which found significant racial disparities would not result in the federal courts reversing a death sentence, so why then should a state high court conduct proportionality review using a systemwide approach? In the majority of states proportionality review was turned into a limited review of individual death sentences, a comparison to one or two or three other sentences which resulted in the predictable affirmance of the death sentence under review. It was especially easy to ignore the constitutional issues if there was no reliable, systematic analysis of the capital case processing system, since there could be no constitutional violation without a factual predicate indicating disparities with a constitutional dimension.

But state high courts were not required to abandon the constitutional principles of proportionality review, so why were so many state high courts eager to eviscerate the process? There is no definitive answer, but by the late 1980s, state high courts considered themselves ill-equipped and unprepared to undertake an empirical review of their state capital punishment systems. These courts did not have spare resources to devote to the task, and judges often did not wish to make the educational investment required to understand the issues. No institutional actor except the Office of the Public Defender was pushing the state high court to undertake systematic proportionality review; the political and institutional pressures were all in the opposite direction. Moreover, in most states the Public Defender had been rendered ineffective by the lack of a centralized administration, the absence of political support, and a severe shortage of funds.[132] They were not strong enough to defend against the attack on proportionality review. The draconian dollar limits imposed upon capital appeals in many states mean that no one defendant has the resources to collect the information required for a systematic analysis of the state's capital punishment system.[133] And if the defense does not press for proportionality review, certainly the attorney general and county prosecutors will not. The prosecution has nothing to gain from systematic proportionality review by the court. Judges, including state high court judges, are overwhelmingly composed of ex-prosecutors.[134] The problem was not that there was no legal theory or principles available to support proportionality review. The patterns show that most state high courts intentionally turned away from support of proportionality review. They did this in two different ways: by repealing or overturning proportionality review entirely or by limiting the universe of cases for comparison.

Getting Rid of Proportionality Review

Six state legislatures repealed their statutory provisions for proportionality review after initially following the *Gregg* mandate.[135] One state, Tennessee, reinstated its proportionality review provision after a repeal in 1992.[136] In two additional states the state high court, on its own initiative, explicitly abandoned the effort to conduct a systematic review of the state's capital case processing system.[137]

States that abandoned proportionality review were not necessarily the states where the procedure was a meaningless exercise. For example, in Wyoming, proportionality review was not a perfunctory exercise prior to repeal. The Wyoming high court systematically examined a large number of cases and carefully considered the issues.[138] Nevada overturned five death sentences as disproportionate prior to repeal, a relatively large number of death sentences to be overturned for such a small jurisdiction.[139]

Limiting the Pool of Cases or Scope of Review

Death only. Some states limited proportionality review by cutting their pool of comparison cases to those in which the sentence of death had actually been imposed.[140] The articulated rationale for this is that a death sentence is unlike any other sentence, therefore a death sentence can only be compared with other death sentences.[141] Courts adopting this approach have thereby concluded that cases which did not result in a death sentence are by definition qualitatively different from the death sentence case under review.[142] Thus, the method fails to account for situations in which the death penalty was not applied.

Cases in which the death sentence was not imposed are irrelevant because the only purpose of proportionality review is to make sure that the death sentence under review belongs with the class of other death sentences. Similarity between cases can also mean nothing more than similarity to only one other death sentence which has been upheld. The proportionality decision in this context, then, is whether this death sentence is internally consistent with the class of other death sentences, [143] or if there is any other case in which the death sentence has been upheld which is similar to the death sentence under review. This process usually results in a statistically meaningless comparison. In California and Texas, states with large death row populations, where the pool of comparison cases using only death sentences could be large, with the possibility of statistically significant results, there is no mandated proportionality review.

Except in states where the death row populations are very large, this limitation essentially reduces proportionality review to a perfunctory exercise. Only one death sentence has been overturned on grounds of disproportionality in all of the jurisdictions which have limited the pool of cases to other death sentences, and that death sentence was overturned relatively soon after *Gregg.*[144]

Courts which adopt this rationale tend to ask whether the case under review is as "heinous," "aggravated," or "serious" as other cases in which the same court has already upheld a death sentence.[145] No similar cases in which defendants escaped the death penalty are considered. This proportionality review exercise, then, groups all the death sentences together and asks if all of the cases in which death was imposed are similar to one another. The principle of proportionality will be upheld if all of these cases resemble one another. The death sentence will be overturned only if the court can identify the case under review as an aberrant judgment, a case in which the circumstances of a murder or the characteristics of the defendant are strikingly dissimilar to those in other death sentences. The circumstances most likely to occasion a substantive legal argument on this basis are those where the death sentence has been imposed upon one codefendant, while an "equally or more culpable" codefendant received life.[146] Typically, however, state court opinions upholding death sentences consist of inflammatory rhetoric, a recitation of horrors designed to appeal to emotions of vengeance and disgust before the court upholds the death sentence. Moderation is rare.

Interestingly, those state supreme courts that only consider the pool of other death sentences typically say little or nothing about their proportionality review procedures. The court may not even cite another case in affirming a death sentence. Courts adopting this approach usually have a small and manageable number of cases immediately after reenactment of the death penalty. Ironically, perfunctory review procedures are usually institutionalized when the number of comparison cases grows, as more people in the jurisdiction are sentenced to death.

Capital convictions. Other state courts have defined the pool of comparison cases as all cases which resulted in a conviction for capital murder but not necessarily a death sentence. The rationale for this approach is that a death sentence should be compared with all cases where there has been an actual legal judgment which could have supported the imposition of the death sentence, that is, all convictions which reached the penalty phase of a capital trial.[147] Cases which have a factual or circumstantial similarity to the case under review are excluded if there was no conviction for capital murder. The justification for this exclusion is that prosecutorial and juror decision-making, and hence trial outcomes, are essentially unpredictable. This pool thus leaves out cases whose facts or circumstances could have supported a capital prosecution, but prosecutors choose not to pursue it.[148]

This initial choice does not result in the same universe in every jurisdiction. Nor does this decision rule mean that all death sentences or capital convictions which have ever been imposed in that jurisdiction will necessarily be included.[149] The pool may also not be comprised solely of jury verdicts at penalty phase. It may include some pleas to capital murder.[150] It may include some death sentences and life sentences imposed by a judge either without a jury or when overruling a jury.[151] It may or may not include death sentences reversed on appeal or the result of penalty phase retrials.[152]

A conviction for death-eligible murder under this rationale appropriately limits the class of similar cases because these are the only cases in which there is both a legal and factual foundation for the death sentence. Or, to put the matter in terms of similar defendants, members of this class are similar because they are the only defendants actually at risk of receiving the death penalty. Proportionality review in the state high court, then, exists for the sole purpose of correcting aberrant death sentences imposed by a jury or judge, after the factual and legal prerequisite for such a judgment has been found to exist. A death sentence may be found disproportionate if other cases with similar facts and circumstances resulted in a life sentence after a conviction for capital murder.[153]

Proportionality Review in Practice: Three States, Three Approaches

Connecticut: Racial Discrimination and the Abuse of Prosecutorial Discretion as a Matter of Statutory Interpretation

Recently, the Supreme Court of Connecticut addressed its state's constitutional issues with respect to capital punishment in depth, carefully examining the standards in other jurisdictions before holding that the statute met state constitutional standards in the case *State v. Ross.*[154] The challenge to the death sentence was not, however, based upon proportionality.[155] The legislature revised the death penalty statute, effective October 1, 1995, prospectively eliminating proportionality review.[156] The legislature presumably took this action to preempt the possibility of the court declaring the statute unconstitutional on grounds of proportionality. The court will, however, continue to conduct proportionality review for those cases in which the homicide occurred before the effective date of the amendment, avoiding issues of ex post facto.

The Supreme Court of Connecticut again addressed proportionality in *State v. Cobb.*[157] The proportionality arguments in *Cobb* were not based upon federal or state constitutional challenges. No empirical evidence or projections concerning the operation of the capital case processing system in the state were presented. The claim was that independent of the state and federal constitutions, the state proportionality review provision required expanding the universe of cases for proportionality review because the death penalty has been applied in a discriminatory manner.[158] Although the court did not consider the matter one of interpretation of state or federal constitutional issues, raising the issue of racial bias suggests that the court was mindful of the fact that this constitutional claim could be brought under proportionality review in the future.[159] The majority commented that evidence similar to that presented under *McCleskey* would be appropriately brought under the general provision for appellate review and such a claim would not necessarily be rejected if the factual basis was analogous to that in *McCleskey.*[160] The implication is that the Supreme Court of Connecticut could and would consider such evidence of bias and rule on the constitutional issue, irrespective of whether the legislature had eliminated proportionality review.

The question of what was and has been the universe of cases in Connecticut is confusing because the court made rulings regarding the universe of cases which were not published and because the universe of potentially similar cases includes crimes committed as far back as 1973, when the capital statute in Connecticut was passed.[161] The universe of cases in *Cobb* includes all capital felony cases which have reached the penalty phase since 1973.[162] In *Ross* the court refused the defendant's request that the universe be expanded to include those cases in which the state clearly could have, but did not, charge the accused with a capital felony and which then resulted in a conviction of not less than first-degree manslaughter.[163]

The court rested its interpretation on the legislative history of the proportionality review provision and held that the legislature did not "contemplate the kind of universe advocated by the defendant, which would necessarily be accompanied by a detailed, complex fact-finding."[164] The court also declined to follow the New Jersey model set out in *Marshall II;*[165] however, the court allowed the defendant to present a post-appeal state habeas corpus petition, including empirical evidence of systematic racial bias in the Connecticut capital punishment system as applied, after creating a reliable factual record at the trial level.[166] In other words, the court will allow the defense to present a factual record based upon a systemwide study of the state capital punishment system. The habeas corpus petition in state court on these issues is pending, and as of this writing no death sentence has been affirmed in Connecticut.

Nebraska: Conflict Between the Supreme Court and Legislature over the Universe of Cases for Proportionality Review

The 1978 Nebraska statute specifies that proportionality review encompasses challenges to systemwide disparities and challenges to possibly discriminatory patterns introduced by the exercise of prosecutorial discretion, including a consideration of prosecutorial charging practices.[167] Since 1979, however, the Nebraska Supreme Court has consistently narrowed the scope of proportionality review. The Nebraska Supreme Court initially interpreted the proportionality review statute as requiring the court to review only cases in which the defendant was found guilty of first-degree murder.[168] The court subsequently narrowed the pool of comparison cases even further to require a review only of death sentences imposed.[169] In other words, the court narrowed the universe of cases on two separate occasions. The most recent decisions of the Nebraska Supreme Court all limit comparison to other death sentences only, directly contradicting the 1978 statutory mandate to consider all potentially capital cases when conducting proportionality review.[170]

The majority opinion in *Williams* noted in dicta that the statutory mandate would violate constitutional principles of separation of powers if interpreted literally because it explicitly required the court to review prosecutorial decision-making in the selection of cases for capital prosecution.[171] And that was the statute's explicit intention. *Williams* did not, however, hold the proportionality review provision unconstitutional on those grounds.[172] Instead the court ignored the legislative mandate and decided to conduct proportionality review by comparing the death sentence under review only with all other convictions for first-degree murder after the effective date of the statute.[173] This compromise did not satisfy all members of the court.[174]

The Nebraska Supreme Court further narrowed the scope of proportionality review in the 1986 case of *State v. Palmer*.[175] The majority in *Palmer* concluded that the appropriate universe of cases for proportionality review was other death sentences.[176] The chief justice of the Nebraska Supreme Court objected not only that the court's decision ignored the legislature's explicit mandate to review all homicide cases which were potentially death-eligible,[177] but also that the court's decision to limit the universe of cases to other death sentences abrogated the primary function of proportionality review.

The purpose of the Nebraska statute requiring proportionality review, L.B. 711, was to ensure that persons were not being arbitrarily sentenced to death. To therefore suggest that we look only at those individuals who may have been discriminated against to determine whether or not they have been discriminated against is an exercise in futility. If one wants to determine whether individuals are being discriminated against in public transportation, one does not merely look at those who are required to sit in the back of the bus and conclude that since everyone in the back of the bus looks alike, there is no discrimination. One, of necessity, must look at who is riding in the front of the bus as well in order to determine whether the persons in the back are being discriminated against. So, too, there is no way that we can determine whether those who are sentenced to death are being discriminated against if we do not examine those cases having the same or similar circumstances which, for whatever reason, did not result in the imposition of a death sentence.[178]

The chief justice then proceeded to present a database and conduct his own proportionality review.[179] The chief justice attached to his opinion a list of 185 homicides in which individuals were involved in the killing of another and convicted, or pled guilty to either first-degree murder, second-degree murder, or manslaughter or less.[180] Of that number he noted that only thirteen, or 7 percent, of these cases resulted in the death penalty being considered.[181] Out of these 185 cases, Chief Justice Krivosha identified 57 homicides involving robberies, of which six, or 10.5 percent, including the case under review, resulted in the imposition of the death penalty.[182] A closer examination of the facts of some of the non-death cases demonstrated to the satisfaction of Chief Justice Krivosha that many of the cases where a life sentence was imposed had not only similar, but nearly identical, fact patterns to the death case on appeal.[183] Therefore the death sentence under review was, in his opinion, disproportionate.[184]

Statistics and Law: The Supreme Court of New Jersey's Implementation of Proportionality Review

The development of the law in New Jersey illustrates the possibilities of what a state high court can do under the rubric of proportionality review. The doctrinal foundation for proportionality review in New Jersey was developed in the five-year period between *State v. Ramseur*[185] in 1987, the case upholding the constitutionality of the New Jersey statute, and *State v. Marshall*[186] in 1992, when the court conducted its first proportionality review using the data and analysis presented to it in the Proportionality Review Project's "Final Report."[187] While the factual and legal issues in New Jersey were not unusual, they were simply not addressed with such careful reasoning elsewhere. Nonetheless, the Supreme Court of New Jersey has not yet reversed any death sentences on grounds of proportionality.[188]

State v. Marshall II is the leading case on proportionality review. Issues which were referred to tangentially in other jurisdictions were fully litigated before the New Jersey court. These issues polarized opinion on the court, although the majority held for the principle of systemwide review and for the commitment to proportionality review based upon comprehensive empirical analysis. The political pressure to abandon or severely restrict proportionality review was present in New Jersey just as it was in other jurisdictions. Even though it was politically costly to do so, the court maintained its initial commitment to the establishment of a process dedicated to protecting the constitutional due process rights of capital defendants. This sustained support for a reliable and comprehensive data-gathering and analysis project has not yet been matched by any other state high court.

Many other state high courts were presented with the identical statutory mandate as New Jersey following *Gregg.*[189] Similarly, New Jersey legal institutions and New Jersey homicide cases incorporate most of the features observed in other jurisdictions.[190] The New Jersey high court addressed the questions which arise again and again in other jurisdictions: what should be the universe of cases; should proportionality review include the review of prosecutorial discretion in charging; how should racial and geographic disparities be examined; what should be the relationship between the authority of the state high court and the legislature; how should the political pressure placed on the court be reduced; and what is the foundation and purpose of proportionality review itself? What other state high courts did, or did not do, as they set about to conduct proportionality review is brought into focus by examining the approach taken by the Supreme Court of New Jersey.

The Proportionality Review Project of the Supreme Court of New Jersey put flesh on the bones of the statutory mandate to conduct proportionality review. Under the direction of the court's special master, David C. Baldus, the Proportionality Review Project established a reliable database and a methodology and procedure for conducting proportionality review. Building on the assembled facts and the technical analysis of the Proportionality Review Project, the court then defined the constitutional foundation for proportionality review. From the beginning of the development of these principles to the conclusion of the first phase of proportionality review marked by *Marshall II,* the court moved against the direction taken by other high courts and contrary to the evolving capital jurisprudence of the U.S. Supreme Court.

The Proportionality Review Project identified the relevant variables affecting capital case processing and analyzed them using the most sophisticated social science methodologies available, while the project itself made substantial contributions to those methodologies.[191] The court educated itself concerning these methods and used the analyses in its proportionality review of Robert Marshall's death sentence.[192] The court chose among alternative formulations of comparison categories, rejecting some, elaborating upon others. At no time was the court the passive recipient of an expert's opinion. The court never shirked its responsibility to define the constitutional dimensions of proportionality for itself in the context of capital punishment.[193]

The methodological contributions of the Proportionality Review Project represent a considerable advance over previously existing methods for tracking case dispositions, and for measuring defendant culpability and the relative aggravation level of murder cases, especially for those cases which did not go to trial as capital cases.[194] The development of the constitutional principles underlying proportionality traces a part of the history of the court itself under the leadership of former Chief Justice Robert N. Wilentz. The court's center held on to proportionality, but it become increasingly embattled, both from within and without, with Justice Garibaldi and Justice Handler increasingly defining independent positions.[195] The death of Chief Justice Wilentz in July 1996 may change these alignments and signal a change in the court's continued commitment to systematic proportionality review.

The early history of proportionality review in New Jersey. In 1982 the New Jersey legislature reinstated capital punishment. Reenactment occurred a decade after the state's former capital punishment statute had been declared unconstitutional by the U.S. Supreme Court, followed by the reluctant concurrence of the state supreme court. It occurred almost two decades after the last execution in New Jersey.[196] The New Jersey capital punishment scheme, like the majority of those now in effect in the thirty-nine other capital jurisdictions, is built upon a structure of statutory aggravating and mitigating factors which are found as facts and then weighed by a specially selected jury during the second stage of a capital trial.

Not all murders are eligible for capital prosecution in New Jersey. As in other states, the county prosecutor in each of the twenty-one separate county jurisdictions has the sole discretionary authority to select which of the potentially death-eligible cases will be subject to capital prosecution through a procedure called the serving of a notice of factors. Throughout the period considered here, the law required both a factual basis for one of the eight enumerated statutory aggravating factors and that the defendant either committed the homicidal act by his own conduct with the requisite intent to kill, or paid another to commit the homicidal act.[197]

The language of the proportionality review provision in New Jersey was taken directly from *Gregg:* the New Jersey Supreme Court shall determine whether the death sentence is "disproportionate to the penalty imposed in similar cases, considering both the crime and the defendant."[198] Proportionality review was created by statute; however, it was always the responsibility of the state high court to determine how proportionality review would be conducted.[199]

The Office of the Public Defender raised proportionality in all capital appeals beginning in 1982. The earliest direct appeals included data from the Public Defender Homicide Study in support of appellate arguments that the operation of the capital case processing system in New Jersey violated constitutional principles of proportionality.[200] The Public Defender consistently argued that proportionality review must encompass an examination of the entire capital case processing system in the jurisdiction and incorporate an analysis of capital case processing by stages. It was an unusual and fortuitous circumstance that the New Jersey Office of the Public Defender had the resources and commitment to begin a systematic study of capital case processing throughout the state prior to the court appointing the special master.[201]

The identification of issues. State v. Ramseur[202] and *State v. Marshall II*[203] frame the constitutional jurisprudence on proportionality review in New Jersey.[204] Although proportionality review had not been mandated by the federal Constitution since *Pulley v. Harris,*[205] or by the New Jersey legislature since 1985,[206] in 1987 the state high court in *Ramseur* stated its commitment to performing thorough and complete examinations of the imposition of the death penalty in the jurisdiction under the rubric of proportionality review: "Proportionality review has a function entirely unique among the review proceedings in a capital proceeding . . . 'It purports to inquire instead whether the penalty is nonetheless unacceptable in a particular case because disproportionate to the punishment imposed on others convicted of the same crime.'"[207] In *Ramseur* the court expressed "some preliminary views concerning this important aspect of the death-penalty review process . . ."[208] Although proportionality review had not yet been institutionalized within the Administrative Office of the Courts in 1987, the court was prescient in delineating the parameters of the impending legal debate within the court and in the larger legal community in New Jersey and elsewhere.

Prior to *Ramseur,* the court identified its concern that prosecutorial discretion could be a possible source of arbitrary or discriminatory patterns in capital charging and sentencing.[209] Then in *Ramseur* the court declared its intention to review prosecutorial decision-making in the selection of cases for capital prosecution. In doing so, it anticipated that it would consider empirical evidence of discrimination based upon race, sex, and socioeconomic status as part of proportionality review.[210] Proportionality review would be statewide. It would include systematic data collection and a statistical analysis of the entire capital case processing system. The court called on the expert advice of statisticians, criminologists, sociologists, and others to help prepare the database.[211]

The process of record gathering. In *Ramseur* the court asked all parties who expected to participate in the appellate review process in future capital cases to "begin gathering data necessary for proportionality review of a death penalty in comparison to similar crimes and defendants. Moreover, these statistics will be helpful in determining whether there is race and gender discrimination in the imposition of the death penalty."[212] The court correctly anticipated that controversy would crystallize around the issue of the universe of cases.[213] This apparently procedural decision in fact determined the scope of proportionality review itself. The controversy was initially resolved by the court in *Marshall II,* with the selection of the universe of cases recommended by the special master. However, the legislature would finally intervene on the side of the attorney general, and attempt to restrict the universe of cases.[214]

In 1991 the court created the Proportionality Review Project and appointed the independent special master in an unprecedented and unexpected order. The July 29, 1988, order[215] gave the special master the authority to collect and analyze data, produce a database and files on individual homicide cases, invite the participation of interested parties, develop a public data file (including a record of dispositions of all relevant homicide cases), conduct hearings, procure expert technical advice, call witnesses, and request public records and any other relevant information. Not only was the special master given broad authority to accomplish a comprehensive, scientifically sound empirical study, but the court appointed as special master a person capable of achieving such a task: Professor David C. Baldus.[216] The special master was specifically ordered to consider and assess the validity and utility of the database and analyses presented to the court in the reports of the Public Defender Homicide Study.[217] To its credit the Proportionality Review Project accomplished all of the tasks enumerated in the order.

The special master was ordered to make recommended findings of fact and recommended conclusions of law regarding proportionality in the administration of cases subject to capital punishment in New Jersey, but not to make any determination concerning the excessiveness or disproportionality of any death sentence imposed in any particular case.[218] The legal determination of proportionality was the province of the court. The special master was to educate the court and provide the court with the factual basis necessary to make an informed decision. The report recommended that the court keep open the database, and that it continue to include death-eligible cases which did not reach penalty phase. The court accepted that recommendation in *Marshall II.*[219]

The Proportionality Review Project conducted research over a four-year period, assembling what is probably the most complete database ever compiled by a court on homicide and capital case processing in a single United States jurisdiction.[220] The 1991 "Final Report" is both an extensive review of all death-eligible cases in the jurisdiction from 1982 to 1990 and an exhaustive proportionality analysis of Robert Marshall's individual death sentence. The attorney general filed an Independent Report containing a series of tables and analyses based upon an expanded data set of 264 death-eligible murder cases.[221] The 246 cases analyzed in detail in the 1991 "Final Report" went to the penalty phase as death-eligible cases or were found to have met the factual criteria for at least one statutory aggravating factor, and hence to have been potentially death-eligible, although the death sentence was either not imposed, not charged, or not even considered by the county prosecutor.[222] Justice Garibaldi took exception to this selection of cases.[223]

During the four years of the Proportionality Review Project the attorney general of New Jersey consistently proposed that proportionality review be limited to death sentences only in its arguments before the courts, in its briefs, and in the proportionality review meetings. The attorney general also brought an independent action asking the court for a declaration that the universe of cases be limited to death sentences only.[224] The high court consistently refused to limit proportionality review to such a restricted category.[225] During the pendency of *Marshall* the attorney general took these arguments to the legislature, where he was successful in persuading the legislature to pass a statute adopting the state's position, declaring that the universe of cases for proportionality review would be limited to death sentences only.[226]

The relevance of the data to systemwide claims of unconstitutional infliction of the death penalty. In *Ramseur* the New Jersey Supreme Court stated its position on discrimination at the outset: "Discrimination on the basis of race, sex, or other suspect characteristics cannot be tolerated . . ."[227] *Marshall II* reaffirmed that commitment and stated it more sharply:

> Were we to believe that the race of the victim and race of the defendant played a significant part in capital sentencing decisions in New Jersey, we would seek corrective measures, and if that failed

> we could not, consistent with our State's policy, tolerate discrimination that threatened the foundation of our system of law.[228]

The first major issue addressed by the *Ramseur* court was whether proportionality review was the appropriate vehicle for examining systemwide defects in the operation of the capital case processing system. The court believed it was, declaring that "proportionality review therefore is a means through which to monitor the imposition of death sentences and thereby to prevent any impermissible discrimination in imposing the death penalty."[229] The *Ramseur* court's declaration did not end the controversy over this issue. In 1992 Justice Garibaldi broke with the *Marshall II* majority on this question.[230]

The *Ramseur* majority then set out its views on the second principal issue in proportionality review, the definition of similar cases.[231] In *Ramseur* the court anticipated what factors would be relevant in developing categories of similar cases and called for guidance from experts in their development.[232] The difference between the complexity of analysis in *Marshall II* and what was previously anticipated in *Ramseur* indicates just how far the court was brought along by the empirical analysis of the special master's "Final Report." In *Marshall II* the facts allowed for a number of comparison categories, and the court went through a separate proportionality analysis for each category. The analysis relied upon by the court in *Marshall II* was far more detailed and case-specific than what could have been anticipated in *Ramseur.*[233]

Racial and geographical disparities and their relation to differences in prosecutorial charging practices. In *Ramseur* the New Jersey high court did not avoid another area of controversy: whether it would be appropriate within the context of proportionality for the court to examine the prosecutor's discretionary selection of cases for capital prosecution.[234] This issue sharply divided other state high courts. In *State v. Koedatich* the court prodded county prosecutors to take action to reduce disparities in capital case charging.[235] The *Koedatich* court strongly suggested that New Jersey should promulgate uniform statewide guidelines for the exercise of prosecutorial discretion in the selection of cases for capital prosecution.[236] In response to this directive, the attorney general and county prosecutors adopted a set of "Guidelines for the Designation for Capital Prosecution."[237] The guidelines directed each county prosecutor to screen all death-eligible homicide cases in the jurisdiction and then decide whether or not a notice of factors should be served in any individual case. The guidelines stated that the goal is to achieve uniform statewide standards for the charging of capital murder: "It is neither desirable nor acceptable to have a capital charging standard dependent upon individual attitudes."[238]

The guidelines' preamble asserts that "race, sex, social or economic religion [*sic*] and/or national origin of a defendant [or victim] has not in the past, nor will in the future be considered in any fashion to determine whether or not a case warrants capital prosecution."[239] The preamble further states that "economic or other resource constraints of their respective offices shall not be a factor in determining whether or not the case warrants capital prosecution nor shall it in any specific case play any role whatsoever in the capital designation decision making process."[240]

The reference to economic or resource constraints is particularly noteworthy.[241] There are several aspects of the costs issue. To begin with, no one disputes that capital cases cost the system considerably more than non-capital cases—for the prosecution, the defense, and the courts. The question of who pays is always relevant. Another aspect of the cost issue is whether prosecutorial charging decisions are influenced by the budgetary constraints of local prosecutors, and/or the relative prosperity of individual counties.[242] A cost issue which did not arise during this period in New Jersey, but which is very much in the forefront elsewhere, is whether the state can effectively limit the defense of capital cases by refusing to authorize adequate funds for indigent capital defense.[243] Related to the defense limitation issue is the question of whether states may prohibit expenditure of funds for the development of a factual basis for a constitutional challenge. In New Jersey the legal costs of developing defense arguments on proportionality were not initially allocated to the county, thereby postponing some of these problems.

Capital murder prosecutions are significantly more expensive to prosecute than cases which do not proceed capitally.[244] In New Jersey the twenty-one county prosecutors are funded by twenty-one separate and autonomous authorities of the county freeholders.[245] Some counties are very rich, while other counties face severe budgetary constraints. The urban counties, such as Essex County, which includes the city of Newark, and Camden County, are characterized by a declining inner-city tax base and high maintenance expenses.[246] The problem of vastly different economic resource distribution among counties is replicated in most large industrial states, the majority of whom now have substantial death row populations.[247]

Homicides themselves are also unevenly distributed across the state.[248] For instance, Essex County reports over 140 homicides a year on average.[249] A significant fraction of these are felony murders. Under the definition of the felony factor in the New Jersey statute, every felony murderer is potentially death-eligible if he committed the homicidal act by his own conduct with the requisite specific intent to kill.[250] During the period studied by the Proportionality Review Project, the Essex County prosecutor alone could have averaged 20 capital murder prosecutions a year for felony murder cases.

On April 6, 1989, the attorney general and the county prosecutors jointly asked the Supreme Court of New Jersey to rule on the appropriate universe of cases for proportionality review.[251] The attorney general and the county prosecutors saw proportionality review as a limited remedy whose purpose was to correct aberrational judgments. In their view, proportionality review was inappropriate for consideration of possible racial bias or other systemwide defects in the operation of the state's capital case processing system, irrespective of whether racial or other disparities were introduced by prosecutorial discretion or other factors.[252]

The Office of the Public Defender took the position that the court must have a sufficiently large database of cases from which to select appropriate categories of similar cases if proportionality review was to be meaningful.[253] The database must include information on cases which were not prosecuted as capital cases so that prosecutorial discretion in charging could be subject to judicial review by the state's highest court. Proportionality review was created, the Public Defender argued, to allow the court to identify and correct systemwide defects, such as disparities related to race or economic factors, which might have been introduced by the exercise of prosecutorial discretion, caprice, or any other extralegal factor.

The attorney general and the county prosecutors maintained that the New Jersey capital punishment system did not exhibit constitutionally impermissible disparities, and that proportionality review was not the mechanism for identifying or correcting such systemwide defects, even if there was evidence of them. They were unpersuaded by data and analysis presented by the Public Defender Homicide Study or the special master's "Final Report," or by studies from other jurisdictions indicating that the exercise of prosecutorial discretion in the selection of capital cases had resulted in evidence of systemwide disparities.[254] The Office of the Public Defender argued there was no reason to think that such systemwide disparities are confined to a single aberrant jurisdiction or a particular period. The preliminary results of its own research suggested that racial and geographic disparities were present in the New Jersey capital case processing system. In *Marshall II,* the high court adopted this position:

> That, we believe, is an acceptable understanding of the intentions of the framers of our Act—that statutory proportionality review

> should seek to ensure that the death penalty is being administered in a rational, non-arbitrary, and evenhanded manner, fairly and with reasonable consistency. That review serves as "a means through which to monitor the imposition of death sentences and thereby to prevent any impermissible discrimination in imposing the death penalty."[255]

Especially noteworthy was the court's willingness to analyze the capital case processing system from its earliest stages, beginning with every indictment for homicide in the state.[256] Even Justice Garibaldi, who took the position that prosecutors' discretionary decisions not to seek the death penalty should not be reexamined, was persuaded that the database must include all cases that the prosecutors declared capital.[257]

The methods of analysis. The 1991 "Final Report" of the Proportionality Review Project describes in detail its methodology for classifying cases as clearly death-eligible.[258] This is a critical methodological decision and one which the special master addressed with care. What facts are sufficient to define the presence of statutory aggravating factors absent a penalty phase determination, and how are these facts established? How are "cases" similar, considering both the "crime" and the "defendant"? The research in New Jersey gave new meaning to the abstraction: "in similar cases, considering both the crime and the defendant."[259] The preparation of detailed narrative summaries of the circumstances of the offense and the procedural history of the case was a crucial part of this methodology. Even with a detailed data collection instrument, maintaining an accurate record of the procedural events and circumstances of the crime was impossible without a narrative description. The narrative description for each case also gave the court concrete and specific facts for its qualitative analyses.

The 1991 "Final Report" addressed the methodological problem of how facts relevant to aggravating and mitigating factors are to be determined absent a penalty phase jury verdict. The methodology developed in New Jersey for classifying cases as death-eligible takes into account the strength of the evidence in the case on the elements of capital murder and is fact-sensitive.[260] This "strength of the evidence" typology sets out what constitutes an overwhelming case, a strong case, a clearly defensible case, and a clearly insufficient case on all of the elements of capital murder, including statutory aggravating factors.[261] An overwhelming case, for example, would include evidence from eyewitnesses or a full confession which completely corroborated all of the elements of capital murder, including the "by his own conduct" requirement, the presence of at least one statutory aggravating factor, and the requisite mens rea under the legal standard in effect at the time.[262] Finding a measure for mens rea in cases which did not result in a jury verdict proved to be one of the Proportionality Review Project's most challenging tasks. A clearly insufficient case, on the other hand, would include eyewitness evidence which only placed the defendant at the scene of the crime, or evidence which was inconclusive or unreliable. Non-penalty phase cases are identified as clearly death-eligible only if there is overwhelming or strong evidence for all of the elements of capital murder.[263]

In another notable methodological advance, the 1991 "Final Report" developed two separate streams of analysis—one for decision-making by juries and another for decision-making by prosecutors, judges, and others.[264] Jury decisions regarding facts and culpability trumped all other decisions. The methodological question was, how to determine facts when a jury was never presented with them, when a jury decision was preempted. A jury finding of intent less than the requisite intent for capital murder, for example, a jury verdict for manslaughter, would automatically exclude a case from the category of death-eligible murder—and thus from proportionality review—no matter how strongly the factual circumstances suggested a basis for death eligibility.

One of the Proportionality Review Project's principal goals was to identify why some cases reach capital trial while others, which meet the "legal" criteria for death eligibility, do not.[265] The project built upon the stage analysis of the earlier reports of the Public Defender Homicide Study, which began with an analysis of cases which dropped out of the capital case processing system. A sharp decline in the number of potentially capital cases at each successive capital case processing stage is typical.[266] Each county prosecutor unilaterally makes decisions about whether to declare a case capital. In almost all jurisdictions, prosecutors are elected and capital case prosecutions are vehicles for keeping the prosecutor in the public eye.[267] New Jersey is exceptional in that neither county prosecutors nor judges are elected. Prosecutors are appointed for five-year terms. Local and party politics, however, play a role in the appointment process.[268]

The 1991 "Final Report" identified a significant race-of-defendant effect which has been replicated by subsequent research of the Proportionality Review Project. This effect was not considered by the court to be a sufficient basis for declaring the death sentence imposed upon Robert Marshall to be disproportionate.[269] In *Marshall* the court expressed its ongoing concern that decision-making by prosecutors could be the cause of racial disparities in capital case processing.[270] The court continues to conduct proportionality analysis with an updated database. The most recent proportionality review research, prepared for *State v. Harris,*[271] yielded significant race effects.[272]

The politics of proportionality review in New Jersey. Conflict between the legislature, the state supreme court, and the attorney general ensued in spite of or perhaps because of the principled commitment of the New Jersey Supreme Court to its Proportionality Review Project. The court was sharply criticized by state legislators, the press, and the New Jersey attorney general on capital punishment issues, particularly proportionality review, during the period from 1982 until 1992. The antagonistic relationship between the attorney general, the state legislature, and the court was influenced by a variety of national and state events, not all of which were related to capital punishment, or to proportionality review, although capital punishment issues were prominent in the five-year period between *Ramseur*[273] and *Marshall II.*[274]

Capital punishment in the late 1980s and early 1990s was a salient political issue which politicians ignored at their peril.[275] There was then and is now no political support for those accused of capital murder and their representatives in the legal system. Moreover, the issues surrounding the cost of the reimposition of the death penalty, which might have caused some members of the public or the legislature to question the reimposition of capital punishment, have never been documented or treated seriously by the public, the press, or the legislature.[276]

The conflict between the New Jersey legislature and the New Jersey Supreme Court over capital punishment was preceded by sharp disagreements on other highly political issues, such as school funding and mandated low-income housing in suburban residential communities.[277] Conflict between the state high court and legislature occurs in many jurisdictions, but the supreme court under the leadership of Chief Justice Wilentz provoked more than the ordinary amount of controversy. It was the Wilentz court's willingness to adopt principled and politically unpopular positions that led to its preeminence among state high courts.

Conflict between the court and the legislature began with a 1985 amendment to the capital punishment statute which retained the proportionality review requirement but removed the provision making such review mandatory in all appeals of death sentences.[278] In its first capital punishment decision, the Supreme Court of New Jersey indicated that it did not intend to have its constitutional jurisprudence on capital punishment dictated by the legislature.[279] The court simply continued to prepare to conduct a proportionality review of every death sentence which was not reversed on other constitutional grounds.[280]

The New Jersey Supreme Court waited five years before holding the revised capital punishment statute constitutional on state and federal grounds.[281] Given the direction of federal constitutional law, the state constitutional holding was the important interpretation. Many state legislators were impatient with this delay and even more antagonized by the fact that the court reversed twenty-six death sentences before upholding the death sentence of Robert Marshall on direct appeal in January 1991.[282]

The impatience of state legislators reared itself at Chief Justice Wilentz's reconfirmation in 1986. In New Jersey, judges are not elected. They are appointed by the governor subject to confirmation by the Judiciary Committee of the New Jersey Senate.[283] The reconfirmation of the chief justice in 1986 was delayed by legislators who were frustrated by the court's independence under his leadership. The court's decisions in capital cases were a large part of the controversy.[284] Legislators, the governor, and state law enforcement officials expressed the view that the court was determined not to enforce the capital punishment statute, even though the court had been unwilling or unable to declare the statute unconstitutional.[285]

In 1988, conflict between the state legislature and supreme court and criticism of the court by the law enforcement community intensified after the court held in *State v. Gerald*[286] that proof of a specific intent to kill, not merely an intent to cause bodily harm, was a prerequisite for a conviction for capital murder.[287] Ironically, the death sentence was reversed on other grounds as well, but this became the general doctrine. The New Jersey legislature and state law enforcement personnel became even more outraged when a series of death sentences were overturned by the court on the basis of *Gerald*.[288] Since before *Gerald* the court has based its constitutional rulings in capital cases on independent state constitutional grounds, leaving no basis for an appeal to or the possibility of reversal by the U.S. Supreme Court.[289]

In the period between 1982 and 1991, public support for capital punishment in the country as a whole stayed high and showed little sign of being eroded, although there was no state poll on the issue in New Jersey from 1982 to 1992.[290] Even if the "public" was not more in favor of capital punishment and executions than they had been in the past, it was clear to New Jersey legislators and others that the U.S. Supreme Court had undergone a substantial doctrinal shift during the intervening decade.[291] The federal courts were not predictably going to interfere with any state supreme court ruling or statute which had the intention or effect of streamlining the process of carrying out executions.[292] Federal remedies became increasingly unavailable to state capital defendants during the period.[293] The Supreme Court of New Jersey was correctly perceived to be the principal impediment to executions being carried out in the state.

An unusual election in November 1991 in which the entire New Jersey Senate and Assembly stood for election resulted in a veto-proof Republican majority in both houses for the first time in twenty-five years. Thereafter, on March 12, 1992, the governor of New Jersey signed into law legislation restricting proportionality review in capital cases to cases in which the death sentence was imposed.[294] The newly elected legislature also directly challenged the independence of the New Jersey Supreme Court by passing a proposed constitutional amendment[295] that overturned the court's holding in *State v. Gerald*.[296]

These actions appeared to be part of a broad conservative agenda of the newly elected members of the legislature,[297] but the court did not change its procedure for conducting proportionality review when the "death only" law was enacted.[298] At some point the court will necessarily conduct proportionality review with the newly reduced comparison category of death sentence cases only, but the practical effect of the amendment may be minimal. In *Marshall II* the court stated its commitment to the larger universe for the consideration of broad constitutional issues such as racial discrimination and arbitrariness in capital sentencing generally.[299]

The 1995 Reenactment in New York: New Rules for the Reimposition of Capital Punishment in the 1990s

The election of Republican Governor George Pataki in 1994 marked a turning point in New York politics.[300] Governor Mario Cuomo was defeated in the 1994 election in part because of his continued opposition to capital punishment, even though he had been elected over pro–death penalty opponents in 1986 and 1990. His defeat in November 1994 followed a campaign in which Pataki kept Cuomo's opposition to the death penalty in the public eye.

Reenactment was a certainty after the election of Governor Pataki, and a reenactment bill was passed less than six months after Pataki took office.[301] The timing of reenactment in New York strongly influenced the structure of the New York statute.[302] Experienced New York prosecutors and defense attorneys watched for twenty years as the number of persons on death row across the nation climbed to over 3,000 and the number of executions passed

300 with relatively little public protest.[303] New York was no longer going to be the exception.

The Importance of New York for Proportionality Review

By 1995 all efforts to enact national legislation addressing the persistent evidence of racial disparities in the application of state capital statutes had been rejected by the U.S. Congress.[304] With no foreseeable prospect of the Congress enacting legislation which would require states to address the constitutional issues raised by the persistent evidence of racial disparities in capital sentencing, the procedures for appellate review included in the New York statute become especially critical. While no one can predict how the New York Court of Appeals will address issues of racial and geographic disparities in capital charging and sentencing, it is certain such disparities will emerge.[305] The statute anticipates that the court will consider the constitutional issues from an empirical perspective.

The New York Court of Appeals is in a position to take advantage of the strides made by the Supreme Court of New Jersey in defining the constitutional parameters for proportionality review under state constitutional law. Like the Supreme Court of New Jersey, the New York Court of Appeals has a long and distinguished history of developing state constitutional doctrine. This court's consideration of the constitutional issues raised by the reenactment of capital punishment in New York will not be perfunctory or evasive. That litigation and the development of state constitutional doctrine on the application of the death penalty in New York are anticipated with great interest in the national legal community.

No participant in the reenactment process in New York, including the state legislators, expects that the initial decision on the constitutionality of the New York statute will be made by a federal court. This is an important difference from the view expressed in many state legislatures in the past. Legislators in states where reenactment occurred prior to *Pulley* and *McCleskey* fully expected the U.S. Supreme Court to rule on the constitutionality of their statute, and they fashioned their statutes for review by the Supreme Court. State legislators copied the Georgia statute because they expected that was the only version of a capital statute which would be upheld by the Supreme Court. No such expectation of imminent review by the U.S. Supreme Court existed in New York in 1995. The New York Court of Appeals will, in all likelihood, be the first and only court to address the constitutional issues regarding the application of the New York statute in this century.

The national and local politics regarding capital punishment changed dramatically between 1976 and 1995, and the effects of these changes are reflected in the structure of the New York statute. The New York statute was designed to build in, to the extent the legislature was willing and able to do so, protections for the due process rights of capital defendants. The statute is structured to preempt protracted litigation on certain issues which have been exhaustively litigated in other states or in the federal courts. Further, and most importantly, the statute is very detailed, with specific provisions on several issues which have been sharpened by extensive adversarial litigation in the state and federal courts throughout the 1980s. This by itself is remarkable. There is no other capital legislation which attempts to preempt litigation to this extent. Many of the provisions in this statute had previously been the subject of highly partisan debate in state and federal courts, in the state legislatures, and before the U.S. Congress.[306] Ironically, however, the specificity of some provisions may increase the likelihood of litigation, rather than preempt it.

Statutory Provisions for Appellate Review and Proportionality Review

The specificity of the appellate review procedures incorporated within the 1995 New York statute is unique. This comprehensive statutory structure, including very detailed rules governing the procedures and substantive aspects of appellate review, means at the very least that litigation under the statute will be governed by new principles. The New York Court of Appeals will first be required to address the statutory provisions under review and their effect and purpose. The legislature's clear intention is that the court of appeals will thoroughly review all constitutional issues, both state and federal, in direct capital appeals.[307]

The New York Court of Appeals has a distinguished history and is known for its independence. The experience of the Proportionality Review Project in New Jersey can save the New York Court of Appeals from time-consuming litigation if the court institutes procedures for maintaining a reliable factual record for proportionality review and the consideration of other constitutional issues raised by racial and geographic disparities in capital case processing.

Although no death sentence has been imposed in New York in 1996, there are already indications of disparities in the policies of local prosecutors. At the time of reenactment some New York prosecutors, most notably the district attorneys in the Bronx and Manhattan, had gone on record as saying they were not in favor of the reenactment.[308] The district attorney from the Bronx, in particular, stated that his constituents did not support the death penalty and that he did not intend to seek it.[309]

All death sentences will be reviewed by the court of appeals, irrespective of whether the defendant requests such a review.[310] This review cannot be waived by the defendant.[311] A provision allows the court to set aside a sentence of death "in the interests of justice," which would encompass a variety of injustices at trial or incapacities of representation.[312]

The statute specifically provides for the court to consider, upon written motion, cases in which the death sentence is imposed on the grounds of improper conduct of a juror or a jury, or newly discovered evidence—grounds which are no longer considered sufficient to reopen a case by the federal courts in habeas corpus proceedings.[313] The statute affords the state the opportunity to appeal from a trial judge's order setting aside the sentence of death, another controversial procedural provision with constitutional implications strongly favoring the prosecution.[314]

The statute also contains provisions governing the court's consideration of evidence of racial disparities.[315] The court of appeals must determine whether the sentence of death was imposed under the influence of any "other arbitrary or legally impermissible factor including whether the imposition of the verdict or sentence was based upon the race of the defendant or [the race of] a victim of the crime for which the defendant was convicted."[316] And the statute has a proportionality review provision which requires the court of appeals to determine whether the sentence of death is "excessive or disproportionate to the penalty imposed in similar cases considering both the crime and the defendant."[317] The proportionality review provision additionally provides that the court shall, "upon request of the defendant . . . review whether the sentence of death is excessive or disproportionate to the penalty imposed in similar cases by virtue of the race of the defendant or a victim of the crime for which the defendant was convicted."[318] The presence of two such provisions means that if the legislature should repeal only the requirement for proportionality review, there would still be a second provision making explicit reference to the court's obligation to consider racial disparities in the application of the statute. In other words, the statute preempts the legislature's removal or limitation of proportionality review.

The statute establishes that the court of appeals, and not another institution, has the authority and responsibility for creating and maintaining a database on capital case processing, including the creation of an accurate record of all murders and their disposition throughout the entire state.[319] The court of appeals has broad authority to set rules and procedures for the review of capital cases.[320] It is noteworthy that the court has not limited its universe of cases to penalty phase trials.

The fact that the statute refers to statistical evidence implies that the New York Court of Appeals intends to rule on the state constitutional issues based upon facts established in a scientifically reliable empirical study of its capital case processing system, similar to the data and analysis prepared for the Supreme Court of New Jersey. The court has already committed to a uniform capital case data report form for systematic data collection. Importantly, the universe of cases is all indictments for first-degree murder, whether disposed of by plea or trial. As part of proportionality review, the court may consider statistical evidence to determine whether the race of the victim or the race of the defendant is having a "significant" impact upon the imposition of the death penalty. The use of the term "significant" implies that the court anticipates a standard multivariate analysis such as that recommended by the U.S. General Accounting Office.[321] Such evidence may be based upon the required data reports submitted and filed with the court, or upon evidence independently gathered by the defense. The specific reference to data independently prepared by the defense implies that the legislature intended the court to consider all relevant empirical evidence. The legislative history supports that interpretation.[322] With this background, empirical findings are not likely to be ignored or dismissed by this court.

These provisions stand in sharp contrast to the proportionality review provisions of any other state. The reference to the collection of data on race is not now included in any other state statute. The New York Court of Appeals called for comments on its proposed rules very soon after enactment.[323] Detailed comments on the proposed rules for data collection and the maintenance of an adequate record for proportionality review were submitted by attorneys with experience with the implementation of proportionality review in New Jersey and other states.[324]

Twenty years ago legislators and lobbyists would not have considered including provisions explicitly stating that the court of appeals can always consider questions "in the interests of justice," or on the basis of newly discovered evidence of innocence. Prior to the present holdings of the U.S. Supreme Court, the assumption would have been that newly acquired evidence of innocence could always be presented, even after appeals were completed. However, given the present capital jurisprudence of the Supreme Court, such provisions have become advisable, if not necessary.[325]

The first capital case probably will not reach the New York Court of Appeals on direct review for at least two or more years. Interlocutory appeals, and even perhaps statistical evidence on the operation of the capital case processing system in New York, may precede the first direct capital appeal. The court of appeals will have the benefit of the experience in Georgia, New Jersey, Connecticut, Pennsylvania, and other jurisdictions. Technical advice on systematic case tracking, the necessity of a clear and concise narrative summary for each case, accessibility to and the appropriate use of the official data set, and other issues have already been the subject of comment. This court will be in a better position to conduct systematic proportionality review than any other state high court has been in the past.

In particular, the New York Court of Appeals will benefit greatly from the expertise of the Proportionality Review Project commissioned by the Supreme Court of New Jersey. The court of appeals seems to recognize its responsibility to maintain an adequate record so that disparities in capital sentencing based upon racial identification and other extralegal factors can be accurately identified and measured. Without such documentation, references to due process protections by legislators and others are an empty litany, performing lip service to the appearance, but not the fact, of justice.

Conclusion

State high courts have been the principal interpreters of state constitutional doctrine in capital jurisprudence since *Gregg*. Overwhelmingly, these institutions have not been staunch guardians of the constitutional rights of capital defendants, or so it would seem from the way in which states have conducted proportionality review. As the state-by-state analysis indicates, vast differences exist among the states on this subject. The national frustration, even rage, over what is perceived to be an intractable crime problem, and its association, in the minds of the public, with minorities in large cities, and the fragility of courts in the face of political pressure seem to make courts unwilling to reverse death sentences on grounds of documented racial or geographical disparities. Such documentation, showing sharp differences in the administration of justice with respect to the death penalty, might well persuade courts of the unconstitutionality of the application of capital punishment within a jurisdiction if they were actually willing to review it. The Supreme Court of New Jersey has been the exception. The Court of Appeals in New York now has the opportunity to follow New Jersey's lead.

In the past few years a few other state supreme courts have also refused to bow to the public's demand for vengeance. Too often, however, it appears that, for the overwhelmingly white and middle-class members of the judiciary, young men, many of them minorities, who have committed murder are the problem, not an allegedly discriminatory criminal justice system. And when, in jurisdiction after jurisdiction, an innocent person is found to have been sentenced to death, it has little or no impact upon the criminal justice system in the state. That an innocent person has been found to be sentenced to death might in another era provoke a reaction of public outrage, but in this period the public and the courts do not seem surprised.

Certainly the large number of people on death row, as well as the sharp increase in the death row population in the period from 1984 to 1996, has influenced the public, the judiciary, and the administration of criminal justice. For the remainder of this century, state high courts and legislatures will be the legal institutions with the primary responsibility of protecting the constitutional rights of criminal defendants. These institutions, though they are beset by political pressures, by changing demographics, and by large and unwieldy caseloads, will, hopefully, create a jurisprudence which they and we can respect and recognize as principled.

Notes

Introduction

1. The benefit of clergy was a provision exempting certain offenders from arrest, attachment, or conviction. Later the benefit of clergy came to be applied to anyone connected with the church, and then to exempt from the death penalty anyone who could read and write. As the law developed, there was such abuse of the privilege that statutes were enacted denying the benefit of clergy for certain crimes. For a discussion of the benefit of clergy and its modification, see Leigh Bienen, "Rape I," 3 *Women's Rts. L. Rep.* 45 (1976); and 18 Eliz. 1, c. 7 (1576).

2. Great Britain no longer has a death penalty. The United States of America is the only Western country to continue the death penalty. The European Union has outlawed capital punishment. Any country joining the European Union must abolish capital punishment. This results in complications with extraditions from the European Union to the United States, since the European Union has refused to extradite any person to a country where he could be subject to the death penalty.

3. New Jersey now has no persons on death row, having abolished the death penalty in 2008. The proportionality review process in New Jersey and more recent developments in the state are described in chapters 2 and 5.

4. In Illinois nineteen men on death row have been exonerated; there have been a total of twelve executions since 1974. A series of highly dramatic exonerations—one involving a man a few days from execution—occurred in Illinois immediately prior to Governor Ryan's commutations. This history is described in detail in chapters 2 and 4. For the most recent information on the status of the death penalty in Illinois, see http://www.icadp.org/.

5. These and the subsequent statistics are from "Death Row U.S.A., Winter 2009," quarterly report of the Criminal Justice Project of the NAACP Legal Defense and Educational Fund, http://www.naacpldf.org/content/pdf/pubs/drusa/DRUSA_Winter_2009.pdf.

6. Texas has executed 423 and still has 358 on death row; Virginia has executed 102 and has 18 on death row. The number of executions in the United States peaked in 1999 with 98 in a single year, followed by 85 in 2000. California has 678 on death row; Ohio, 181; Florida, 402; Pennsylvania, 226. See "Death Row U.S.A., Winter 2009," *supra* note 5, at 1, 10, and 34 et seq.

7. The total number of death row inmates known to the Legal Defense and Educational Fund, as of January 1, 2009, was 3,297: 45 percent white, 42 percent black, 11 percent Latino/Hispanic, the remainder unknown; 98 percent male. Id. 1.

8. The federal Uniform Crime Reporting system defines murder as the willful, non-negligent killing of one human being by another. The most recent figure for 2004 showed

16,137 murders in the United States, a decrease of 3.3 percent from the prior year. The number of murders in the United States has been steadily decreasing, perhaps as a result of the aging of the population, perhaps as a result of an abeyance in the drug wars or the gang wars, or for some other reason, such as the high rate of incarceration of young men, especially young African Americans, in the age cohort most likely to commit murder. See "Crime in the United States, Murder" (content updated Feb. 17, 2006), tbl. 3, and other tables and figure, http://www.fbi.gov/ucr/cius2007 (data tables).

9. There is a federal death penalty and the military courts have the authority to sentence to death, but the numbers are very small in comparison to the number convicted and executed under state capital punishment systems. There are nine persons on death row who have been sentenced under the Code of Military Justice. "Death Row U.S.A., Winter 2009," *supra* note 5, at 35. See also chapter 5.

10. In New Jersey when the Supreme Court of New Jersey began to build its database of murders eligible for capital prosecution in the years since reenactment, it found there were over five hundred cases the State Bureau of Identification, the official state crime-reporting agency, did not have in their records. They knew nothing about them. Ironically, the files of the Clerk of the Court in the late nineteenth century may have been more consistent and transparent, and easier to use, even if they were only accessible in one physical place. See chapter 2.

11. For a summary of the history of the death penalty in Illinois, with particular emphasis upon the decisions of the Illinois Supreme Court after reinstatement, see chapter 4.

12. The Illinois Capital Punishment Reform Study Committee was created by the state legislature in 2003, after the Ryan commutations and in part because of the discovery of so many innocent men on death row in Illinois. The author is a member of this committee. For further information on the committee and to see its annual reports, see http://www/icjia.org/public/index.cfm?metasection=dpsrc.

13. The Illinois Supreme Court has repeatedly affirmed that it does not and does not intend to conduct proportionality review. See chapter 4. The court seems to pride itself on this fact.

14. The details for all of the states are reported in "Death Row U.S.A.," *supra* note 5.

15. The Illinois budget for fiscal 2008 included $16 million for the Capital Litigation Trust Fund. That figure represents a fraction of the cost of administering and implementing the death penalty in Illinois. It does not include the court costs and administrative costs of administering capital trials and appeals. Nor does it include special allocations to the Department of Corrections or the police to maintain death row, or extra costs to the police, e.g., the cost of special crime lab testing, and the segregation of persons charged and convicted of capital crimes. The defense in the Aubrey Tucker case tried in Lawrence County in early 2007 cost the Capital Litigation Trust Fund $571,033.53 through fiscal 2007, and that was three months *before* trial. The report estimates that the preparation for the trial in that case and the trial itself cost $1.14 million. See Illinois Coalition to Abolish the Death Penalty, "Death Penalty Reform in Illinois: Five Years of Failure: 2008 Annual Report," http://www.icadp.org/docs/ICADPannualreport08.pdf.

16. About two thirds of all murders in the United States are committed with a firearm. See "Crime in the United States, Murder," *supra* note 8.

17. The abolition of the death penalty in New Jersey was preceded by years of advocacy and study. See the summary of the history of the death penalty in New Jersey in chapters 2 and 5.

Chapter 1

The chapter epigraph is from Georg Büchner, *Leonce and Lena, Lenz, Woyzeck* 100 (Michael Hamburger, trans., University of Chicago Press, 1972) (1836).

1. For a detailed description of the legislative history of this reimposition, including an analysis of newspaper articles at that time, see the Woodrow Wilson School Policy Conference Final Report, "A Decade of Capital Punishment in New Jersey" (unpublished), presented to the New Jersey Assembly Judiciary Committee at the public hearing on ACR No. 20, Mar. 16, 1992, and to the New Jersey Senate Judiciary Committee at the public hearing on S. 549, Mar. 23, 1992.

This report also includes research papers which discuss and analyze the New Jersey Supreme Court jurisprudence on proportionality review and capital punishment, a summary of national and state public opinion polls on capital punishment, a discussion of recent U.S. Supreme Court cases, the racial composition of the national death row population, and the status of proportionality review in other states.

2. Empirical research conducted by the Public Defender Homicide Study was presented to the New Jersey Supreme Court in two reports: Leigh B. Bienen et al., "The Reimposition of Capital Punishment in New Jersey: Preliminary Report" (1987; unpublished); see *State v. Ramseur,* 524 A.2d 188, 212 (N.J. 1987) (first interpretation of the reenacted capital punishment statute); and Leigh B. Bienen et al., "The Reimposition of Capital Punishment in New Jersey: Interim Report" (1988; unpublished); see *State v. Koedatich,* 548 A.2d 939, 953–55 (N.J. 1988); see also Leigh B. Bienen et al., "The Reimposition of Capital Punishment in New Jersey: Felony Murder Cases," 54 *Alb. L. Rev.* 709, 711 n. 6 (1990) [hereinafter "Felony Murder Cases"].

For the principal findings of these reports, see Leigh B. Bienen et al., "The Reimposition of Capital Punishment in New Jersey: The Role of Prosecutorial Discretion," 41 *Rutgers L. Rev.* 27 (1988) [hereinafter "Prosecutorial Discretion"]; see "Felony Murder Cases," *supra* note 2 (analyzing subset of felony murders).

3. Partly in response to reports describing the research of the Public Defender Homicide Study, the New Jersey Supreme Court, in an order dated July 29, 1988, appointed Professor David C. Baldus as special master to collect a database and establish an appropriate methodology for proportionality review in New Jersey. David C. Baldus is the Joseph B. Tye Professor of Law at the University of Iowa College of Law. With colleagues, he had conducted two empirical studies of the Georgia capital punishment system after *Furman v. Georgia,* 408 U.S. 238 (1972). These studies formed the factual basis for the statistical arguments presented in *McCleskey v. Kemp,* 481 U.S. 279 (1987). For a description of this work and litigation, see David C. Baldus et al., *Equal Justice and the Death Penalty: Legal and Empirical Analysis* (Boston: Northwestern University Press, 1990).

The order that created the Proportionality Review Project and appointed Professor Baldus as the special master is reprinted in "Prosecutorial Discretion," *supra* note 2, at 371 appendix E. The order gave the special master the authority to collect and analyze data, produce a database and files on individual homicide cases, invite the participation of interested parties, develop a public data file, including a record of dispositions of all relevant homicide cases, conduct hearings, procure expert technical advice, call witnesses, and request public records and any other relevant information. The work of the Proportionality Review Project is described in detail in *State v. Marshall II,* 613 A.2d 1059 (N.J. 1992).

4. For three years, the Proportionality Review Project met regularly with the interested parties to discuss the legal and factual issues raised by the search for all homicide cases in the jurisdiction since reenactment and the identification of those cases which were death-eligible

under the New Jersey capital statute, as that statute continued to be interpreted by the court. For a summary of all New Jersey Supreme Court reversals of death sentences through *State v. Moore,* 585 A.2d 864 (N.J. 1991), see "Felony Murder Cases," *supra* note 2, at 713 n.12. For a discussion of the history of the death penalty in New Jersey and in British common law, see id. at 722. For a history of capital punishment in New Jersey, see "Prosecutorial Discretion," *supra* note 2, at 46–70.

5. The project's "Final Report" is a major accomplishment of data collection and represents a significant advance in the research methodology for the study of capital punishment systems. First, and perhaps most importantly, the project identified and screened every homicide case to reach final disposition in the jurisdiction from the reimposition of capital punishment on Aug. 6, 1982, through 1989. It began with the State Police (SBI) list of 2,300 persons arrested for a homicide offense between 1982 and 1988, and supplemented that list with 500 more cases identified by the Administrative Office of the Courts, and another 200 cases identified by the Public Defender Homicide Study. This is the most complete and accurate data set on homicide dispositions and capital case processing assembled to date in a single U.S. jurisdiction. The Administrative Office of the Courts and the Public Defender together identified a total of 600 cases which were not recorded in the official files of the State Police. The State Police reports, which were missing almost one-fifth of the cases, serve as the basis for the Federal Bureau of Investigation's Uniform Crime Reports, the data set used by many homicide researchers and frequently referred to by journalists and other commentators. The 600 cases missing from the FBI crime reports all involved formally charged homicide offenses which went to final disposition at the trial court stage.

The project screened over 3,000 New Jersey homicide cases from 1982 to 1990, compiled basic information on over 1,300 intentional homicides, and presented the New Jersey Supreme Court with a detailed factual and legal analysis of those cases which either went to the penalty phase of a capital trial or were sufficiently aggravated that there existed a factual basis for at least one statutory aggravating factor, although the death sentence was not imposed or, in some cases, not considered. The frequencies and percentages for homicide cases and capital prosecutions by county cited in this essay are from that database.

6. 613 A.2d 1059 (N.J. 1992). David C. Baldus, "Death Penalty Proportionality Review Project Final Report to the New Jersey Supreme Court" (Sept. 24, 1991) [hereinafter "Final Report"]. This report, including its technical appendices and descriptions of the data set, can be obtained upon written request from John P. McCarthy Jr., Assistant Director, Administrative Office of the Courts, CN 982, Justice Complex, Trenton, N.J. 08625.

In its statistical analysis, the "Final Report" found a significant race effect:

> The Supreme Court did not request the Proportionality Review Project to undertake an analysis of arbitrariness and discrimination in New Jersey's capital charging and sentencing system. We were asked, however, to develop a reliable data base with which the parties could address those issues if they chose to do so . . . We included race variables in the culpability models to ensure that variables for legitimate case characteristics were not carrying any possible race effects . . . We consider these results to be strictly preliminary . . . Our analysis of the penalty-trial sentencing decisions suggests that black offenders may be at greater risk of receiving a death sentence than similarly situated white and Hispanic defendants . . . The data in table 18 suggest that, on average, after controlling for the aggravation level of the cases, black defendants may have a 19-percentage point higher risk ($p = .0001$)

> of receiving a death sentence than do other defendants . . . The model we developed to explain which cases advanced to a penalty trial showed no race of defendant effects. It did suggest, however, that cases with white victims may be at greater risk of advancing to a penalty trial than cases involving black or Hispanic victims. ("Final Report," at 100–103 (internal footnotes omitted))

In *Marshall II,* 613 A.2d 1059 (N.J. 1992), the court adopted the recommendations of the "Final Report" and is continuing data collection. The governor of New Jersey has since signed legislation that restricts proportionality review in capital cases to cases in which the death sentence was imposed, 1992 N.J. Laws ch. 5 ("Proportionality review under this section shall only consist of a comparison of similar cases in which a sentence of death has been imposed under subsection c. of this section"). Principles of ex post facto prevented this provision from having a retrospective effect upon the *Marshall* case.

7. The legal history of proportionality review in New Jersey can be found in *State v. Marshall (I),* 586 A.2d 85 (N.J. 1991) (first death sentence to be upheld on direct appeal by the New Jersey Supreme Court).

8. As of Mar. 1, 1993, thirty-seven death sentences have been imposed by New Jersey trial courts. "Prosecutorial Discretion," *supra* note 2, at 363, appendix C, lists all death sentences imposed, the county in which they were imposed, and the race of the defendant and victim, beginning on May 17, 1983. On that date, the first death sentence since reenactment was imposed on Thomas Ramseur. The listing continues through Jan. 25, 1988, when the death sentence was imposed on Anthony Difrisco.

In thirty-two cases the death sentences were reversed; Raymond Kise's death sentence was reversed by the Warren County trial court on Apr. 15, 1987; Dominick Schiavo died on death row. As a result, 34 of the 37 death sentences were set aside. Three people remain on death row in New Jersey: Robert Marshall, whose death sentence was upheld on direct appeal on Jan. 24, 1991; the court later held that his death sentence was not disproportionate on July 28, 1992. John Martini's death sentence was upheld on Feb. 9, 1992. Marko Bey's death sentence was upheld on July 28, 1992. Both cases are before the New Jersey Supreme Court.

9. For a review of empirical studies of the imposition of the death penalty with regard to race, see "Prosecutorial Discretion," *supra* note 2, at 100–158. For more recent data in regard to felony murders, see Samuel R. Gross and Robert Mauro, *Death and Discrimination: Racial Disparities in Capital Sentencing* 44–45 (1989) (cited in "Felony Murder Cases," *supra* note 2, at 737 n.112).

10. Death Penalty Information Center, "Chattahoochee Judicial District: The Buckle of the Death Belt" (1991). With the support of the Southern Christian Leadership Conference, this organization (based in Washington, D.C.) reports statistics on the imposition of the death penalty in Chattahoochee and Atlanta.

11. Michael Kroll, "Justice on the Cheap: The Philadelphia Story" (1992), Death Penalty Information Center. This article reports statistics on the imposition of capital punishment in Philadelphia, Allegheny County, and all Pennsylvania. www.deathpenaltyinfo.org/node/744.

12. Joe McGinniss, *Blind Faith* (1989). The book remained on the *New York Times* Best Seller List for nineteen weeks in 1989, hitting number one. NBC-TV also made the book into a television miniseries, also entitled *Blind Faith.*

13. *Payne v. Tennessee,* 111 S.Ct. 2597 (1991) (Eighth Amendment erects no per se bar prohibiting a capital sentencing jury from considering victim impact evidence).

Chapter 2

The author gratefully acknowledges the continuing support of the Northwestern University School of Law and its Research Funds, and the unflagging assistance of the law school staff. Special thanks to Sarah Hager, Marcia Lehr, and Juana Haskin.

1. The cited work summarizes some of the early studies of race and the death penalty after Wolfgang's work: "The Impact of Race in Pre-*Furman* Studies: 1900–1959"; "The Impact of Race in Pre-*Furman* Cases: 1960–1970," pp. 103–18 in Bienen et al. (1988). Race had been linked with different rates of homicide and the imposition of the death penalty prior to Wolfgang's work, but the study at that time brought issues of race to the forefront (see also the "race of victim" studies cited in Bienen, 1996, 149–50 n. 66).

2. This research resulted in two publications, and also got me my first job out of law school, as a research attorney for a large, quantitative study of sexual assault in Philadelphia. The African monographs on homicide are Bienen (1974) and Bienen (1976).

3. There was another military coup in July 1975, deposing Gowon, and the subsequent military government handed over power to a civilian government in October 1979.

4. The law was enacted in 1970 and still in effect: the Robbery and Firearms Decree of 1970. It was amended at various times, in 1971, 1972, and 1977, and then replaced with a very similar provision in 1984 (An Act to Make Comprehensive Provisions for Matters Relating to Armed Robbery, 1984).

5. The Western State of Nigeria in 1972 had a similar legal structure to New Jersey: a largely autonomous state legal system, with its own court structure, layered within a larger federal system. In 1972 questions concerning the conflicting authority of the civil and religious courts were not an issue, at least not in the homicide cases I was studying, and not in the Western State of Nigeria. Nor were they an issue for the Armed Robbery Tribunal in Western Nigeria.

6. My recollection is that there was little radio, and no television except a small, tedious, state-run network. The dominant role of the newspapers in reporting all political and international news, and especially crimes, was similar to the role played by newspapers in Chicago in the early twentieth century (see Bienen and Rottinghaus, 2002, 456–60).

7. The language of the decree incorporated in the statutory law reads:

> If [any offender] wounds or uses any personal violence to any person, the offender shall be liable upon conviction under this Act to be sentenced to death. The sentence of death imposed may be executed by hanging or causing such offender to face firing squad as directed by the Governor. The Governor of each State is empowered to set up a tribunal for the trial of offences under this Act. The Act provides for a conviction to be subject to be confirmed or disallowed by the Governor of a State. No civil proceedings shall be or be instituted in any court for or on account of or in respect of any act, matter or thing done or purporting to be done under this Act by the Governor of a State or by any member or officer of a tribunal constituted under this Act. (An Act to Make Comprehensive Provisions for Matters Relating to Armed Robbery, 1984)

8. The 1984 version of the statute does not require that the person "in the company of" the armed robber who wounds be sentenced to death. The 1990 version of the same statute states that any offender "in company with" any person shall upon conviction be sentenced to death (Criminal Code Act, 1990).

9. The 1990 statute does not mention public executions; the 1984 statute specifies hanging or firing squad (see note 7, *supra*).

10. This essay does not address the complex and very interesting questions involving traditional Muslim law, Sharia, and the death penalty. In 1999 the Sharia courts were empowered across northern Nigeria under the new penal legislation to impose the death penalty for sexually related offenses (*zina*). The Sharia does provide for executions, including public executions, and death sentences have been handed down by Sharia, at least four recently (Amnesty International, 2006, "Nigeria"; United Nations High Commissioner for Refugees).

11. If an answer was required of the accused—"Where were you on Saturday night when the victim was stabbed?"—then an interpreter would be brought in and that question was asked and answered in a language the accused understood. Then the trial would go back to being a conversation among the lawyers and judges.

12. The most comprehensive report on the death penalty in Nigeria concluded that it did not deter additional armed robberies: "The introduction of [the] death penalty for armed robbery in Nigeria, which was targeted at reducing the increasing cases of armed robbery in the country, did not result in any remarkable reduction in armed robbery cases" (Ilo, 2004). This same report lists 487 persons on death row, including 11 women, as of July 2003 (p. 71). A government report in July 2005 recommended that the death penalty be applied to juveniles and that state governors should execute people on death row to relieve congestion in the prisons (see Amnesty International, 2005, "Appeal for the Abolition of the Death Penalty in Africa").

13. Sentences by tribunals are generally severe, particularly for armed robbery and treason, which carry a mandatory death sentence with no right to appeal. Some of the death sentences are carried out in public, even though public execution has been outlawed in Nigeria. In July 1991, Amnesty International reported that a total of fifteen armed robbery convicts were publicly executed in three states and were witnessed by hundreds of spectators (Africa Watch, 1991).

14. Ralph Hudson, a forty-three-year-old white male whose crime was committed in Atlantic County, was executed on January 22, 1963, according to the New Jersey Department of Corrections. There have been no executions in New Jersey since 1963.

15. The then Chief Justice Weintraub's concurring opinion was particularly noteworthy: "My point is the doctrines of the Federal Supreme Court have led to an impossible situation, I believe the case method should be replaced by a rule-making process in which the Federal Supreme Court can meet regularly with representatives of State Supreme courts, to become aware of their problems, to benefit from their experience, and to adopt rules of prospective application" (*State v. Funicello,* 1972, Weintraub, C.J., concurring).

16. The then governor of New Jersey, Brendan Byrne, had kept his promise to veto any legislation reenacting the death penalty in 1978, and he was reelected in 1978. As a judge he had declared the pre-*Furman* New Jersey capital punishment statute unconstitutional. He was prevented from being reelected by a term-limits provision in the New Jersey Constitution (New Jersey Constitution). See also Waldron (1978). For a history of capital punishment in New Jersey and the reenactment in 1982, see Bienen et al. (1988, 66–70).

17. By 1982 the majority of states had reenacted the death penalty, and the executions had begun again with the death by firing squad of Gary Gilmore in 1977, under the authority of a Utah statute, which provided for death by firing squad at the election of the defendant.

18. Particularly note, in tbl. 1, the columns "Date Death Penalty Reenacted," "Date First Death Sentence Affirmed," "Date of First Execution," and "Years from Reenactment to First Death Sentence Afirmed."

19. When the New Jersey state legislature was enacting the Criminal Code which included the possibility of reenacting capital punishment, with the specter of the first execution in

decades, the provision in the code which attracted the most vocal opposition was the decriminalization of certain forms of consenting sexual conduct (see Sullivan, 1978).

20. For a detailed description of the litigation surrounding the *Marshall* case, see "Statistics and Law: The Supreme Court of New Jersey's Implementation of Proportionality Review," 183–212 in "The Proportionality Review of Capital Cases by State High Courts After *Gregg:* Only 'the Appearance of Justice,'" *Journal of Criminal Law and Criminology* 87: 130–314 (discussed in Bienen, 1998a, 1998b).

21. See also McGinniss (1991).

22. "It might be the best Supreme Court in the country—state or federal," said Harvard law professor Laurence H. Tribe, as quoted in Rosen (1984). See also Hoffman (1996).

23. Robert Marshall was sentenced to death, and his co-conspirator, Robert Cumber, who let a man use his phone to set up the killing, got a thirty-year life sentence. Cumber, now sixty-eight and nearly blind, was released recently after former Governor Richard J. Codey granted him clemency in the final days of his stay in office.

24. In spring 2005 Robert Marshall's death sentence was overturned by the Third Circuit Court of Appeals on grounds of the incompetence of his private trial counsel. The Ocean County prosecutor announced that they were not going to prosecute him again for capital murder in the spring of 2006. The attorney general of New Jersey did appeal the Third Circuit ruling by filing a writ of certiorari on the last day of eligibility (Vaughan, 2006).

25. "At the end of an emotional 40-minute hearing in Toms River, Superior Court Judge Wendel Daniels gave Marshall the toughest sentence he could: life imprisonment with no parole for 30 years. The 66-year-old Marshall, who faced execution by lethal injection until the federal courts overturned that sentence, could be eligible for parole in December 2014—30 years from his arrest for arranging the murder of his wife, Maria, in 1984" (Schwaneberg, 2006). The Ocean County prosecutor recommended that sentence (id.). The Ocean County prosecutor tried the case in Atlantic County because of the publicity surrounding the crime.

26. "In the summer of 1986 Robert N. Wilentz was very nearly fired. By then he had been Chief Justice for seven years, the point at which the [New Jersey] Senate considers whether to give a judge a lifetime appointment" (Hoffman, 1996, 6–7). The New Jersey Supreme Court held the death penalty statute constitutional in *State v. Ramseur* (1987), soon after Chief Justice Wilentz's confirmation. The first capital conviction was not affirmed, however, until the first *Marshall* case (*State v. Marshall,* 1991). *Marshall II* affirmed the death sentence of Robert Marshall after proportionality review (*State v. Marshall II,* 1992).

27. This was typical. Legislators often expected executions to start soon after reenactment.

28. See also discussion of *Pulley v. Harris* (1984, 189).

29. This chapter provides a history of the proportionality review project in New Jersey prior to the appointment of Professor Baldus and the order appointing him as special master (see also "The Reimposition of Captial Punishment in New Jersey," *Rutgers Law Review* 41, 1 (1988), appendix E, Order of July 29, 1988, 371–72). For the history of proportionality review after the appointment of the special master, see Bienen (1996, 159–212).

30. The Wilentz era ended in 1996, when the chief justice resigned for reasons of illness, dying a few months later in July 1996. Deborah T. Poritz, the former attorney general and governor's counsel, was immediately appointed and confirmed as the new chief justice.

31. In January 2006, the interim governor of New Jersey signed into law a bill requiring an immediate moratorium on executions and creating a Study Commission to study the economics, ethics, effects, and possible alternatives to the death penalty and report back to the legislature by November 15, 2006. A new study of the cost of capital prosecutions by the

New Jersey Policy Perspective said capital trials cost an average of $162,960, compared with $46,560 for non-capital trials (see Forsberg, 2005).

32. See, e.g.:

> The Legislature finds and declares that [b] The experience of this State with the death penalty has been characterized by significant expenditures of money and time; [c] The financial costs of attempting to implement the death penalty statutes may not be justifiable in light of the other needs of this State; [d] There is a lack of any meaningful procedure to ensure uniform application of the death penalty in each county throughout the State; [e] There is public concern that racial and socioeconomic factors influence the decisions to seek or impose the death penalty; [f] There has been increasing public awareness of cases of individuals wrongfully convicted of murder, in New Jersey and elsewhere in the nation; [g] The Legislature is troubled that the possibility of mistake in the death penalty process may undermine public confidence in our criminal justice system; [h] The execution of an innocent person by the State of New Jersey would be a grave and irreversible injustice. (An Act Creating a Study Commission on the Death Penalty and Imposing a Moratorium on Executions and Amending P.L. 1983, 1984)

33. The attorney general of New Jersey has supervisory authority over the twenty-one county prosecutors in New Jersey. See Consultation with and Supervision over County Prosecutors; Uniform Enforcement of Criminal Laws (2006): "The Attorney General shall consult with and advise the several county prosecutors in matters relating to the duties of their office and shall maintain a general supervision over said county prosecutors with a view to obtaining effective and uniform enforcement of the criminal laws throughout the State." Illinois does not provide that the attorney general of Illinois shall have supervisory authority over the independently elected state's attorneys.

34. As of spring 2006 only thirteen people are on death row in New Jersey, more than twenty years after reenactment, and there have been no executions in New Jersey since 1963. There have been 1,016 executions in the country as a whole since *Gregg* (National Association for the Advancement of Colored People Legal Defense and Education Fund, 2006). http://www.naacpldf.org/content/pdf/pubs/drusa/DRUSA_Spring_2006.pdf.

35. See also the discussion in Bienen (1996, 235, nn. 401–3) and Bienen (1998a, 1998b, 197–209). And see Warden (2005, 389–91).

36. Only recently has the Illinois State's Attorneys Association issued a set of guidelines for the prosecution of capital cases, and those have only recently been published and made public. The New Jersey county prosecutors published their guidelines in 1989 (see Bienen et al., 1990, 791–93, "Appendix B: Prosecutor's Guidelines for Designation of Homicide Cases for Capital Prosecution").

37. In 2003 there were a total of 896 murders reported by the Illinois State Police, and 696 were from Cook County. The collar counties around Cook also account for a sizable fraction, e.g., Kane County and Lake County had 21 and 15 murders, respectively, in 2003. Other counties, such as DuPage (6 murders in 2003), have a strong pro–death penalty culture.

38. The present mayor of Chicago, Richard M. Daley, was the state's attorney in Cook County from 1980 to 1989 and was elected mayor in 1989. He was a member of the Illinois State Senate from 1972 to 1980 and a supporter of capital punishment.

39. See also Warden (2005, 391–410); and in numerous articles and newspaper accounts.

40. See, e.g., a 2003 Roper poll showing that 60 percent of those asked supported a

moratorium on executions to allow government to reduce the chances that an innocent person would be put to death (survey, Jan. 15–16, 2003, telephone interview with 1,010 national adults). The same survey showed 64 percent in favor of the death penalty for individuals convicted of serious crimes such as murder. Survey questions 29 and 21, respectively.

41. See also Sarat (2005, 1–33).

42. The nearly perfect storm was the Rolando Cruz case that brought professor Lawrence Marshall into the vortex, but the Cruz case had too many ambiguities, too much baggage, and too many recent memories about the brutal murder of a child for that case to capture the public imagination the way the *Porter* case did. The defendant himself, Rolando Cruz, was not sufficiently credible to prevent another jury from finding him guilty. At his third trial the judge directed a verdict of acquittal (see Warden, 2005, 400–401 and nn. 80–84).

43. See also *People v. Porter* (1995).

44. See the *Tribune* and *Reader* sources cited in Warden and elsewhere.

45. See also Warden (2005, 405–9). As a state legislator, George Ryan had voted for the death penalty to be reinstated and then voted for it to be expanded (id., 388).

46. See also Wolfgang (2002).

47. The highly publicized hearings before the Prisoner Review Board in October 2002, consisting of testimony about the underlying crimes by victims' families, alienated many, including the *Chicago Tribune,* which in an editorial called for Governor Ryan not to commute all death sentences.

48. The act was filed without the signature of the governor and after an amendatory veto was overridden. The Illinois Study Committee Act does not contain the sweeping declarations of the New Jersey law.

49. *Baze v. Rees,* No. 07-5439 (U.S. S. Ct., cert. granted, Sept. 25, 2007), decision at 553 U.S. 35 (2008).

50. Discussing *Taylor v. Crawford* (June 26, 2006), Fernando J. Gaitan Jr., J.

51. See also Denno (1997) and Denno (1994).

52. See also discussion in Denno (2002, n. 345 and surrounding text).

53. New Jersey, for example, specified lethal injection as the method of execution shortly after reenactment in 1982, years before the first death sentence was upheld.

54. Denno (2002) provides a state-by-state survey of the methods and drugs used, includes tables describing when individual states adopted lethal injection, and if there are protocols specifying procedures and participants.

55. See statutory language in the compilation of each state provision, e.g., Arkansas, Ohio, Oregon, or Arizona. The Arizona regulations declare that the procedure is "not painful" (id., 207).

56. While observing this process in New Jersey I wrote a fictional account of the hiring and training of such a person, and his socialization into the task of killing for the state (see Bienen, 1998b).

57. See also Bandura (1999).

58. "The high percentage of botches in Texas appeared to be partly attributable to the dearth of written procedures provided to the executioners concerning how to perform an execution. Originally, these 'procedures' listed little more than the chemicals to be used (in incorrect order or application) and a vague account of the content of the syringes. Moreover, there was no information specifying the nature and extent of the qualifications that executioners should have in order to perform an execution [internal footnote omitted]" (Denno, 2002, 111).

59. Tim Robbins's film *Dead Man Walking,* based upon the 1993 book by Helen Prejean, grossed more than $39 million in the United States alone, and was nominated for and won numerous awards (see Internet Movie Database, 1995).

60. U.S. District Judge Jeremy Fogel in San Jose, California, has scheduled a two-day hearing in September 2006 to review California's lethal injection protocol, which prompted the state in February to call off the scheduled execution of Michael Morales (Weinstein, 2006a).

61. The challenge via habeas corpus was based upon the fact that the defendant would be decapitated by the hanging because he weighed 409 pounds. The case became moot when Washington changed its method of execution to lethal injection.

62. Dr. Orin F. Guidry, president of the American Society of Anesthesiologists, has strongly urged members of his 40,000-member organization to "steer clear" of any participation in executions. "Lethal injection was not anesthesiology's idea, American society decided to have capital punishment as part of our legal system and to carry it out with lethal injection. The legal system has painted itself into this corner, and it is not our obligation to get it out" (American Society of Anesthesiologists, 2006). The president of the association said he was prompted to issue that message when the federal judge in Missouri ordering a halt to lethal injections said that a board-certified anesthesiologist needed to be responsible for the mixing of drugs in the lethal injection process (Weinstein, 2006b).

63. See also Weinstein (2006a).

64. "A federal judge in San Jose has effectively halted the practice [of lethal injection] in California, after state officials said they could not satisfy his orders to have medical personnel take part in executing rapist-killer Michael Morales last week. Despite a widespread assumption that it is painless, courts around the country are weighing similar challenges from prisoners who contend that the most common method of lethal injection can still lead to physical suffering" (Bailey, 2006, and subsequent articles in this same paper on the *Morales* case).

Chapter 3

The chapter epigraph is from Mary Douglas, *Purity and Danger: An Analysis of Concepts of Pollution and Taboo* (London and New York: Routledge, 1984), 40.

1. See American Veterinary Medical Association, "AVMA Guidelines on Euthanasia" 1 (2007), http://www.avma.org/issues/animal_welfare/euthanasia.pdf [hereinafter "AVMA Guidelines"]. In another anomaly, the Animal Welfare Act, which governs the humane treatment of animals by the federal government, notably excludes rats, mice, and birds, the animals most often used in medical experiments, from its protocols for euthanasia. See 7 U.S.C. 2131(1), 2132(g) (2007).

2. "AVMA Guidelines," *supra* note 1, at 1.

3. Id.

4. Id. at 2 (internal footnote omitted). The AVMA cautions that:

"[1.] The guidelines are in no way intended to be used for human lethal injection. [2.] The application of a barbiturate, paralyzing agent, and potassium chloride delivered in separate syringes or stages (the common method used for human lethal injections) is not cited in the report. [3.] The report never mentions pancuronium bromide or Pavulon, the paralyzing agent used in human lethal injection." Id. at title page.

5. Id. at 22.

6. Id. The guidelines contain a detailed annotation of 223 scientific sources, such as "anesthesia for reptiles" (n. 198); "[a] humane killing trap for lynx (Felis lynx): the Conibear 330 with clamping bars" (n. 159); and "the use of a shotgun for emergency slaughter or euthanasia of large mature pigs" (n. 117). Id. at 23–27 nn. 117, 159, and 198.

7. Id. at 22.

8. Id.

9. See id. at 28–36. "Appendix 1—Agents and methods of euthanasia by species" distinguishes between "acceptable" (those that consistently produce a humane death when used as the sole means of euthanasia) and "conditionally acceptable" methodologies. Id. at 28–29. "Appendix 2—Acceptable agents and methods of euthanasia" classifies agents, such as barbiturates and carbon dioxide, according to "Mode of action," "Rapidity," "Ease of performance," "Safety for personnel," "Species suitability," and "Efficacy and comments." Id. at 30–31. "Appendix 3—Conditionally acceptable agents and methods of euthanasia" classifies agents and methods, such as chloral hydrate and electrocution, according to the same categories as appendix 2. Id. at 32–34. Finally, "Appendix 4—Some unacceptable agents and methods of euthanasia" lists agents or methods along with comments as to why the agent is unacceptable, such as: "Air embolism may be accompanied by convulsions, opisthotonos [a muscle spasm causing the head, neck, and spine to be arched backwards], and vocalization. If used it should be done only in anesthetized animals"; and "Cyanide poses an extreme danger to personnel and the manner of death is aesthetically objectionable." Id. at 35–36.

10. Id. at 28–29. The *Code of Federal Regulations* defines a penetrating captive bolt as "[a] stunning instrument" which "delivers bolts of varying diameters and lengths through the skull and into the brain." 9 C.F.R. 301.2, 313.15 (2007). The Food Safety and Inspection Service, an agency of the U.S. Department of Agriculture, has approved the penetrating or non-penetrating captive bolt as an accepted humane practice for the slaughtering of livestock intended for human consumption. See id.

11. See "AVMA Guidelines," *supra* note 1, at 12, 36.

12. Id. at 15.

13. Id. at 22.

14. Id. at 1.

15. See Brief for Michael Morales, Michael Taylor, Vernon Evans Jr., and John Gary Hardwick Jr., as Amici Curiae Supporting Petitioners at 21, *Baze v. Rees,* 2007 WL 3407042 (Ky. Nov. 13, 2007) (No. 07-5439).

16. For example, a Tennessee state commission, relying on medical expert Dr. Mark Dershwitz, recommended replacing its present three-drug practice of lethal injection with a single large dose of a barbiturate. Its advice went unheeded. Id.

17. See, e.g., Deborah W. Denno, "When Legislatures Delegate Death: The Troubling Paradox Behind State Uses of Electrocution and Lethal Injection and What It Says About Us," *Ohio St. L.J.* 63, 233 (2002) [hereinafter "Legislatures"].

18. See, e.g., id. at 207–60.

19. See, e.g., id. at 249–52. South Dakota has more than two pages of protocols, but only a few lines apply to the actual killing as opposed to the various preparations (mostly relating to the person to be killed) and the disposal of the body after the killing. Id. The enumeration of who may witness the execution is also a focus of South Dakota's protocol. Id. at 250; see also S.D. Codified Laws 23A-27A-35 (2007).

20. See "Legislatures," *supra* note 17, at 116–17; Deborah W. Denno, "The Lethal Injection Quandary: How Medicine Has Dismantled the Death Penalty," 76 *Fordham L. Rev.* 49, 95 (2007) [hereinafter "Quandary"].

21. See generally "Legislatures," *supra* note 17.

22. Id. at 207. Without the persistence of Professor Denno and her students, the protocols would never have come to light.

23. Id. at 113–14; Linda L. Emanuel and Leigh B. Bienen, "Editorial: Physician Participation in Executions: Time to Eliminate Anonymity Provisions and Protest the Practice," 135 *Annals of Internal Medicine* 922, 922–24 (2001), available at http://www. annals.org/cgi/

reprint/135/10/922.pdf. The first oath of a doctor is the Hippocratic Oath: "In whatsoever houses I enter, I will enter to help the sick, and I will abstain from all intentional wrongdoing and harm." Robert Jay Lifton, *The Nazi Doctors: Medical Killings and the Psychology of Genocide* vii (1986). The question of with whom the medical doctor at an execution has the doctor-patient relationship raises a dozen more questions of what the doctor's role is, could be, or should be in the state's administration of death. See Atul Gawande, "When Law and Ethics Collide: Why Physicians Participate in Executions," 354 *New England Journal of Medicine* 1221, 1229 (2006), available at http://content.nejm.org/cgi/reprint/354/12/1221.pdf.

24. Leigh B. Bienen, "Not Wiser After Thirty-Five Years of Contemplating the Death Penalty," 42 *Studies in Law, Politics and Society* (2008). Dr. Orin F. Guidry, president of the American Society of Anesthesiologists, recommends that the 40,000 members of his organization become well-informed on the subject of lethal injection and then "steer clear" of any participation in those executions. "The legal system has painted itself into this corner, and it is not our obligation to get it out." Id. at n. 61 (citing Orin F. Guidry, "Message from the President: Observations Regarding Lethal Injection," American Society of Anesthesiologists, June 30, 2006, available at http://www.asahq.org/news/asa news063006.htm.

25. "Quandary," *supra* note 20, at 82–88. In the event that there is not an institutional physician willing to participate in an execution, New Jersey's former protocol allowed for a doctor to be hired on a contractual basis. "Legislatures," *supra* note 17, at 229.

26. It took a court order in Missouri to bar executions from being carried out by a doctor who had been banned from practice and sued for malpractice twenty times. See Brief for Michael Morales, Michael Taylor, Vernon Evans Jr., and John Gary Hardwick Jr., as Amici Curiae Supporting Petitioners, *supra* note 15, at 13–16. This doctor, who admitted to being dyslexic and to mixing up dosages, had carried out fifty-four executions in Missouri. Id. at 14. Missouri is not the only jurisdiction that relied on his incompetence. This is the person the federal government chose to consult when designing its execution method. Id. at 15–16.

27. "Quandary," *supra* note 20, at 89; see also Ga. Code Ann. 17-10-38 (West 2007) (stating "no state agency, department, or official may, through regulation or otherwise, require or compel a physician to participate in the execution of a death sentence"); S.D. Codified Laws 23A-27A-32 (2008) ("The person administering the intravenous injection need not be a physician, registered nurse, licensed practical nurse, or other medical professional licensed or registered under the laws of this or any other state"). Moreover, Alabama, Delaware, Florida, Georgia, New Hampshire, New Jersey, Oregon, and South Dakota have statutes that explicitly "provide that lethal injections do not constitute the practice of medicine." "Quandary," *supra* note 20, at 89; see Ala. Code 15-18-82.1(f) (2007) ("Prescription, preparation, compounding, dispensing, and administration of a lethal injection shall not constitute the practice of medicine, nursing, or pharmacy"); see also Del. Code Ann. tit. 11, 4209(f) (2007); Fla. Stat. Ann. 922.105 (West 2007); Ga. Code Ann. 17-10-38 (West 2006); N.H. Rev. Stat. Ann. 630:5 (2007); N.J. Stat. Ann. 2C:49-3 (repealed by L. 2007, c. 204, § 7, effective Dec. 17, 2007); Or. Rev. Stat. Ann. 137.4732 (West 2007); S.D. Codified Laws 23A-27A-32 (2008).

28. "Legislatures," *supra* note 17, at 251; see S.D. Codified Laws 23A-27A-32.

29. "Legislatures," *supra* note 17, at 234–40. The "setup procedure" provides an entire page of instructions which includes the placement of clamps near the "Y" injection site, "the flow of solution to be controlled by the Flo-Trol clamp," and the standard drugs used (saline solution, potassium chloride, Pavulon, and sodium pentothal). Id. at 237.

30. The concern with sterilization is part of the obsession with "cleanliness" seen in some of these protocols.

There are two notable differences between our contemporary European ideas of defilement and those of, say, primitive cultures. One is that dirt avoidance for us is a matter of hygiene or aesthetics and is not related to our religion . . . The second difference is that our idea of dirt is dominated by the knowledge of pathogenic organisms. The bacterial transmission of disease was a great nineteenth-century discovery. It produced the most radical revolution in the history of medicine. So much has it transformed our lives that it is difficult to think of dirt except in the context of pathogenicity. Douglas, *supra,* at 36.

31. "Legislatures," *supra* note 17, at 226.

32. Id.

33. Death Penalty Information Center, "Number of Executions by State and Region Since 1976" (Sept. 28, 2007), http://www.deathpenaltyinfo.org/article.php?scid=8& did=186.

34. "Quandary," *supra* note 20, at 95–96.

35. "Legislatures," *supra* note 17, at 116–17; see also "Quandary," *supra* note 20, at 95–98.

36. "Legislatures," *supra* note 17, at 227.

37. Id. at 226.

38. Id. at 227.

39. Id. at 226.

40. Id.

41. See "Legislatures," *supra* note 17, at 137, tbl. 8 (listing thirty-one problematic executions).

42. "Uncomfortable facts which refuse to be fitted in, we find ourselves ignoring or distorting so that they do not disturb these established assumptions . . . An anomaly is an element which does not fit in a given set or series." Douglas, *supra,* at 38.

43. According to Douglas:

> Ritual focuses attention by framing; it enlivens the memory and links the present with the relevant past. In all this it aids perception. Or rather, it changes perception because it changes the selective principles. So it is not enough to say that ritual helps us to experience more vividly what we would have experienced anyway. *It is not merely like the visual aid which illustrates the verbal instructions for opening cans and cases. If it were just a kind of diagrammatic map or diagram of what is known it would always follow experience.* But in fact ritual does not play this secondary role. It can come first in formulating experience. It can permit knowledge of what otherwise would not be known at all. It does not merely externalize experience, bringing it out into the light of day, but it modifies experience in so expressing it. This is true of language. There can be thoughts which have never been put into words. Once words have been framed the thought is changed and limited by the very words selected. So speech has created something, a thought which might not have been the same. (Id. at 65 (emphasis added))

44. "Quandary," *supra* note 20, at 92.

45. 465 F. Supp. 2d 972, 979 (N.D. Cal. 2006).

46. See "Quandary," *supra* note 20, at 56; *Morales,* 465 F. Supp. 2d at 979.

47. *Morales,* 465 F. Supp. 2d at 978–81; see also Henry Weinstein, "Ruling Halts State Method of Execution; A Judge Says California's Injection Procedure Is Cruel and Unusual," *Los Angeles Times,* Dec. 16, 2006, at A1. The court in *Morales* found "inconsistent and unreliable record-keeping." 465 F. Supp. 2d at 979. There existed "no contemporaneous records showing that all of the sodium thiopental in the syringes was actually injected." Id.

Testimony revealed that in at least several executions some of the sodium thiopental was not injected. Id. Moreover, large doses of sodium thiopental (an addictive substance) are unaccounted for, because they were purportedly taken for training exercises; however, the exercises were unreliably documented and the substance was not returned to the pharmacy. Id. at 979 n. 9. Team members admitted their inability to follow simple directions provided by the manufacturer of sodium thiopental, among other failures. Id. at 980.

48. *Morales,* 465 F. Supp. 2d at 980.

49. 428 U.S. 153 (1976) (holding that the death penalty does not automatically violate the Eighth Amendment).

50. "Legislatures," *supra* note 17, at 139 tbl. 9; see also Death Penalty Information Center, http://www.deathpenaltyinfo.org (accessed Mar. 31, 2008).

51. "Legislatures," *supra* note 17, at 256.

52. Id. at 139–41 tbl. 9. It took Stephen Peter Morin eleven minutes to die. Id. at 139. Justin Lee May's death took nine minutes. Id. at 140.

53. Id. at 255.

54. Id. Similarly, the Tennessee protocols instruct the warden to announce that "the sentence of_______has been carried out. Please exit to the rear at this time." Id.

55. See, e.g., id. at 249–50. "Senior ranking officers should do the actual strapping of the inmate to the gurney. An IV will be put in both arms, with one intended as a back-up . . . *The inmate will not be sedated before hand.* The inmate can wear regular inmate clothing or "dress outs" if they can obtain them. The inmate will wear shoes. . . . Curtains or blinds should be in place." Id. (emphasis added).

56. Id. at 218–19.

57. Id.

58. In New York, the regulation stating that the procedure should be "done over" if it fails has its own number: C.13(b). Id. at 245. "If the inmate is still alive, the physician will inform the security supervisor that the inmate is still alive. The security supervisor will announce to the witnesses that the inmate is still alive and that in accordance with the law, the lethal injection procedure shall be repeated." Id.

59. Lifton, *supra* note 23, at 254–60. "The choice of killing substance and the injection technique had a specific development in Auschwitz. There was considerable experimentation with other substances—benzine, gasoline, hydrogen peroxide, evipan, prussic acid (cyanide), and air—all injected into the vein." Id. at 257. Later the gas chamber and the crematoria supplanted phenol injections for mass killings. Id.

60. Id. at 256 (internal quotations omitted).

61. Id. at 254. "They were so careful to keep the full precision of a medical process—but with the aim of killing. That was what was so shocking." Id. (quotation attributed to an Auschwitz prisoner doctor).

62. Id. at 257.

63. Id. at 254. A Polish non-Jewish prisoner doctor, Marek P., vividly described how deadly injections were given in the same hospital room where he routinely assisted with surgical operations:

> This time there was a table prepared with syringes. The phenol was in a bottle. There was cotton—everything you needed for an injection. There was also alcohol, as with ordinary injections—and rubber tourniquets. There was just one table . . . and the right hand [of the victim] was put out on a kind of support table [to hold the arm steady], as with a regular intravenous injection, [and] the rubber tourniquet on the arm to apply the pressure to make the vein visible—all in the usual way . . . Mengele [who

performed this killing] then rubbed alcohol on the spot, just under the elbow, that he was using for the injection, and then injected the phenol . . . He did it as though he were performing regular surgery. (Id. at 257–58 (ellipses in original))

64. Id. at 258.

65. Id.

66. Id. "The concentrated aqueous solution of phenol that was developed proved inexpensive, easy to use, and absolutely effective when introduced into the heart ventricle . . . causing death within fifteen seconds . . . The execution was performed by driving the long needle into the fifth [rib] space." Id. (internal quotations omitted). Attention to cost is a matter of concern in the United States as well. North Carolina's regulations note the cost of each item in the execution supply list, concluding that the total is $346.51. "Legislatures," *supra* note 17, at 246.

67. Lifton, *supra* note 23, at 259:

> At that point two Jewish prisoner assistants brought a victim into the room (sometimes victims were brought in two at a time) and positioned him or her on a footstool, usually so that the right arm covered the victim's eyes and the left arm was raised sideways in a horizontal position. Sometimes one's right hand was at the back of one's neck, with the left behind the shoulder blade; and sometimes victims were blindfolded with a towel. The idea was for the victim's chest to be thrust out so that the cardiac area was maximally accessible for the lethal injection, and for him or her to be unable to see what was happening. (There is also mention of a position in which the right arm was placed so that the hand was in one's mouth, not over the eyes, so that one stifled one's own cries.) (Id. (parentheses in original))

68. "Quandary," *supra* note 20, at 95:

> States have never been forthcoming about how they perform lethal injections; remarkably, however, unless prompted by litigation, they now reveal less than ever before. States likely withhold crucial details because, almost invariably, the more data states reveal about their lethal injection procedures, the more those states demonstrate their ignorance and incompetence. The result is a perpetual effort by states to maintain secrecy about all aspects of the execution. (Id. (internal footnote omitted))

69. See Marc Santora et al., "Dictator Who Ruled Iraq with Violence Is Hanged for Crimes Against Humanity," *New York Times,* Dec. 30, 2006, stating that Saddam Hussein's "hanging was carried out with such haste that an ad hoc air at times overshadowed the historical import" of the event.

70. Sudarsan Raghavan, "Saddam Hussein Is Put to Death: Former Iraqi President Hanged Before Dawn in Baghdad to Divided Reaction," *Washington Post,* Dec. 30, 2006, at A1.

71. See Santora et al., *supra* note 69.

72. See id.

73. See id.

74. During the Inquisition the preparations, ceremonies, and celebration of Mass associated with executions were known as the "auto da fe." See Joseph Perez, *The Spanish Inquisition: A History* 154–67 (Janet Lloyd, trans., Yale University Press, 2002). An integral part of this historical public event was for large crowds to stay up all night and then follow those to be executed to a special location, where they were garroted and then burned alive. Id.

75. August Spies, Michael Schwab, Samuel Fielden, Albert R. Parsons, Adolph Fischer,

George Engel, Louis Lingg, and Oscar W. Neebe were found guilty of the murder of Mathias J. Degan on May 4, 1886, in the city of Chicago. *Spies v. People* (*The Anarchists' Case*), 12 N.E. 865 (Ill. 1887). Neebe was sentenced to fifteen years, and the other prisoners were sentenced to death. Id. Spies, Parsons, Engel, and Fischer were executed in Chicago on November 11, 1887. Paul Avrich, *The Haymarket Tragedy* 388–92 (1984). Lingg committed suicide a day before the executions occurred. Id. at 375–78. Governor Altgeld pardoned Schwab, Neebe, and Fielden on June 26, 1893. Id. at 421–23.

76. Avrich, *supra* note 75, at 388–92. The convictions for homicide-by-conspiracy and the sentences of death imposed by the criminal court of Cook County had been upheld in a long and unprecedented opinion by the Illinois Supreme Court. See *Spies,* 12 N.E. at 865. Counsel for the defendants petitioned the U.S. Supreme Court on a writ of error to review the judgment of the Supreme Court of Illinois. Avrich, *supra* note 75, at 335. After two days of hearing arguments, the U.S. Supreme Court handed down a unanimous decision that it lacked jurisdiction in the case because no federal issue was presented. Ex parte *Spies,* 123 U.S. 131, 181 (1887).

77. Avrich, *supra* note 75, at 381, 388.

78. Id.

79. Id. at 392.

80. Id.

81. Id. The line drawing of the execution scene shows the four men on the scaffold plus six other people: one woman, two uniformed officers, and three others standing beside those about to be executed. Id. at illus. 30.

Descriptions of preparations for the hangings and the hangings themselves, including drawings and reports of the last words and movements of those executed, were widely reported by national and local newspapers for whom special seats were set aside. Id. at 392. Similarly, under present protocols, places for the press are typically reserved among the "witnesses." See, e.g., "Legislatures," *supra* note 17, at 250 (citing South Dakota protocols which allow for at least one member of the news media).

82. Avrich, *supra* note 75, at 392–93.

83. Id. at 393.

84. See id.

85. Id.

86. Id.

87. Id.

88. Id.

89. Runners carried the news of their deaths from the jail to specially prepared bulletin boards and to the newspaper offices on Dearborn Street, announcing: "the law [is] vindicated." Id. at 394. The anticipated riot and civil disorder after the executions did not occur. Id. at 383–85.

90. See, e.g., "Legislatures," *supra* note 17, at 213 (Florida protocols provide general procedures for the prisoner's last meal and his last statement); id. at 245 (North Carolina protocols provide for the inmate to be given the opportunity to speak and pray with the chaplain and to record a final statement). The Texas Department of Criminal Justice maintains an elaborate website for the public on its death row population. Texas Department of Criminal Justice, "Executed Offenders" (Sept. 26, 2007), http://www.tdcj.state.tx.us/stat/executedoffenders.htm. The last words of those executed are one of the details included. Id. Many like Gary Graham have maintained their innocence until the end. Id.

91. "Legislatures," *supra* note 17, at 208.

92. Avrich, *supra* note 75, at 393. The line drawing of the hanging scene shows the shrouds tied at the bottom like modern body bags. Id. at illus. 30.

93. See discussion *supra* notes 58–67 and accompanying text.

94. According to Douglas:

> Danger lies in transitional states, simply because transition is neither one state nor the next, it is undefineable. The person who must pass from one to another is himself in danger and emanates danger to others. The danger is controlled by ritual which precisely separates him from his old status, segregates him for a time and then publicly declares his entry to his new status . . . The whole repertoire of ideas concerning pollution and purification are used to mark the gravity of the event and the power of ritual to remake a man. (Douglas, *supra,* at 97)

In the case of lethal injection, the transition to death occurs when the condemned is executed, which creates fear in those present.

95. "Legislatures," *supra* note 17, at 246.

96. Id. at 209.

97. See, e.g., Cal. Prob. Code 4653 (West 2007); 755 Ill. Comp. Stat. Ann. 35/9(f) (West 2007); Ky. Rev. Stat. Ann. 311.639 (West 2007). No statement as to whom the protocol is administered is given. Similarly, states have carefully crafted their statutes and regulations to distinguish an advanced medical directive for the removal of life support from euthanasia or assisted suicide. See, e.g., Ky. Rev. Stat. Ann. 311.637 (West 2007); N.J. Stat. Ann. 26:2H-77(a) (West 2007).

98. "Legislatures," *supra* note 17, at 230.

99. Id. at 230–31.

100. Id. at 231.

101. "AVMA Guidelines," *supra* note 1, at 21.

102. Or. Rev. Stat. Ann. 411-365-0260(2)(i) (West 2007).

103. See U.S. Const. amend. VIII.

104. Historically, the United States has replaced its various capital punishment methods (hanging, the gas chamber, the electric chair) because of public perceptions of unnecessary cruelty associated with each method. See, e.g., Allen Huang, "Hanging, Cyanide Gas, and the Evolving Standards of Decency: The Ninth Circuit's Misapplication of the Cruel and Unusual Clause of the Eighth Amendment," 74 *Or. L. Rev.* 995 (1995); Annulla Linders, "The Execution Spectacle and State Legitimacy: The Changing Nature of the American Execution Audience, 1833–1937," 36 *Law & Soc'y Rev.* 607 (2002).

105. See generally Ellyde Roko, Note, "Executioner Identities: Toward Recognizing a Right to Know Who Is Hiding Beneath the Hood," 75 *Fordham L. Rev.* 2791 (2007).

106. See id.

107. For example, New Jersey's former protocol stated "the team nurse shall not, under any circumstances, advise any person other than the Commissioner of the Department of Corrections of the identity of the syringe carrying the lethal medication." "Legislatures," *supra* note 17, at 232.

108. Id. at 221.

109. A lawsuit has recently been filed by the mother of a prisoner who was executed in a botched procedure that lasted for eighty-six minutes. See Erica Blake, "Family Sues over Botched Ohio Execution: 2006 Procedure Lasted 86 Minutes," *The Blade* (Toledo, Ohio), July 3, 2007, available at http://toledoblade.com/apps/pbcs.dll/article?AID=/20070703/NEWS02/707030342/-1/NEWS.

110. U.S. Const. amend. VIII.

111. Apparently, in Kentucky the protocols for lethal injection are exempt from review under the state's administrative procedures act. See "Quandary," *supra* note 20, at 115; *Bowling v. Kentucky Department of Corrections,* No. 06-CI-00574, slip op. at 8 (Ky. Cir. Ct. Dec. 27, 2006) (stating that public review would create a substantial obstacle to capital punishment). It is not clear what legal implications follow from that ruling.

112. Denno, "Legislatures," *supra* note 17, at 220.

113. See, e.g., Avrich, *supra* note 75, at 393 (noting the presence of a physician with a clock for each of the persons hanged in the Haymarket executions).

114. See, e.g., Blake, *supra* note 109.

115. In several of the botches it was clear the drugs were not reaching their destinations. See "Legislatures," *supra* note 17, at 139 tbl. 9.

116. Id. at 214–19.

117. Id. at 218–19. The regulations do specify that the drugs are to be prepared by a contract physician. Id. at 218.

118. Id. at 219.

119. See, for example, Connecticut, a state with few on death row and where a challenge to capital punishment is in process; the state has detailed protocols for executions which are unlikely to ever happen. "Legislatures," *supra* note 17, at 210–12. See also Thomas Kaplan and Alison Leigh Cowan, "Arguing Against the Death Penalty, in a Gym near Connecticut's Death Row," *New York Times,* Dec. 14, 2007, at B1; Connecticut's death row inmates claim that Connecticut's death penalty discriminates against minorities.

120. See N.J. Stat. Ann. 2C:49-1 (West 2007) (repealed by L. 2007, c. 204, § 7, effective Dec. 17, 2007); "Legislatures," *supra* note 17, at 229–34. This is the first repeal of a death penalty statute in more than fifty years. Governor Jon S. Corzine, "Remarks on Eliminating Death Penalty in New Jersey" (Dec. 17, 2007), http://www.newjersey.gov/governor/news/news/approved/20071217b.html.

121. Leigh B. Bienen, "The Proportionality Review of Capital Cases by State High Courts After *Gregg:* Only 'the Appearance of Justice.'" 87 *J. Crim. L. & Criminology* 130, 209 (1996) (providing a general history of the death penalty in New Jersey).

122. David Von Drehle, "New Jersey: A Death Penalty Trend?" *Time,* Dec. 17, 2007, available at http://www.time.com/time/nation/article/0,8599,1695334,00.html.

123. "Legislatures," *supra* note 17, at 229. To its credit, New Jersey required a medical team for the procedure (including two state physicians and a registered nurse), specified for the use of morphine and a sedative forty-five minutes prior to the execution, and was the only state not to include a paralytic drug in its protocols. Id. at 292–32; see also *supra* notes 20–28, 58–67, and accompanying text for a discussion on the use of paralytic drugs.

124. "AVMA Guidelines," *supra* note 1, at 11.

125. Id.

126. Being executed, like being murdered, is the ultimate non-act where the person subjected to it has no control, and in the case of lethal injection is immobilized and prone, rendered completely passive. Thus, the repeated references to the person being strapped down and prevented from speaking or moving are efforts to give the illusion of control, over the person to be executed and over the situation. As an example, New Mexico procedures bizarrely require the condemned to lie down on a table on his back and then be strapped down at the ankle, wrist, chest, below and above the knees, and across the stomach. See "Legislatures," *supra* note 17, at 240.

127. The evolving standards of decency now incorporated in the jurisprudence of the Eighth

Amendment to the U.S. Constitution encompass the social and cultural aspects of the death penalty. The kind of public celebrations and bodily defilements associated with lynching and hangings in our past would be as unacceptable today as the lynching and hangings themselves.

Chapter 4

The chapter epigraph is from *People v. Bull,* 705 N.E.2d 848 (Ill. 1998) (Harrison, J., concurring in part, dissenting in part).

1. "[S]ome form of meaningful appellate review is an essential safeguard against the arbitrary and capricious imposition of death sentences by individual juries and judges . . . Meaningful appellate review is an indispensable component of the Court's determination that the State's capital sentencing procedure is valid." *Pulley v. Harris,* 465 U.S. 37, 59 (1984) (Stevens, J., concurring).

2. See, e.g., *infra* notes 101–9 and accompanying text; Larry W. Yackle, "The American Bar Association and Federal Habeas Corpus," 61 *Law & Contemp. Probs.* 171 (1998); Symposium, "Capital Punishment: Is There Any Habeas Left in This Corpus?" 27 *Loy. U. Chi. L.J.* 523 (1996).

3. Elected trial judges are under intense political pressure to impose death sentences, and even to override jury sentences of life. "Not surprisingly, given the political pressures they face, judges are far more likely than juries to impose the death penalty." *Harris v. Alabama,* 513 U.S. 504, 521 (1995) (Stevens, J., dissenting). For specific examples of the role played by the death penalty in the outcome of many judicial elections, see Stephen B. Bright and Patrick J. Keenan, "Judges and the Politics of Death: Deciding Between the Bill of Rights and the Next Election in Capital Cases," 75 *B.U. L. Rev.* 759 (1995).

4. The decisions of actual jurors in the penalty phase of capital cases in fourteen states was the subject of extensive and detailed analysis by the Capital Jury Project. The recent findings of this project confirm that jurors are confused about instructions, and that they bring misinformation and misconceptions, and their irrational fear of the defendant's imminent release, into the decision of life or death. The research demonstrates how much more is known about juror decision-making and how much juror attitudes have changed since the U.S. Supreme Court decided *Witherspoon v. Illinois,* 391 U.S. 510, in 1968. See William J. Bowers and Benjamin D. Steiner, "Death by Default: An Empirical Demonstration of False and Forced Choices in Capital Cases," 77 *Tex. L. Rev.* 605 (1999); William J. Bowers et al., "Foreclosed Impartiality in Capital Sentencing: Jurors Predispositions, Attitudes, Guilt-Trial Experience, and Premature Decision Making," 83 *Cornell L. Rev.* 1476 (1998). In Illinois, a challenge to the comprehensibility of capital jury instructions resulted in the federal district court finding that jurors were inadequately guided by these instructions. This result was later overturned by the Seventh Circuit. See *United States ex rel. Free v. Peters,* 806 F. Supp. 705 (N.D. Ill. 1992), rev'd, 12 F.3d 700 (7th Cir. 1993).

5. See also Michael L. Radelet et al., "Prisoners Released from Death Rows Since 1970 Because of Doubts About Their Guilt," 13 *T.M. Cooley L. Rev.* 907 (1996).

6. 720 Ill. Comp. Stat. Ann. 5/9-1 (West 1993 & Supp. 1998).

7. The results appeared in a five-part series of articles by Ken Armstrong and Maurice Possley. See "The Verdict: Dishonor," *Chicago Tribune,* Jan. 10, 1999, at 1; "The Flip Side of a Fair Trial," *Chicago Tribune,* Jan. 11, 1999, at 1; "Prosecution on Trial in DuPage," *Chicago Tribune,* Jan. 12, 1999, at 1; "Reversal of Fortune," *Chicago Tribune,* Jan. 13, 1999, at 1; "Break Rules, Be Promoted," *Chicago Tribune,* Jan. 14, 1999, at 1.

8. See *infra* notes 27–44 and accompanying text. Nor has the legislature responded to appeals from the defense bar to amend the procedures or functioning of the Illinois capital case processing system.

9. Recently, for example, Justice Miller wrote the following:

> Justice Harrison frequently chooses, as he does in this case, to impugn the integrity of other members of the court and to impute improper motives to those with whom he disagrees . . . Baseless and unfounded imputations of improper motives to those members of the court who support a majority opinion are unjustified and demean the court . . . When rancor eclipses reason, the quality of the debate is diminished, the bonds of collegiality are strained, and the judicial process is demeaned. (*People v. Bull,* 705 N.E.2d 824, 845 (Ill. 1998) (Miller, J., concurring specially))

10. See Council of State Governments, 31 *The Book of the States* 133–35 (1996–97). Only Connecticut, New Jersey, and Delaware do not elect prosecutors. See Leigh B. Bienen, "The Proportionality Review of Capital Cases by State High Courts After *Gregg:* Only 'the Appearance of Justice.'" 87 *J. Crim. L. & Criminology* 130, 206 n. 269 (1996).

11. See Alan H. Gray and Courtenay Edelhart, "Judge Rules Cruz Innocent: Finally, 'The Whole Case Just Fell Apart,'" *Chicago Tribune,* Nov. 4, 1995, at 1.

> For retired Illinois State Police Maj. Ed Cisowski, the acquittal of Rolando Cruz on Friday at his third trial was vindication for 10 years of doubt. For lawyer Scott Turow, it offered a fresh blast of hope for his client, Alejando Hernandez, who like Cruz, has also been convicted of the murder of 10-year-old Jeanine Nicarico of Naperville. For Illinois Atty. Gen. Jim Ryan, who was deeply involved in the case for years as a three-term DuPage County state's attorney, it was a bitter pill he reluctantly swallowed while expressing regrets the "nightmare" will continue for the victim's family. But for the Cruz family, it was a moment of triumph and tears. They hugged one another and wept for five or more minutes in the Wheaton courtroom after the verdict was rendered before being ushered out by bailiffs. Less than an hour later, Cruz left the DuPage County Jail carrying plastic bags of belongings in both hands and was immediately engulfed again by weeping family members. (Id.)

12. In one of his appeals, the Seventh Circuit summarized the factual and legal history of the case as follows:

> John Wayne Gacy is a serial killer. Between 1972 and 1978 he enticed many young men to his home near Chicago for homosexual liaisons. At least 33 never left . . . The discovery of so many skeletons, several with rags stuffed in the victims' mouths, created a national sensation. Gacy regaled the police with stories about his exploits, which he attributed to "Jack," an alternative personality. A jury convicted Gacy in March 1980 of 33 counts of murder, rejecting his defense of insanity. The same jury sentenced Gacy to death for 12 of those killings, the only 12 that the prosecution could prove had been committed after Illinois enacted its post-Furman death penalty statute . . . Opinions in this case already exceed 200 pages. We spare readers further recapitulation and turn directly to the four arguments Gacy has culled from more than 100 raised at one or another stage of this litigation, now 14 1/2 years old. Gacy has in this sense already escaped the 12 judgments of execution, for judge and jury cannot decide whether a

> murderer will die, but only how soon. (*Gacy v. Welborn,* 994 F.2d 305, 306 (7th Cir. 1993))

On May 10, 1994, Gacy was the second person to be executed in Illinois—twenty years after some of his victims were murdered. See NAACP Legal Defense and Educational Fund, "Death Row U.S.A., Fall 1998," at 11 [hereinafter "Death Row U.S.A., Fall 1998"].

13. See Ted Gregory and Christi Parsons, "The Surprise Decision: Edgar's Power Halts Execution of Garcia," *Chicago Tribune,* Jan. 17, 1996, at 1. The defendant, a battered woman who killed her spouse, asked to be executed.

14. Interestingly, a Scripps Howard poll conducted shortly after the execution of Karla Faye Tucker showed a significant drop in support for capital punishment:

> A new Scripps Howard Texas Poll found 68 percent of Texans favor capital punishment, down a whopping 18 percentage points from a 1994 survey, the last time the Texas Poll questioned people about their views on the subject.
>
> That is the lowest approval rating the Texas Poll has found in a decade and perhaps the lowest since the 1960s, when executions were carried out by electrocution. A 1953 Gallup Poll found that 63 percent of Texans supported the punishment scheme, and a 1966 poll found only 42 percent favored it. (Kathy Walt, "Death Penalty's Support Plunges to a 30-Year Low; Karla Faye Tucker's Execution Tied to Texans' Attitude Change," *Houston Chronicle,* Mar. 15, 1998, at A1)

Assessing public attitudes toward court and judicial acts has always been difficult at best, and not because polling information was lacking or inaccurate. For an excellent summary of the then-major studies of attitudes toward courts, see Austin Sarat, "Studying American Legal Culture: An Assessment of Survey Evidence," 11 *L. & Soc'y Rev.* 427, 466–69 tbl.3 (1977).

15. See Rick Pearson, "Death Row Case Likely in Ryan's Hands Now: Execution Delay Puts Enoch Case in New Term," *Chicago Tribune,* Nov. 27, 1998, at 4.

16. See Bienen, *supra* note 10, at 166 tbl.1.

17. Telephone interview with Office of Communications, Department of Corrections, Springfield, Illinois (Feb. 1, 1999); see also "Death Row U.S.A., Fall 1998," *supra* note 12, at 15, 29–30. Illinois accounted for 2.32 percent of all executions in the United States. See "Death Row, U.S.A., Fall 1998," *supra* note 12, at 15.

18. See generally 720 Ill. Comp. Stat. Ann. 5/9-1 (West 1993 & Supp. 1998).

19. Id. 5/9-1(b)(6)(c).

20. For example, the aggravating factor for drive-by shootings became effective in 1995. See Ill. Pub. Act 88-678, § 10 (1994), available in *Ill. Legis. Serv.* (West 1994) (codified at 720 Ill. Comp. Stat. Ann. 5/9-1(b)(15) (West 1993 & Supp. 1998)).

21. 720 Ill. Comp. Stat. Ann. 5/9-1(d) (West 1993 & Supp. 1998).

22. The Supreme Court of New Jersey was exceptional in immediately declaring its intention to review discrepancies introduced by prosecutorial charging practices, irrespective of their origin. See *State v. Koedatich,* 548 A.2d 939 (N.J. 1988); Leigh B. Bienen et al., "The Reimposition of Capital Punishment in New Jersey: Felony Murder Cases," 54 *Alb. L. Rev.* 709, 732–35 (1990). In addition, in *State v. Marshall,* 613 A.2d 1059 (N.J. 1992), and *State v. Ramseur,* 524 A.2d 188 (N.J. 1987), the court took it as axiomatic that it had the authority and duty to review prosecutors' charging decisions in the selection of cases for capital prosecution. See generally Bienen, *supra* note 10, at 196–202.

23. See James R. Acker and Charles S. Lanier, "Statutory Measures for More Effective Appellate Review of Capital Cases," 31 *Crim. L. Bull.* 211, 215 n.13 (1995) ("Arbitrariness

and discrimination continue to plague the administration of death penalty legislation, and researchers in many different jurisdictions have identified prosecutorial decision making as a primary cause of these problems"). The recent dispute in New York between Governor George Pataki and Bronx County prosecutor Robert Johnson is an unusual and special illustration of the issue. See *Johnson v. Pataki,* 691 N.E.2d 1002 (N.Y. 1997). Governor Pataki removed Johnson as prosecutor in a potentially death-eligible case involving the murder of a police officer when Johnson refused to charge the suspect with capital murder. A series of lawsuits followed. The New York Court of Appeals, in a split decision, held that the governor did have the authority to take the case away from Johnson and appoint a special prosecutor in his place. See id. at 1003.

24. The issue has taken a variety of forms in different states. See Bienen, *supra* note 10, at 222–62 (appendix A as published in the original version, summarizing state laws regarding proportionality review); see also Symposium, "The New York Death Penalty in Context," 44 *Buff. L. Rev.* 283 (1996). For a detailed description of disparities in prosecutorial charging practices in Pennsylvania, see Tina Rosenberg, "The Deadliest D.A.," *New York Times Magazine,* July 16, 1995, at 22. The article describes how the district attorney in Philadelphia sought the death penalty in every death-eligible case, while in Allegheny County, which has similar demographics, the prosecutor selected among cases for capital prosecution, producing a much lower rate of capital prosecution.

25. This analysis is articulated in Justice Ryan's dissent in *People ex rel. Carey v. Cousins,* 397 N.E.2d 809, 822–23 (Ill. 1979). The federal district court later cited the argument with approval in *United States ex rel. Silagy v. Peters,* 713 F. Supp. 1246, 1258–59 (C.D. Ill. 1989) (granting relief and declaring statute unconstitutional), rev'd, 905 F.2d 986 (7th Cir. 1990). For a formulation of this argument based upon an analysis of 1,017 homicide cases, see Michael L. Radelet and Glenn L. Pierce, "Race and Prosecutorial Discretion," 19 *L. & Soc'y Rev.* 587 (1985). For a generalized variation on the same argument, see Leigh B. Bienen, "A Good Murder," 20 *Fordham Urb. L.J.* 585 (1993). This issue is also at the core of the New York dispute between Governor Pataki and District Attorney Johnson. See *supra* note 23.

26. See *People v. Lewis,* 430 N.E.2d 1346 (Ill. 1981) (*Lewis I*). The Illinois capital statute was upheld against a number of constitutional challenges in *Lewis I,* the first case which brought a death penalty case to the Illinois Supreme Court. The statute had previously been found constitutional by a divided court, on an appeal from a writ of mandamus, on the narrow issue of how the penalty was to be presented. See *People ex rel. Carey v. Cousins,* 397 N.E.2d 809 (Ill. 1979). The state high court had invalidated an earlier capital statute that had attempted to bypass jury sentencing by creating a streamlined procedure with the death sentence being imposed by a three-judge panel. See *People ex. rel. Rice v. Cunningham,* 336 N.E.2d 1 (Ill. 1975).

27. *Cousins,* 397 N.E.2d at 809.

28. See, for example, Chief Justice Goldenhersh's concurring opinion in *Lewis I,* 430 N.E.2d at 1363.

29. The trial court entered an order declaring section 9-1(d) of Illinois' capital punishment statute unconstitutional. This section stated that "[w]here requested by the State, the court shall conduct a separate sentencing proceeding to determine the existence of factors" warranting the imposition of capital punishment. 38 Ill. Rev. Stat. 9-1(d) (West 1977).

The basis for the trial court's holding section 9-1(d) invalid was that the section "vests the prosecution with unlimited discretion to trigger death sentence proceedings," and thereby permits the death penalty to be "wantonly and freakishly imposed." For this reason the section was viewed as contravening the due process clause, the prohibition of cruel and unusual punishments found in the Eighth Amendment to the Constitution of the United States, and the separation of powers provision of article II, section 1, of the Constitution of Illinois. *Cousins,* 397 N.E.2d at 811.

30. The challenge to the prosecutor's discretion was based in part upon an analogy to a series of decisions challenging the constitutionality of the prosecutor's unilateral authority to remove a juvenile case to adult court. See *Cousins,* 397 N.E.2d at 811–13 (discussing *People v. Bombacino,* 280 N.E.2d 697 (Ill. 1972); *People v. Handley,* 282 N.E.2d 131 (Ill. 1972)). The Juvenile Court Act, 705 Ill. Comp. Stat. Ann. 405/1-1 to 405/1-16 (West 1993 & Supp. 1998), was subsequently amended to reduce the degree of prosecutorial discretion in this area. See *Cousins,* 397 N.E.2d at 813.

31. *People ex rel. Carey v. Cousins,* 397 N.E.2d 809 (Ill. 1979). *Cousins* reached the Illinois Supreme Court on a writ of mandamus; a death sentence imposed on an individual after a capital trial was not being challenged. See id. at 811. Consequently, the multitude of factual wrinkles that often create unique interpretations of constitutional issues in capital cases were not present. See *infra* notes 50–51 (discussing the *Silagy* case). The majority in *Cousins* noted that the broad challenges to the constitutionality of the statute were premature because the case arose on a writ of mandamus addressed to the limited question of whether placing the sole power to request the death penalty in the prosecutor usurped the sentencing function of the court. See *Cousins,* 397 N.E.2d at 815.

32. See *Cousins,* 397 N.E.2d at 814–15 (discussing *Gregg v. Georgia,* 428 U.S. 153 (1976)). The majority noted that the same argument was made and rejected in *Gregg.* See *Cousins,* 397 N.E.2d The arguments in *Gregg* addressed the broader question of arbitrariness introduced by unreviewable prosecutorial discretion. It will always be the prosecutor who decides whether to seek the death penalty, however, whether that decision is reviewed, reviewable, or subject to external guidelines in addition to the statutory aggravating factors themselves. But see id. at 821 (Ryan, J., dissenting) (challenging the majority's view that the Georgia statute upheld in *Gregg* was analogous). The four dissenting justices argued that the fact that the prosecutor alone could request the death penalty was an encroachment upon the judiciary's exclusive prerogative to sentence. See id. at 824.

33. Quoting the Illinois Constitution, Justice Ryan wrote: "'The legislative, executive and judicial branches are separate. No branch shall exercise powers properly belonging to another . . .' I agree with this contention and would hold that section 9-1(d), which confers upon the prosecutor the discretion to determine whether or not a sentencing hearing shall be held, violated article II, section 1, of the Illinois Constitution of 1970." Id. at 816–17 (Ryan, J., dissenting). The Nebraska Supreme Court made the same argument in *State v. Williams,* 287 N.W.2d 18, 29 (Neb. 1979). For a general discussion of this issue, see Bienen, *supra* note 10, at 180–83 and n. 173.

34. See *Cousins,* 397 N.E.2d at 817 (Ryan, J., dissenting) (citing *People v. Montana,* 44 N.E.2d 569 (Ill. 1942), and other precedent). The argument was that, by possessing the unilateral power to request the death penalty, the prosecutor thereby was approving the penalty in advance of the judicial branch, usurping judicial autonomy by choosing among the appropriate penalties set by the legislature. See *Cousins,* 397 N.E.2d at 819 ("When the decision to prosecute has been made, the process which leads to acquittal or to sentencing is fundamentally judicial in nature").

35. See id. at 819 (Ryan, J., dissenting): "Any attempt by the legislature to confer upon the prosecutor authority to exercise any part of the sentencing function or the authority to limit, interfere with, or to condition the exercise of the judicial function upon a request by the prosecutor is a violation of the doctrine of separation of powers as contained in article II, section 1, of the Illinois Constitution of 1970."

36. In New Jersey, prior to upholding the constitutionality of the statute itself, the state supreme court required prosecutors to reveal both the intention to seek the death penalty and the nature and sufficiency of the grounds for statutory aggravating factors at a specified time well prior to the guilt phase of the capital trial. See *State v. McCrary*, 478 A.2d 339 (N.J. 1984).

37. *Cousins*, 397 N.E.2d at 822 (Ryan, J., dissenting) (citations omitted). Justice Ryan continued:

> Some prosecutors may look to [the statutory aggravating and mitigating factors] for guidance. Others may consider some of the listed factors controlling and disregard the remaining, while others may totally ignore these sections . . . There can be no doubt that under this statute some offenders will be chosen as candidates for the death penalty by one prosecutor, while other offenders with similar qualifications will be spared, not as a result of mercy, but because of the uneven application of the law due to the lack of statutory direction to the prosecutor. There will inevitably be cases where there will be no reasonable basis for the distinction between one on whom the penalty of death is imposed and another who is passed over. There will be no reasonable explanation for the distinction between the two convicted offenders except that, because of the personal belief or office policy of one State's Attorney, one offender was chosen as a candidate for the penalty of death, whereas for similar reasons personal to another prosecutor, an equally culpable offender was spared. (Id. (Ryan, J., dissenting) (citations omitted))

Similar concerns over county-by-county disparities in charging decisions were expressed by the Supreme Court of New Jersey in *State v. Koedatich*, 548 A.2d 939 (N.J. 1988). See also Rosenberg, *supra* note 24.

38. *Lewis I*, 430 N.E.2d 1346, 1357–62 (Ill. 1981). *Lewis I* was the first constitutional challenge to reach the Illinois Supreme Court through an appeal from the imposition of a death sentence after a capital trial. Although the Illinois Supreme Court did not set aside the death sentence in 1981, the federal district court later set it aside on grounds not related to the constitutionality of procedures for imposing the death penalty. On retrial, Cornelius Lewis was again sentenced to death. On a subsequent petition for habeas corpus, the federal district court issued a writ vacating the second death sentence. See *United States ex rel. Lewis v. Lane*, 656 F. Supp. 181 (C.D. Ill. 1987). The federal appellate court affirmed. See *Lewis v. Lane*, 832 F.2d 1446 (7th Cir. 1987). At the next retrial, the jury did not impose the death sentence. In 1988 Lewis was sentenced to life plus a term of years. The history of the case is reviewed in *People v. Lewis*, 547 N.E.2d 599, 600–601 (Ill. App. Ct. 1989).

39. See *Lewis I*, 430 N.E.2d at 1357–62. The challenge was based on the argument that defendants were being pressured to plead guilty to escape the death penalty.

40. See id. at 1366 (Clark, J., concurring):

> If we were to decide now, four years after the passage of the act, and after so many persons sit on death row, that the act is unconstitutional, a great disservice to the stability of the law would be perpetrated by this court . . . Secondly, striking down the death penalty statute at this point on the ground that the statute violated the [s]tate constitutional separation of powers principle would prevent the U.S. Supreme Court from considering this case or any other capital case arising in Illinois.

Justice Moran also concurred. See id. at 1367.

41. "It would be blatant folly for this court to acquiesce in the execution of Cornelius Lewis without disclosing that four of the judges comprising the present court, either now or

in the past two years, have viewed the death penalty statute as unconstitutional." Id. at 1370 (Simon, J., dissenting). Justice Simon noted that two earlier Illinois capital statutes had been struck down, one on federal grounds in *Moore v. Illinois,* 408 U.S. 786 (1972), and one on state grounds in *People ex rel. Rice v. Cunningham,* 336 N.E.2d 1 (Ill. 1975). See *Lewis I,* 430 N.E.2d at 1371 (Simon, J., dissenting). "So we are faced with the strange spectacle of this court still adhering to the *Cousins* decision although a majority of its judges have stated that it does not represent the correct conclusion." *Lewis I,* 430 N.E.2d at 1373 (Simon, J., dissenting).

42. "The 102 counties in Illinois potentially present 102 different death penalty policies. Executions cannot depend on geography." Id. at 1376 (Simon, J., dissenting).

43. Simon wrote, "A majority of four of the present Justices have said and continue to adhere to the view that they believe the statute is unconstitutional because it allows prosecutors too much discretion in choosing whether to seek the death penalty and that this may result in arbitrary application of the statute. Three of these Justices [Ryan, Goldenhersh, and Clark], however, relying on the doctrine of *stare decisis,* have refused to follow their previously dissenting viewpoint after four other members of the court, one of whom [Justice Thomas E. Kluczynski] is no longer a member, ruled in favor of the constitutionality of the statute." *People v. Silagy,* 461 N.E.2d 415, 433 (Ill. 1984) (Simon, J., concurring in part and dissenting in part) (citations omitted).

44. See *People v. Lewis,* 473 N.E.2d 901 (Ill. 1984) (*Lewis II*). There were allegations of ineffective assistance of counsel, prosecutorial misconduct, and the suppression of exculpatory evidence, as well as frontal challenges to the Illinois capital case processing scheme. The court rejected all of the defendant's arguments, relying on its own prior jurisprudence. See id. at 914.

45. The court referred to "A Compilation and Comparison of Statistics Concerning Application of the 1977 Illinois Death Penalty and Murder Statute in Felony Murder Cases." See id. at 913. (The Northwestern University School of Law Library was not able to obtain a copy of this report or examine its data, despite numerous calls to agencies and courts.) In *Lewis II,* the court also rejected proportionality review. See id. at 913–14. Two justices dissented on the incompetence of counsel issue. See id. at 914. Dissenting Justice Simon restated his view that the death penalty statute and this death sentence were unconstitutional. See id. at 920.

46. It is not clear from the opinion what "statistics" or "data" on proportionality were presented. See id. at 913. But compare *State v. Marshall,* 613 A.2d 1059 (N.J. 1992) (presenting a detailed review of data and evidence).

47. See *United States ex rel. Lewis v. Lane,* 656 F. Supp. 181 (C.D. Ill. 1987). A habeas petition on behalf of Cornelius Lewis under those circumstances probably would be precluded today on procedural grounds. See generally Yackle, *supra* note 2.

48. *Lewis v. Lane,* 832 F.2d 1446 (7th Cir. 1987). The 1979 version of the Illinois capital statute provided that non-slayer participants in a felony murder could not be sentenced to death. See id. at 1454 n.2. The circuit court found that the state withheld material evidence regarding the defendant's prior convictions and knowingly made false representations to the court and the petitioner's counsel. See id. at 1454–58. The court set aside the defendant's death sentence and did not reach the issue of the constitutionality of the statute as applied. See id. at 1458. The number and length of these appeals is an example of how many years, and the amount of diligence and skill on the part of the defense, were required for the evidence of prosecutorial misconduct to be brought before the court.

49. *People v. Silagy,* 461 N.E.2d 415, 433–35 (Ill. 1984) (Simon, J., concurring in part and dissenting in part). On federal habeas review, the federal district court declared the

Illinois capital statute unconstitutional on the ground of arbitrariness, but the court of appeals reversed. See *Silagy v. Peters,* 905 F.2d 986 (7th Cir. 1990), aff'g in part and rev'g in part *United States ex rel. Silagy v. Peters,* 713 F. Supp. 1246 (C.D. Ill. 1989).

50. "The refusal by the defendant to make any record in the sentencing hearing that can provide a basis for his automatic appeal denies this court any meaningful role in the [s]tate's decision to impose the death penalty and turns our reviewing role into a sham." *Silagy,* 461 N.E.2d at 436 (Simon, J., concurring in part and dissenting in part). Compare *Commonwealth v. McKenna,* 383 A.2d 174, 181 (Pa. 1978) ("The waiver rule cannot be exalted to a position so lofty as to require this court to blind itself to the real issue—the propriety of allowing the State to conduct an illegal execution of a citizen").

Dissenting Justice Simon also disagreed with the majority's view that *Cousins* stated the law until the U.S. Supreme Court ruled otherwise, commenting that "[a] person should not be put to death in order to perpetuate the doctrine of stare decisis." *Silagy,* 461 N.E.2d at 434. He further pointed out, citing Justice Harlan's separate opinion in *Oregon v. Mitchell,* 400 U.S. 112 (1970), that courts have always been able to reexamine the basis of their constitutional decisions: "I believe it is a violation of due process to execute a person on the basis of a statute that the majority of this court currently believes is unconstitutional, but that three Justices making up the majority support only because of the doctrine of stare decisis." *Silagy,* 461 N.E.2d at 435. Justice Simon considered it reversible error to allow the defendant to defend himself at the capital penalty phase when he presented no mitigating evidence; the defendant's right to represent himself was outweighed by society's interest in "ensuring that the death penalty is only imposed rationally and consistent with our values and traditions." Id. at 437.

51. See *Silagy,* 461 N.E.2d at 422 (citing *People v. Gaines,* 430 N.E.2d 1046, 1059 (Ill. 1981)). The defense claimed that, had it known that all of the psychiatric testimony introduced in the guilt phase on the issue of insanity would be automatically admitted at the penalty phase toward proof of future dangerousness, it would have restricted or limited the presentation of psychiatric evidence in the guilt phase. See *Silagy,* 461 N.E.2d

52. *People v. Albanese,* 473 N.E.2d 1246 (Ill. 1984).

53. See id. at 1264 ("The holding in *Cousins* is the law of this [s]tate unless it is reversed by a United States Supreme Court holding that our statute is unconstitutional").

54. Were the present U.S. Supreme Court to consider the constitutionality of the Illinois capital sentencing scheme as applied, the outcome would be predictable after *McCleskey v. Kemp,* 481 U.S. 279 (1987). Nor would habeas corpus offer the defendant relief. See James S. Liebman, "More Than 'Slightly Retro': The Rehnquist Court's Rout of Habeas Corpus Jurisdiction in *Teague v. Lane,*" 18 *N.Y.U. Rev. L. & Soc. Change* 537 (1990–91); Note, "The Evolution of the Supreme Court's Retroactivity Doctrine: A Futile Search for Theoretical Clarity," 80 *J. Crim. L. & Criminology* 128 (1990).

55. See *Albanese,* 473 N.E.2d at 1264 (Ryan, C. J., specially concurring):

> To date, the Supreme Court has not seen fit to grant certiorari in any of the cases in which this court has upheld the imposition of the death penalty . . .
>
> There are 39 capital cases now pending in this court. We cannot wait until the Supreme Court finally passes on our statute before reviewing these cases. We have reviewed 37 capital cases since the *Cousins* decision prior to this term of court. If we would have reviewed no capital cases after *Lewis,* the first case in which the imposition of the death penalty was affirmed, and if we would have waited for a decision of the Supreme Court in that case on

> the validity of the statute, we would now have a backlog of 75 capital cases. That figure would no doubt exceed 100 before *Lewis* finally works its way to the Supreme Court by way of habeas corpus.
>
> Besides the judicial-administration consideration of the backlog problem, common decency requires that we review these cases as rapidly as possible. Of the 37 capital cases we have reviewed prior to this term of court, the penalty of death has been vacated in 20 of those cases. Those individuals upon whom the death penalty will not be imposed deserve to know their fate as soon as possible. It would be unconscionable to needlessly subject them to the uncertainty of their fate until the Supreme Court finally passes on the constitutionality of our statute.

56. Id. at 1265–66 (Clark, J., specially concurring) (citing his own concurring opinion in *People v. Lewis,* 430 N.E.2d 1346, 1365–66 (Ill. 1981)).

57. See *Albanese,* 473 N.E.2d at 1267 (Simon, J., concurring in part and dissenting in part). Justice Simon also noted that

> [a]t present, however, three members of this court, having expressed their belief that the death penalty statute of this State offends the Federal Constitution, refuse because of stare decisis to join me in invalidating that statute. They have thereby exalted stare decisis to a position above the Constitution, and allowed a doctrine having no constitutional basis or significance to override the affirmative constitutional guarantees of due process. The result is a clear violation of the supremacy clause.
>
> Second, application of stare decisis in this context violates the State supremacy doctrine . . .
>
> Moreover, this court has specifically acknowledged that the doctrine of stare decisis must yield to State constitutional considerations. (Id. at 1267–68)

58. Id. at 1263 (Simon, J., concurring in part and dissenting in part).

59. The summary in this paragraph is derived from a telephone interview with Shelton Green, chief, Homicide Task Force, Cook County Public Defender's Office (Dec. 8, 1998).

60. Death qualification is the practice of questioning jurors specifically on their attitudes toward the death penalty prior to a capital trial. See *Witherspoon v. Illinois,* 391 U.S. 510 (1968). Death qualification was initially designed to remove jurors who were fundamentally opposed to the death penalty for religious reasons. Subsequently, the purpose of death qualification has been described as assuring that "high degree of objectivity, sensitivity, fairness, and impartiality essential to determine criminal guilt and sentence." *Ross v. Oklahoma,* 487 U.S. 81 (1988). A long legal battle, based upon substantial scientific evidence documenting that death-qualified juries were more "conviction prone," culminated in *Lockhart v. McCree,* 476 U.S. 162 (1986), in which the U.S. Supreme Court rejected that scientific evidence.

61. Some aggravating factors will be apparent from the indictment; others will not. For example, the presence of the felony-murder factor, that the murder was committed during the course of one of the predicate felonies, would require that the predicate felony be charged in the indictment. That the victim was under twelve years of age, or that there were two victims, would also be information often included in the indictment. Other statutory aggravating factors, on the other hand, such as the fact that the shooting was a drive-by shooting, would not be stated in the indictment. Similarly, non-slayer participants in the crime are not eligible for the death penalty, but the state does not typically identify or charge one defendant as the principal in the indictment.

62. In New Jersey, for example, the issue of the timing of the prosecutor's notice to the defense of the decision to seek the death penalty was resolved even before the state high court upheld the statute. See *State v. McCrary,* 478 A.2d 339 (N.J. 1984); Leigh B. Bienen et al., "The Reimposition of Capital Punishment in New Jersey: The Role of Prosecutorial Discretion," 41 *Rutgers L. Rev.* 27, 73 (1988) (discussing the *McCrary* case in the context of other early cases before the Supreme Court of New Jersey). As in Illinois, the argument centered on the lack of power in the judiciary because of the doctrine of separation of powers to review prosecutorial discretion in the selection of cases for capital prosecution. The Supreme Court of New Jersey, however, considered the review of prosecutorial discretion in the selection of cases for capital prosecution to be fundamental. This separation of powers argument is clearly articulated in *State v. Koedatich,* 548 A.2d 939 (N.J. 1988). In *Koedatich,* the attorney general of New Jersey argued that the New Jersey Supreme Court would violate the doctrine of separation of powers if it reviewed patterns introduced by differences in prosecutorial charging practices. The court categorically rejected that position. See id. at 955. The County Prosecutors' Association adopted "Guidelines for the Selection of Cases for Capital Prosecution" after *Koedatich.* The guidelines are reprinted in Bienen et al., *supra* note 22, at 791–93.

63. The summary in this paragraph is derived from a telephone interview with Ronald S. Safer, chief, Criminal Division, United States Attorney's Office, Northern District of Illinois (Dec. 9, 1998).

64. See 21 U.S.C. § 848(e)-(r) (1994).

65. See 18 U.S.C. §§ 3591–98 (1994).

66. Nonstatutory aggravating factors include victim impact testimony (which is limited to testimony from the victim's immediate family), evidence that the crime was "vile" or "heinous" (neither of which are statutory aggravating factors under the federal statute), and the future dangerousness of the defendant.

67. See 18 U.S.C. § 3593(a) (1994); 21 U.S.C. § 848(h)(1) (1994).

68. *State v. Marshall,* 586 A.2d 85, 222 (N.J. 1991) (Handler, J., dissenting). Justice Handler of the New Jersey Supreme Court added that

> [t]he Administrative Office of the Courts [in New Jersey] has estimated that the death penalty will cost over $7 million per year in court expenses . . .
>
> [T]he Supreme Court [of New Jersey] itself has consumed untold hours and expended enormous effort in deciding capital cases on direct appeal . . . The Court's opinions in capital cases alone cover more than 2,000 pages in the printed official reports of the Court's decisions, almost twenty-five percent of all the Court's decisional work-product for that period. (Id.)

Justice Handler further noted studies in other jurisdictions that suggested that "the price of death is exorbitant." Id.

69. See Bienen, *supra* note 10, at 169 tbl.2.

70. See id.

71. See NAACP Legal Defense and Educational Fund, "Death Row U.S.A., Winter 1998," at 15, 29, 30 [hereinafter "Death Row U.S.A., Winter 1998"]. The total number of death row inmates nationwide as of January 1, 1998, was 3,365. See id. at 1. http://www.naacpldf.org/content.aspx?article=29.

72. See Bienen, *supra* note 10, at 166 tbl. 1. This was neither an exceptionally short nor long period of time in comparison to other states.

73. For figures as of January 1, 1998, see "Death Row U.S.A., Winter 1998," *supra* note

71. California, Texas, and Florida, for example, have larger death row populations. For a comparison of states over time, see Bienen, *supra* note 10, at 166 tbl. 1, 169 tbl. 2.

74. Figures are for January 1, 1998. See "Death Row U.S.A., Winter 1998," *supra* note 71.

75. The information in this section is derived from two unpublished manuscripts (on file with author) compiled by the Illinois Office of the State Appellate Defender, Supreme Court Unit: Relief Granted in Death Penalty Cases in the Illinois Supreme Court (listing cases from 1979 to May 1996); and List of Illinois Supreme Court Opinions in Death Penalty Cases (listing cases from 1979 to May 1997).

76. See Brief and Appendix Amicus Curiae of the Coalition Concerned About the Execution of the Innocent on Behalf of Ronald Kliner at 12, *People v. Kliner,* 750 N.E.2d 850 (Ill. 1998) (No. 81314) (brief filed by Locke E. Bowman, Jean Maclean Snyder, and MacArthur Justice Center, University of Chicago Law School) (on file with author) [hereinafter MacArthur Justice Center Brief]. The Illinois Supreme Court had issued 327 opinions in death penalty cases by May 1996. Some cases were reviewed more than once. See MacArthur Justice Center Brief, *supra,* 11–12 nn. 6 and 7; List of Illinois Supreme Court Opinions in Death Penalty Cases, *supra* note 75.

77. According to data from the Illinois Coalition Against the Death Penalty, fifty-six persons sentenced to death have been removed from death row after resentencing. See MacArthur Justice Center Brief, *supra* note 76, at 12 n. 7.

78. See, e.g., *People v. Johnson,* 538 N.E.2d 1118 (Ill. 1989). The court, in granting relief, found that the offenses (murder, attempted murder, and armed robbery) were the result of extreme emotional disturbance; the defendant had been fired from his job and previously had led a relatively blameless life. Thus, "the retributive and deterrent functions of the death penalty will not be served by putting [the defendant] to death." Id. at 1131.

79. See *Bracy v. Gramley,* 81 F.3d 684 (7th Cir. 1996), rev'd, 117 S. Ct. 1793 (1997). After receiving bribes, Judge Maloney rendered acquittals from the bench in two murder cases; in another case, he handed down a verdict for voluntary manslaughter only, acquitting the defendant of felony murder. These verdicts might well have put Judge Maloney in a position where he felt that he needed to impose a death sentence to appear impartial to federal investigators. The *Bracy* defendants' trial before Judge Maloney coincided with the bribe negotiations in one case and closely followed another murder case that was later proven to have been fixed. The defense attorney asked for a postponement to prepare mitigating evidence at penalty phase. This request was refused. Apparently, the defense attorney appointed by Judge Maloney did not know that the penalty phase of the capital trial would follow immediately upon the guilt phase and that additional and different preparation was required. "It is impossible to say with confidence that Judge Maloney did not deliberately select a less experienced lawyer to represent Petitioner due to a corrupt motive, such as a desire to insure a guilty verdict and a death sentence in a high profile case." *Bracy,* 117 S. Ct. at 1799 n.11.

80. *Bracy,* 81 F.3d at 688.

81. Id. (citation and quotation omitted). For the cases discussing the standard for judicial bias and the relevant empirical research, see Peter David Blanck, "The Appearance of Justice Revisited," 86 *J. Crim. L. & Criminology* 887 (1996); Symposium, "The Appearance of Justice: Juries, Judges and the Media Transcript," 86 *J. Crim. L. & Criminology* 1096 (1996).

82. *Bracy,* 81 F.3d at 690 (citing Ill. S. Ct. R. 56(a)(1)).

83. The Seventh Circuit majority was influenced by the fact that "[a] principled acceptance of [the defendant's] argument would thus require the invalidating of tens of thousands of civil and criminal judgments, since Judge Maloney alone presided over some 6,000 cases during the course of his judicial career and he is only one of eighteen Illinois judges who have been

convicted of accepting bribes." Id. at 689. Significantly, Judge Maloney sentenced more people to death than any other judge in Cook County. See Ian Ayres, "The Twin Faces of Judicial Corruption: Extortion and Bribery," 74 *Denv. U. L. Rev.* 1231, 1247 (1997).

84. Blanck, *supra* note 81, at 913.

85. "We do not make light of judicial corruption. It has tainted the judicial system of Illinois, caused unjust acquittals, jeopardized convictions, tarnished the legal profession, and raised profound doubts not only about the state's method of selecting judges but also about the entire political culture of the state." *Bracy,* 81 F.3d at 691.

86. "The knowing use of perjured testimony by the prosecution, although a very serious infringement of the constitutional rights of a criminal defendant, is not an automatic basis for a new trial. There must be a reasonable likelihood that the violation affected the verdict." Id. at 693–94 (citations omitted).

87. Id. at 696 (Rovner, J., dissenting).

88. Id. at 698 (Rovner, J., dissenting) (quoting *Tumey v. Ohio,* 273 U.S. 510, 532 (1927)). Judge Rovner argued that the proof that Judge Maloney was motivated by his bribe-taking to favor the prosecution would more than satisfy that standard, and would consequently constitute "good cause" to grant the petition to permit discovery. See id.

In a similar case involving a corrupt judge, the then chief justice of the New Jersey Supreme Court noted:

> Society invests its leaders with many powers. No power is greater, nor its responsibilities more awesome, than that given a judge. The power to render final judgment is limited only by the law and the judge's conscience. Society gives this power on condition that judges be independent, trusting them and no one else. Respondent sold this power, he sold his judgments, he sold his independence. He not only betrayed his trust, he betrayed New Jersey's tradition of judicial honesty: in the more than 35 years since the creation of our new court system, consisting now of more than 300 judges, only one other judge has been indicted. (*In re Coruzzi,* 472 A.2d 546, 549 (N.J. 1984) (opinion of Wilentz, C.J.))

In a manner similar to Judge Maloney, Judge Coruzzi let it be known that payment to the judge would result in a noncustodial criminal sentence. The judge even persuaded prosecutors not to object to reconsideration of sentence. When caught with a $12,000 bribe in his jacket pocket, after being taped while accepting the bribe, Judge Coruzzi said that a crazy person had given him the money and he had no idea why. See *State v. Coruzzi,* 460 A.2d 120, 129 (N.J. Super. Ct. App. Div. 1983). This widely reported incident prompted a courthouse wag to quip: "How do you spell Coruzzi? With two z's and 12 G's."

89. *Bracy,* 117 S. Ct. at 1798 and n. 9.

90. *Bracy,* 81 F.3d at 688.

91. *Bracy,* 117 S. Ct. at 1799.

92. See *People v. Hawkins,* 690 N.E.2d 999 (Ill. 1998).

93. On the facts of this case, there was no reason merely to speculate about the judge's motivation because the judge himself initiated the return of the bribery money: "[The intermediary] told the [defendant going to trial] that the fix might not go through, that there may have been a leak regarding the fix from the El Rukns to the FBI, and that the judge was scared." Id. at 1002. The circuit court entered an order vacating the verdict and convictions and ordered a new trial. Id. The Illinois Supreme Court upheld the lower court, finding that the defendants' convictions did not remove the taint introduced into the trial by the bribe: "Having determined that due process was lacking in the criminal proceedings, it is

impossible for this court to know whether the verdict would have been the same if rendered by an uncorrupted judge." Id. at 1007. The Hawkins opinion also refers to a second murder case before another judge also convicted of bribery. That case was remanded by the Seventh Circuit for a hearing on whether a bribe to acquit the codefendant implicated the result for the defendant who was convicted. See id. at 1009 (discussing *Cartalino v. Washington,* 122 F.3d 8 (7th Cir. 1997)). For further discussion of these distinctions, see Ayres, *supra* note 83, at 1231.

94. *Hawkins,* 690 N.E.2d at 1002.

95. Id. at 1006 ("Where surrender of a fundamental constitutional right is concerned, our inquiry cannot be focused upon the 'clean hands' of the defendant").

96. Id. ("That defendants may have contributed to the corruption of an impartial fact finder is immaterial to our immediate inquiry of whether they were denied a fair trial").

97. These include Collins, Bracy, Hooper, Tatoni, Gacho, Fields, Hawkins, and Cobb. Some of these death sentences were set aside on other grounds. See telephone interview with Marcia Lehr, Northwestern University School of Law librarian, and with Marty Carlson, Illinois appellate public defender, Capital Litigation Division (Mar. 25, 1998).

98. See Dirk Johnson, "After Censure, Chief Justice of Illinois Quits," *New York Times,* May 3, 1997, at A11 ("Facing possible impeachment for trying to use his position to escape speeding tickets, James Heiple resigned today as chief of the Illinois Supreme Court. He remains on the court as a justice"). Compare also "Pennsylvania Senate Convicts a State Justice," *New York Times,* Oct. 5, 1994, at A19:

> Pennsylvania's Senate convicted a State Supreme Court Justice on impeachment charges today and voted to remove him permanently from the bench.
>
> The Senate convicted the Justice, Rolf Larsen, on a vote of 44 to 5, finding that his decisions on whether to hear cases had been based on recommendations from a lawyer who was a political supporter. The allegations against Judge Larsen had continued for years before he was impeached.

See Michael deCourcy Hinds, "Bitter Feud Among Justices Rocks Pennsylvania Court," *New York Times,* Dec. 12, 1992, at 8; David Lauter, "Pa. High Court in Turmoil," *Nat'l L.J.,* June 27, 1983, at 1; Vicki Quade, "Unfit Justice?: Pennsylvania's 'Sordid Affair,'" 69 *A.B.A. J.* 885 (1983).

99. "After 9 Years in Prison, Woman Is Acquitted in Husband's Death," *New York Times,* Jan. 24, 1998, at A16.

100. According to the *New York Times,*

> The jury of eight women and four men, who deliberated for about ten hours, received the case on Thursday after an emotional display in the courtroom by the woman, Susie Mowbray, who burst into tears and shouted, "I didn't do it! . . ."
>
> In 1988, she was convicted of murder and sentenced to life in prison. But she was released last year after serving nine years when an appeals court ruled that prosecutors had suppressed blood evidence contradicting their homicide theory. (Id.)

101. See Don Terry, "DNA Tests and a Confession Set Three on the Path to Freedom in 1978 Murders," *New York Times,* June 15, 1996, at 6.

102. On Nov. 13–15, 1998, 1,500 people attended the first national Conference on Wrongful Convictions and the Death Penalty at the Northwestern University School of Law. The conference assembled in one place 27 men and 2 women, 16 African Americans and 9

whites, who had been sentenced to death but later had been found to have been wrongly convicted of capital crimes and wrongly sentenced to death. National and international coverage of the conference was extensive, including full-length programs on ABC's *Nightline* and other national news, and press from Sweden, South Africa, and Switzerland. The 29 men and women who attended the conference and spoke about their cases were less than half of the 75 people who have been exonerated after having been sentenced to death. Many of these people had served decades on death row. See, e.g., Rick Bragg, "In Prison for Three Decades, Man Is Rid of Bars, Not Fears," *New York Times,* Nov. 23, 1998, at A5.

Those present at the Northwestern conference included Randall Dale Adams, incarcerated for over a decade, whose case was brought to the attention of the public through the film *The Thin Blue Line.* Many of those who were later found to be innocent were convicted on the basis of false confessions, perjured testimony, and corrupted trials where they were inadequately represented, usually by publicly paid defense counsel. Panelists and speakers addressed a variety of death penalty topics, including technical questions of federal habeas corpus, the methods for investigating wrongful convictions, the analysis and interpretation of DNA evidence, jury decision-making, grassroots mobilization, executive clemency and parole boards, a proposed moratorium on executions, and many other topics. Tapes of panel presentations and a schedule of the conference are available from Teach'Em, 160 East Illinois St., Suite 300, Chicago, IL 60611.

103. For an analysis and documentation of false confessions in capital cases, see Richard A. Leo and Richard J. Ofshe, "The Consequences of False Confessions: Deprivation of Liberty and Miscarriages of Justice in the Age of Psychological Interrogation," 88 *J. Crim. L. & Criminology* 429 (1998); Richard J. Ofshe and Richard A. Leo, "The Decision to Confess Falsely: Rational Choice and Irrational Action," 74 *Denv. U. L. Rev.* 979 (1997).

104. See MacArthur Justice Center Brief, *supra* note 76, at 11 (nine cases). The most recent (tenth) case is Anthony Porter, who served sixteen years on death row and came within days of being executed. Pam Belluck, "Class of Sleuths to Rescue on Death Row," *New York Times,* Feb. 5, 1999, at A16.

In the MacArthur Justice Center Brief, the amici, a coalition of religious leaders, bar associations, the ACLU, and a number of individuals, asked the court to appoint a special commission to study this issue. In Illinois, more people have been released from prison because they were wrongfully convicted than have been executed:

> Unfortunately, it appears that Illinois, of all the states in the nation, may be in the greatest danger of perpetrating such a miscarriage of justice . . . [Of the] documented 21 cases nationwide in the past four years in which a death row inmate was freed after either a retrial and acquittal or a prosecutorial decision to drop charges as a result of new developments . . . seven—fully one third—are from Illinois. (MacArthur Justice Center Brief, *supra* note 76, at 9–10 (annotating cases and years these defendants spent on death row))

105. See Armstrong and Possley, "The Verdict: Dishonor," *supra* note 7, at 1 (detailing such behavior in the first of a five-part series, "How Prosecutors Sacrifice Justice to Win").

106. In four of the cases, a confession by the actual killer was discovered or overheard inadvertently. See MacArthur Justice Center Brief, *supra* note 76, at 23; see also id. appendix II (Erroneous Illinois Death Sentences and Convictions).

107. See Terry, *supra* note 101, at 6.

> [A] team of lawyers, a teacher, investigators and students cared very much. In court today were three young women, senior journalism majors at

> Northwestern University . . . who along with their professor, David Protess, and a black private investigator, Rene Brown, spent the last six months going through mountains of files and tracking down witnesses in crack houses and prisons. Mr. Brown had been working on the case off and on since 1980, when one of the initial trial lawyers sought his help. (Id.)

108. See Fox Butterfield, "1954 Murder Still Roiling Both Sides in Cleveland," *New York Times,* Mar. 23, 1998, at A10; see also Cynthia L. Cooper and Sam Reese Sheppard, *Mockery of Justice: The True Story of the Sheppard Murder Case* (1995).

A recent *New York Times* article reports that the Ohio Supreme Court ordered the case involving Sam Sheppard be reopened over the strong objection of the original prosecutor. See Editorial, "Injustices in the Sheppard Case," *New York Times,* Dec. 4, 1998, at A30.

109. See *State v. Marshall,* 586 A.2d 85, 223 (N.J. 1991) (Handler, J., dissenting) (citation omitted):

> One commentator, remarking on the Kansas legislature's rejection of the death penalty, largely because of the tremendous drain of resources that the state would suffer, has noted: "The enormous effort and complex jurisprudence in [capital] cases have produced genuine distortions in the criminal justice systems of states that actively pursue capital punishment.
>
> There may also be an intellectual drain on our criminal-justice system attributable to the enormous commitment of resources and efforts to capital-murder prosecutions. The . . . [Supreme Court of New Jersey] has, I think, failed to anticipate or acknowledge the strength of the gravitational pull of capital-murder jurisprudence on the criminal law itself, as well as on the general administration of criminal justice.

110. See *Bracy v. Gramley,* 117 S. Ct. 1793, 1795 n. 2 (citing *Ohio v. McGettrick,* 531 N.E.2d 755 (Ohio 1998); *In re Brennan,* 483 N.E.2d 484 (N.Y. 1985)).

111. See Adam Nossiter, "Ex-Gov. Hunt of Alabama Cleared by Pardon Board: U.S. Attorney Plans Inquiry on the Decision," *New York Times,* June 12, 1997, at A18:

> Guy Hunt, the former Governor whose criminal conviction while in office in 1993 stood out even in the rough-and-tumble world of Alabama politics, was exonerated today by the state pardon board he largely appointed . . .
>
> "The courts at every turn have upheld the conviction, and now this panel of friends in high places have let him off," said State Representative Paul Parker, a Democrat from Hartselle. "If it had been me or you, we'd still be sitting in the jail house. It makes a mockery of our system . . ."

112. For arguments about whether the courts should make a distinction between extortion and bribery in cases of judicial corruption, see generally Ayres, *supra* note 83. The article discusses the academic literature on bribery and extortion and closes with the observation that the issues raised by judicial corruption also apply to issues of juror or prosecutorial corruption. See id. at 1232 n.12. This same article begins with a description of the author's own appearance before Judge Maloney with a motion for recusal due to extortion. See id. at 1231.

113. See Belluck, *supra* note 104, at A16.

114. See *People v. Porter,* 489 N.E.2d 1329, 1332–33 (Ill. 1986).

115. See Walter Berns and Joseph Bessette, "Why the Death Penalty Is Fair," *Wall Street Journal,* Jan. 9, 1998, at A16:

> Rather than being arbitrary and capricious, the system now in place serves as a filter, reserving the death penalty for the worst offenders. This is demonstrably the case in Illinois[:]

20% of those on the Illinois death row committed murders during the commission of a rape or sexual assault, compared with well under 1% of all murderers;

10% of the condemned committed murders during a burglary or home invasion, compared with less than 1% of all murders;

13% of the condemned had murdered a child, compared with 4% of all murders;

37% of the condemned committed murders involving more than one victim, compared with 4% of all murders . . .

There are no barroom brawls here, no domestic disputes that got out of hand, no "heat of passion" crimes that are so common among homicides in the U.S.

116. See, e.g., Marcia Coyle, "Suit: Death Defense Is a Sham," *Nat'l L.J.,* Dec. 21, 1998, at A1 (discussing legal attacks in the Florida Supreme Court on both the public and private death row counsel systems in that state).

117. See Ken Armstrong and Maurice Possley, "Illinois Courts May End Secrecy: State's Chief Justice Wants Prosecutorial Abuses Made Public," *Chicago Tribune,* Feb. 3, 1999, at 1:

> The Chief Justice of the Illinois Supreme Court on Tuesday proposed significant changes designed to remove the secrecy that has shrouded prosecutorial misconduct in scores of Illinois court rulings. Responding to a five-part series in the Tribune [see *supra* note 7] that detailed more than 300 convictions reversed in Illinois because of prosecutorial misconduct, Chief Justice Freeman argued that prosecutors who commit misconduct be more frequently identified by name in court and that all such cases be sent directly to attorney disciplinary officials.

Chapter 5

The chapter epigraph is from *State v. Marshall,* 613 A.2d 1059, 1064 (N.J. 1992).

1. 428 U.S. 153 (1976).

2. *Roberts v. Louisiana,* 428 U.S. 325 (1976); *Woodson v. North Carolina,* 428 U.S. 280 (1976); *Jurek v. Texas,* 428 U.S. 262 (1976); *Proffitt v. Florida,* 428 U.S. 242 (1976).

3. The term "capital case processing system" will be used in this article to refer to the set of laws, rules, and procedures governing the prosecution of capital cases within a single state. Within each state, local prosecutors are subject to jurisdictional boundaries, usually—but not always—termed counties. The legal authority of prosecutors may, but does not always, correspond to sharp demographic differences.

Those challenging the reinstituted capital statutes presented empirical evidence of racially and geographically based discrepancies in capital case processing, whether the result of intentional discrimination or passive systemic discrimination, in order to establish the factual foundation for a constitutional challenge to the restructured state capital punishment systems.

4. 408 U.S. 238 (1972).

5. 433 U.S. 584 (1977).

6. These statutes are discussed in appendix A of the published version of this article in the *Journal of Criminal Law and Criminology.* All references to appendix A, appendix B, and appendix C of this article refer to the version published in 87 *J. Crim L. & Criminology* 130–314 (1996).

7. This statute required the state supreme court to review each death sentence to determine

"if the sentence imposed is excessive compared with the sentence imposed in similar cases." Ga. Code Ann. 27-2537(c)(3) (1983). Justice White rephrased the provision as "whether the sentence of death is excessive or disproportionate to the penalty imposed in similar cases, considering both the crime and the defendant." *Gregg v. Georgia,* 428 U.S. 153, 212 (1976) (White, J., concurring). Justice White's formulation was typically incorporated into state statutes at the time of reenactment.

8. The Georgia statute, which controlled discretion by introducing a structure of aggravating and mitigating factors, was upheld in *Gregg* while the statutes which attempted to eliminate arbitrariness by introducing a mandatory system for imposing capital punishment were struck down. Compare *Gregg v. Georgia,* 428 U.S. 153, 206 (1976) (upholding Ga. Code Ann. 27-2534.1 et seq.) with *Roberts v. Louisiana,* 428 U.S. 325, 336 (1976) (striking down statute which totally removed jury discretion) and *Woodson v. North Carolina,* 428 U.S. 280, 305 (1976) (same).

9. A controlled empirical study of death penalty decision-making in four state high courts (California, Louisiana, New Jersey, and Ohio) from 1980 to 1988 found judicial voting behavior to be significantly related to several variables: age and seniority of the justice, party affiliation, institutional effects, state environmental characteristics, and other variables. These states were chosen to maximize variation in institutional features and to provide regional representation. Melinda Gann Hall and Paul Brace, "Toward an Integrated Model of Judicial Voting Behavior," 20 *American Politics Quarterly* 147 (1992).

10. See "The Appearance of Justice: Juries, Judges, and the Media Transcript," 86 *J. Crim. L. & Criminology* 1096 (1996) [hereinafter "Justice Transcript"]. Recent empirical research supports the proposition that in capital cases, judges in state supreme courts are influenced by the prospect of not being elected or retained.

> Under restricted conditions, elected justices in state supreme courts adopt a representational posture. District-based elections, close margins of victory, approaching the end of a term, conditioning from previous representational service, and experience in seeking reelection influence liberal justices to join conservative majorities in death penalty cases in Texas, North Carolina, Louisiana, and Kentucky . . . Instead of public policy goals driving judicial decisions, basic self-interest may also be an important consideration to the state supreme court justice when rendering decisions. (Melinda Gann Hall, "Electoral Politics and Strategic Voting in State Supreme Courts," 54 *Journal of Politics* 427, 442–43 (1992))

11. See generally Peter David Blanck, "The Appearance of Justice Revisited," 86 *J. Crim. L. & Criminology* 887 (1996).

12. Courts are especially sensitive to charges of racial bias when the decision makers in the criminal justice system are overwhelmingly white, and those receiving the "justice" are blacks or other racial minorities. See "Justice Transcript," *supra* note 10, at 1113.

13. 465 U.S. 37 (1984).

14. There are thirty-nine reenacting jurisdictions. Twenty incorporate some form of a proportionality review provision in their statute, and in three other states the state supreme court has imposed proportionality review.

15. Nationally, there is a close correlation between the method of selection of justices of a state supreme court and that court's affirmance rate in death penalty appeals. For the period 1977–87, death penalty affirmance rates varied among state supreme courts according to manner of judicial selection as follows: executive appointment, 26.3 percent; uncontested retention elections, 55.3 percent; nonpartisan contested elections, 62.9 percent; partisan

contested elections, 62.5 percent; legislative appointments, 63.7 percent. Gerald F. Uelmen, "Elected Judiciary," in *Encyclopedia of the American Constitution* 170, 171 (Leonard W. Levy et al., eds., supp. 1, 1992).

16. 481 U.S. 279 (1987).

17. Sometimes the credibility of the court can be damaged when a judge attempts to maintain the appearance of justice. Recently a furor was created at a New Jersey sentencing proceeding held after the penalty phase trial had resulted in a hung jury when a victim's outraged family confronted an unrepentant defendant.

> Before sentencing Johnson [the defendant], Judge Hoffman chastised him as "the man who made car jacking a household word" and blasted him for committing crimes that caused suffering for the victim, her family and residents throughout the state. "The devastating impact that this crime had, not only on the people of this community, but also on the citizenry of this state, must be considered in imposing sentence," Hoffman said . . . Hoffman loaded up maximum prison terms against Johnson by imposing separate, consecutive terms . . . Under the sentence, the defendant faces life plus 100 years in prison and cannot become eligible for parole until he has served 80 years behind bars. (Jim O'Neil, "Emotions Seethe as Shollar Killer Gets Life Plus, Curses Her Family," *Star-Ledger* (Newark), May 9, 1995, at 1)

See also comments of Judge Hoffman, "Justice Transcript," *supra* note 10, at 1126–27.

18. See comments of Judges Yaskin and Cordell, "Justice Transcript," *supra* note 10, at 1133–35.

19. See *infra* "Statistics and Law: The Supreme Court of New Jersey's Implementation of Proportionality Review."

20. See *State v. Marshall,* 613 A.2d 1059, 1063 (N.J. 1992). The opinions in *Marshall* describe the history and development of the Proportionality Review Project in New Jersey. The order appointing the special master delegated to the court's own expert the authority and the responsibility to collect and analyze data on all homicide cases in the state since the reimposition of capital punishment. See Order, reprinted in Leigh B. Bienen et al., "The Reimposition of Capital Punishment: The Role of Prosecutorial Discretion," 41 *Rutgers L. Rev.* 27, 371 (1988).

21. 428 U.S. 153 (1976).

22. 408 U.S. 238 (1972). These opinions have generated a very large literature. See Michael L. Radelet and Margaret Vandiver, *Capital Punishment in America: An Annotated Bibliography* (1988) (listing 971 books and articles as of June 1, 1988). For example, Robert Weisberg, "Deregulating Death," 1983 *Sup. Ct. Rev.* 305 (1984). Commentary has not been confined to professional legal publications. Economists, criminologists, systems analysts, and other social scientists have also studied the relationships between patterns of homicide, demographic variables, and the imposition of capital punishment. See, e.g., Isaac Ehrlich, "The Deterrent Effect of Capital Punishment: A Question of Life and Death," 65 *American Economic Review* 397 (1975); Lawrence R. Klein et al., "The Deterrent Effect of Capital Punishment: An Assessment of the Estimates," in National Research Council, *Deterrence and Incapacitation: Estimating the Effects of Criminal Sanctions on Crime Rates* 336–60 (Alfred Blumstein et al., eds., 1978); and James A. Fox and Michael L. Radelet, "Persistent Flaws in Econometric Studies of the Deterrent Effect on the Death Penalty," 23 *Loy. L.A. L. Rev.* 29 (1989).

23. This article will not address the reimposition of capital punishment on the federal level. However, the possibility of a relatively large number of federal capital prosecutions allows for

arguments of disproportionality in the application of the federal death penalty, especially if the disparities are based upon regional differences in prosecutorial charging practices and result in racial differences.

24. *Furman,* 408 U.S. at 240–57 (Douglas, J., concurring); id. at 306–10 (Stewart, J., concurring); id. at 310–14 (White, J., concurring).

25. The relative infrequency with which the death penalty is imposed is such that "there is no meaningful basis for distinguishing the few cases in which it is imposed from the many cases in which it is not." *Furman,* 408 U.S. at 313 (White, J., concurring).

26. New Jersey, for example, has approximately 500 homicides a year. In the immediate post-reenactment period there were never more than 50 capital trials in a year, and never more than 10 death sentences imposed. See appendix B tbls. B1, B17. Even Texas, the state with the largest number of executions, executes a small proportion of those sentenced to death and a smaller proportion of those convicted of capital murder. See tbl. 1.

27. The holding in *Furman* was grounded in the cruel and unusual punishment clause of the Eighth Amendment to the U.S. Constitution, so *Furman* did not frame the constitutional principle in terms of proportionality. See, e.g., *Furman,* 408 U.S. at 240.

28. *Furman,* 408 U.S. at 309 (Stewart, J., concurring).

29. Justice White's expectation was that the statutory enumeration of aggravating and mitigating circumstances for the jurors would sufficiently guide their discretion so that it could "no longer be said that the penalty [of death] is being imposed wantonly and freakishly . . ." *Gregg v. Georgia,* 428 U.S. 153, 222 (1976) (White, J., concurring). The decision-making of post-*Gregg* capital jurors is the subject of an interdisciplinary study involving personal interviews with penalty phase jurors in fourteen states. See William S. Geimer and Jonathan Amsterdam, "Why Jurors Vote Life or Death: Operative Factors in Ten Florida Death Penalty Cases," 15 *Am. J. Crim. L.* 1 (1987–88); William J. Bowers, Capital Jury Project, "Models of Decision Making Among Sentencing Jurors," NSF SES-9013252 (National Science Foundation Law and Social Science Program 1993). The research findings of this project have been reported in Theodore Eisenberg and Martin T. Wells, "Deadly Confusion: Juror Instructions in Capital Cases," 79 *Cornell L. Rev.* 1 (1993); William Bowers, "Capital Punishment and Contemporary Values: People's Misgivings and the Court's Misperceptions," 27 *Law & Soc'y Rev.* 157, 169–70 (1993).

30. Ga. Code Ann. 27-2534.1 (1973).

31. "Some form of a meaningful appellate review is an essential safeguard against the arbitrary and capricious imposition of death sentences by individual juries and judges . . . Meaningful appellate review is an indispensable component of the Court's determination that the State's capital sentencing procedure is valid." *Pulley v. Harris,* 465 U.S. 37, 59 (1984) (Stevens, J., concurring).

32. The majority of the twelve states whose mandatory capital punishment schemes were declared unconstitutional in 1976 responded by enacting statutes similar to the Georgia statute upheld in *Gregg.* For example, the post-*Gregg* South Carolina statute includes a proportionality review provision virtually identical to the Georgia provision. S.C. Code Ann. 16-3-25 (Law. Co-op. 1985); *State v. Shaw,* 255 S.E.2d 799, 803–4 (1979) ("The statutory death penalty complex adopted by the General Assembly in 1977 [S.C. Code Ann. 16-3-25] is constitutionally indistinguishable from the statutory complex approved by the United States Supreme Court in *Gregg*").

33. See *Pulley v. Harris,* 465 U.S. 37, 71 (1984) (Brennan, J., dissenting) ("Indeed, despite the Court's insistence that such review is not compelled by the Federal Constitution, over 30 States now require, either by statute or judicial decision, some form of comparative proportionality review" (citation omitted)).

34. *Pulley,* 465 U.S. at 37, held that proportionality review by the state high court was not required by the federal Constitution. Arguments regarding proportionality are important in clemency proceedings. See Hugo Adam Bedau, "The Decline of Executive Clemency in Capital Cases," 18 *N.Y.U. Rev. L. & Soc. Change* 255 (1990–91).

35. See online appendix B.

36. According to Bienen et al.:

> Both "legal" and "extra-legal" factors can influence sentencing decisions concerning the death penalty. Legal factors reflect legally relevant influences or "official-normative descriptions of the criminal justice system," such as the offender's prior criminal record, statutory aggravating or mitigating characteristics, and official charges. Extra-legal factors "refer to perceived characteristics of the offender that are legally irrelevant to the imposition of sentence," such as race, gender, and socio-economic status. (Bienen et al., *supra* note 20, at 101 (citing John Hagan, "Extra-Legal Attributes and Criminal Sentencing: An Assessment of a Sociological Viewpoint," 8 *L. & Soc'y Rev.* 357, 358 (1974))

The relevance and relationship of the race of the victim and the race of the defendant has been particularly controversial. See David C. Baldus et al., "Reflections on the 'Inevitability' of Racial Discrimination in Capital Sentencing and the 'Impossibility' of Its Prevention, Detection, and Correction," 51 *Wash. & Lee L. Rev.* 359 (1994).

37. The U.S. General Accounting Office emphasizes this distinction in its evaluation of empirical studies of state capital punishment systems. U.S. General Accounting Office, "Death Penalty Sentencing: Research Indicates Pattern of Racial Disparities" 3–5 (1990) [hereinafter 1990 GAO Report]. Studies which examine a system under controlled conditions are empirically sound. Id.

38. See Bienen et al., *supra* note 20, at 332 (diagramming stages in capital case processing). See online appendix B for a typical systems approach to capital case processing.

39. This view ignores the fact that the law routinely quantifies human suffering, degradation, and grief in the civil context with similar results. Tort judgments that put a dollar value on a victim's loss, suffering, and grief are acceptable in our culture. The tort law framework accounts for intentionality and malice, increasing the amount of money damages awarded when the intention to cause suffering or injury has been proved. Standard risk analysis is routinely applied in the prediction of accidents and projection of liability in situations involving loss of life such as airplane accidents and equipment failures, and in analyzing other social advancements such as advancement in education. See William Feinberg and Stephen Mason, "Identification and Estimation of Age-Period-Cohort Models in the Analysis of Discrete Archival Data," in 10 *Sociological Methodology* (K. Schuessler, ed., 1979), 1–67.

40. In 1996 state high courts are typically the administrative center for the entire state's court system, with the responsibility for coordinating and reviewing case loads, dispositions, and the allocation of judges and other staff, following the leadership of the federal courts. See, e.g., Scott Gilbert and Patricia Lombard, Federal Judicial Center, "A Report to the Conference of Chief Circuit Judges and Circuit Executives: An Analysis of Disposition Times for Capital Habeas Corpus Petitions" (1995) (on file at State Documents Section, Northwestern University School of Law Library); David Rauma and Donna Stienstra, Federal Judicial Center, *The Civil Justice Reform Act Expense and Delay Reduction Plans* (1995). Ironically, the U.S. Supreme Court, the same court which rejected systems analysis in the context of capital case processing, accepted the reliability of regression analysis as an adequate method of statistical proof in employment cases in *Bazemore v. Friday,* 478 U. S. 385 (1986). See David C. Baldus et al.,

"Law and Statistics in Conflict: Reflections on *McCleskey v. Kemp,*" in *Handbook of Psychology and Law* 251–71 (Dorothy K. Kagehiro and William S. Laufer, eds., 1992).

41. "The Court has said that 'one of the most important functions any jury can perform in making . . . a selection (between life imprisonment and death for a defendant convicted in a capital case) is to maintain a link between contemporary community values and the penal system." *Gregg v. Georgia,* 428 U.S. 153, 183 (1976) (opinion of Stewart, J.) (citing *Witherspoon v. Illinois,* 391 U.S. 510, 519 n.15 (1968)).

42. Compare *Gregg,* 428 U.S. at 153, with *Furman v. Georgia,* 408 U.S. 238 (1972). The history of the Supreme Court of New Jersey's initial ruling on the state's death penalty statute offers an example of how state high courts resented and resisted rulings from the U.S. Supreme Court on the constitutionality of state capital punishment schemes. Prior to the decision in *Furman,* there were intimations of what was to come. In *State v. Forcella,* 245 A.2d 181 (N.J. 1968), the Supreme Court of New Jersey held that the system of allowing defendants to plead non vult and avoid the death sentence did not violate the U.S. Supreme Court opinion in *United States v. Jackson,* 390 U.S. 570 (1968). After keeping the appeal for three years, the U.S. Supreme Court reversed the holding in a memorandum opinion ordering the New Jersey Supreme Court to set aside the capital punishment system in New Jersey at the time. *Funicello v. New Jersey,* 403 U.S. 948 (1971). In the case overturning the death penalty sentencing scheme in New Jersey, the then chief justice wrote an eloquent concurring opinion outlining the tensions between federal and state judicial authorities on matters of constitutional law:

> The case before us dramatizes the failure to provide direction and suggests the Federal and State Judiciaries cannot meet their responsibilities unless some rules are changed . . . My point is the doctrines of the Federal Supreme Court have led to an impossible situation . . . I believe the case method should be replaced by a rule-making process in which the Federal Supreme Court can meet regularly with representatives of State Supreme Courts, to become aware of their problems, to benefit from their experience, and to adopt rules of prospective application . . . (*State v. Funicello,* 286 A.2d 55, 60, 62, 67–68 (N.J. 1972) (Weintraub, C.J., concurring))

43. *Gregg,* 428 U.S at 196–98.

44. Ironically, however, the jury only decides questions of fact. The other decision makers in a capital case processing system—prosecutors and judges—have the responsibility for interpreting law, which makes them a more logical focus of appellate review, since they would be responsible for interpreting the new rules imposed upon juror decision-making. The strictures imposed upon jury decision-making discussed in *Gregg* needed first to be implemented by legislatures and then interpreted by prosecutors and appellate courts. For a graphic representation of the interactive relationship between trial judges and jurors, see Peter David Blanck, "What Empirical Research Tells Us: Studying Judges' and Juries' Behavior," 40 *Am. U. L. Rev.* 775, 783 fig. 1 (1991).

Moreover, the Supreme Court generally addresses errors in legal interpretation. Factual decisions by jurors are usually thought to be beyond the scope of appellate review. The legislature's decision to structure the decision-making of jurors by defining statutory aggravating and mitigating factors could be characterized as no more than offering guidance to jurors on how to sort the facts. On the other hand, the decisions of prosecutors and the decisions of judges are based on professional judgment and interpretations of law, an appellate court's traditional province.

In many state jurisdictions the issue of separation of powers, and whether the state high court could regulate the exercise of prosecutorial discretion, was controversial. For example, the attorney general of New Jersey argued that it would violate the doctrine of separation of powers for the New Jersey Supreme Court to review prosecutorial decision-making. The New Jersey Supreme Court rejected this argument, first in *State v. Koedatich,* 548 A.2d. 939, 955 (1988), and then in *State v. Marshall,* 613 A.2d. 1059, 1070–73 (1992) (*Marshall II*). In response to *Koedatich,* the New Jersey County Prosecutors Association adopted "The Prosecutor's Guidelines for Designation of Homicide Cases for Capital Prosecutions," reprinted in Leigh B. Bienen et al., "The Reimposition of Capital Punishment in New Jersey: Felony Murder Cases," 54 *Alb. L. Rev.* 709, 791–93 (1990).

45. The emphasis upon jury decision-making in *Gregg* may be partly explained by the fact that systems analysis at that time was not routinely applied to decisions within the legal sector.

46. *Gregg's* emphasis upon juror decision-making strongly influenced the direction of social science research. See, e.g., William J. Bowers, "The Capital Jury Project: Rationale, Design, and Preview of Early Findings," 70 *Ind. L.J.* 1043 (1995); Symposium, "The Capital Jury Project," 70 *Ind. L.J.* 1033 (1995).

47. For a graphic illustration, see Baldus et al., *supra* note 40, at 261, fig. 13.3.

48. See *infra* tbl. 1.

49. See, e.g., *Hazelwood School District v. United States,* 433 U.S. 299 (1977); *International Brotherhood of Teamsters v. United States,* 431 U.S. 324 (1977).

50. This is how the majority opinion in *Marshal II* explained the principle:

> The best way to understand the concept of proportionality review is to understand its origin . . .
>
> . . . Justice Stewart's plurality opinion in *Gregg* cited two features of Georgia's scheme that would guide and channel the exercise of sentencing discretion. Georgia's statute had a bifurcated procedure for deciding a defendant's guilt first and sentencing later, and also provided for the further safeguarding of meaningful appellate review of every death sentence . . .
>
> . . . Simply stated, the substantive or offense-oriented proportionality review looks to whether the punishment of death is excessive for a particular offense, while procedural or offender-oriented review examines whether, when compared to factually similar cases involving the same offense, a defendant's death sentence is excessive. The kind of proportionality review that asks whether the death penalty is "generally" imposed is an Eighth Amendment inquiry into substantive proportionality—does the punishment fit the crime? . . . That type of substantive review is best perceived in the context of cases such as *Coker v. Georgia* and *Enmund v. Florida* . . .
>
> . . . Another approach to proportionality review is to "inquire instead whether the penalty is nonetheless unacceptable in a particular case because disproportionate to the punishment imposed on others convicted of the same crime" . . . Proportionality review, "although clearly no panacea, . . . often serves to identify the most extreme examples of proportionality among similarly situated defendants." That, we believe, is an acceptable understanding of the intention of the framers of our Act—that statutory proportionality review should seek to insure that the death penalty is being administered in a rational, non-arbitrary, and evenhanded manner, fairly and with reasonable consistency. That review serves as a means through which to monitor the imposition of death sentences and thereby prevent any impermissible discrimination in imposing the death penalty. (*State v. Marshall,* 613 A.2d 1059, 1068–70 (N.J. 1992) (citations omitted))

51. For some jurors' own descriptions of their decision-making processes and responses in capital cases, see Leigh B. Bienen, "Helping Jurors Out: Post-Verdict Debriefing for Jurors in Emotionally Disturbing Trials," 68 *Ind. L.J.* 1333, 1346–48 (1993). See also William J. Bowers, Capital Jury Project, *supra* note 29; William J. Bowers et al., "In Their Own Words: How Capital Jurors Explain Their Life or Death Sentencing Decisions (Nov. 7, 1992)" (Capital Jury Project Working Paper no. 7); William J. Bowers et al., "In Their Own Words: How Capital Jurors Explain Their Life or Death Sentencing Decisions (May 26, 1992)" (Capital Jury Project Working Paper no. 6); Marla Sandys, "The Life or Death Decisions of Capital Jurors: Preliminary Findings from Kentucky" (paper presented at the annual meeting of the American Society of Criminology, San Francisco, Nov. 27, 1991). A jury's decision to sentence a defendant to death is not only a determination of fact, although it may have a factual predicate in the finding of guilt and the finding of the existence of statutory aggravating and mitigating factors.

52. See Linda A. Foley and Richard S. Powell, "The Discretion of Prosecutors, Judges and Juries in Capital Cases," *Criminal Justice Review* 16, 19–22 (Fall 1982) (finding, post-*Furman,* that extralegal factors continued to influence prosecutors and judges in Florida capital cases).

53. 465 U.S. 37 (1984). See David C. Baldus et al., *Equal Justice and the Death Penalty: A Legal and Empirical Analysis* 22–24 (Boston: Northeastern University Press, 1990) (outlining state legislative responses to *Furman*). Note that several state legislatures reenacted capital statutes almost immediately after *Furman* and before *Gregg.* See, e.g., the date of reenactment in Florida, Arkansas, Indiana, Oklahoma, Utah, *infra* tbl.1.

54. 481 U.S. 279 (1987).

55. The Supreme Court in *Pulley* noted:

> The issue in this case, therefore, is whether the Eighth Amendment . . . requires a state appellate court, before it affirms a death sentence, to compare the sentence in the case before it with the penalties imposed in similar cases if requested to do so by the prisoner . . . In some States, such as Florida, the appellate court performs proportionality review despite the absence of a statutory requirement; in others, such as California and Texas, it does not. (*Pulley,* 465 U.S. at 43–44)

56. Justice Brennan noted that if the defendant had not been sentenced to death in California an appellate court would have been required to undertake proportionality review, but there was no such requirement for a death sentence. "Ironically, although the California death penalty statute reviewed in this case does not require comparative proportionality review, most other felony sentences in the State are subject to a mandatory, and highly complex, system of comparative review. California therefore accords greater protection to felons who are imprisoned."

57. Id. at 44–54. The length of time to final decision in *Pulley* may have contributed to its boomerang effect. The defendant was initially arrested on July 5, 1978. By the time the final decision was handed down on July 23, 1984, six years had passed and the mood of the Court had changed. The dissent noted that the states could continue to require proportionality review under their statutory provisions or as a matter of state constitutional law:

> Indeed, despite the Court's insistence that such review is not compelled by the Federal Constitution, over 30 states now require, either by statute or judicial decision, some form of comparative proportionality review before any death sentence may be carried out. By itself, this should weigh heavily on the side of requiring such appellate review. (Id. at 71 (Brennan, J., dissenting) (footnote omitted))

58. State constitutions became an important independent source of constitutional guarantees in the 1980s and will continue to be so in the 1990s. See, e.g., Stewart G. Pollock, "State Constitutions as Separate Sources of Fundamental Rights," 35 *Rutgers L. Rev.* 707 (1983). State constitutional provisions have been particularly important in the capital jurisprudence of New Jersey. See, e.g., *State v. Ramseur,* 524 A.2d 188, 314 (N.J. 1987) (Handler, J., dissenting).

59. "Whether in the exercise of statutory proportionality review or our constitutional duty to assure the equal protection and due process of law, we cannot escape the responsibility to review any effects of race in capital sentencing." *State v. Marshall,* 613 A.2d. 1059, 1112 (1992) (*Marshall II*) (citing N.J. Const. art. VI, 5(c)). In *Marshall II,* the court explicitly said that it was not following *McCleskey.* Id. at 1109–13.

60. 481 U.S. 279 (1987).

61. See Baldus et al., *supra* note 36, at 364–76. The decision has generated considerable comment. See, e.g., Robert A. Burt, "Disorder in the Court: The Death Penalty and the Constitution," 85 *Mich. L. Rev.* 1741 (1987); Randall L. Kennedy, "*McCleskey v. Kemp:* Race, Capital Punishment, and the Supreme Court," 101 *Harv. L. Rev.* 1388 (1988); David J. Macher, Note, "*McCleskey v. Kemp:* Race, Statistics and the Death Penalty," 15 *W. St. U. L. Rev.* 179 (1987).

62. See Michael L. Radelet and Glenn L. Pierce, "Choosing Those Who Will Die: Race and the Death Penalty in Florida," 43 *Fla. L. Rev.* 1 (1991); Michael L. Radelet and Glenn L. Pierce, "Race and Prosecutorial Discretion in Homicide Cases," 19 *Law & Soc'y Rev.* 587 (1985).

63. Warren McCleskey's death sentence had been subjected to the mandatory provisions of the Georgia proportionality review statute and been upheld as proportionate by the Georgia Supreme Court.

64. And, again,

> The second type of error in capital punishment occurs when we execute someone whose crime does not seem so aggravated when compared to those of many who escaped the death penalty. It is in this kind of case—which is extremely common—that we must worry whether, first, we have designed procedures which are appropriate to the decision between life and death and, second, whether we have followed those procedures. (John Kaplan, "The Problem of Capital Punishment," 1983 *Ill. L. Rev.* 555, 576 (1983))

65. The research conducted by Baldus and his colleagues on the Georgia capital case processing system is set out in Baldus et al., *supra* note 53, and discussed in Bienen et al., *supra* note 20, at 147–56.

> The most recent study of the Georgia system by Baldus and his colleagues represents an extremely thorough and sophisticated perspective on the death sentencing process that both supports and builds upon previous research conducted elsewhere by the authors. Moreover, the authors have addressed, and in many cases denounced, in detail the methodological criticisms of their study that were raised in *McCleskey v. Zant* [580 F. Supp. 338 (N.D. Ga. 1984) (*McCleskey I*)] and *McCleskey v. Kemp* [753 F.2d. 877 (11th Cir. 1985) (*McCleskey II*)] . . . Indeed, the Baldus study simply replicates with a more sophisticated methodology the result found in the numerous prior studies summarized here. Race is not a neutral variable. It may be as significant as the presence of an additional statutory aggravating factor. Id. at 157 (footnotes omitted).

66. The 1990 book by Professor Baldus and his colleagues sets out in detail the lower court

history of *McCleskey* and the research methodology employed in the study which provided the factual basis for the defendant's legal arguments. See Baldus et al., *supra* note 53, at ch. 4, 6, and 10.

67. However, Professor Baldus points out: "Social science research is relevant to death penalty decision-making because these institutions purport to be rational, principled, and guided by facts. And when the facts are in dispute, the basic idea is that the side with the better evidence should carry the day." David C. Baldus, "Keynote Address: The Death Penalty Dialogue Between Law and Social Science," 70 *Ind. L.J.* 1033 (1995). Under the *McCleskey* standard, what would be necessary to demonstrate such an intent has been the subject of much speculation by persons representing capital defendants. Would first-person statements by prosecutors or legislators be necessary? Would the prosecutor, judge, or juror, an alleged racist, have to make statements in a public forum, such as a newspaper? Some of the most avowedly racist legislation in the history of the country would not meet the criteria set out in *McCleskey,* e.g., laws establishing literacy requirements for voting and a poll tax, which were race-neutral on their face, but whose purpose was to disenfranchise blacks and maintain the political power of white minorities. Nor would explicitly racist provisions such as the exclusion of blacks from jury service meet the *McCleskey* criteria.

The U.S. Supreme Court's growing impatience with arguments based upon racial discrimination in capital sentencing was observable prior to 1987 and unmistakable after *McCleskey,* although many respected academic studies consistently document the so-called "race of victim" effects in capital case processing across jurisdictions. See, e.g., Baldus et al., *supra* note 53 (Georgia); Barry F. Nakell and Kenneth A. Hardy, *The Arbitrariness of the Death Penalty* (1987); Steven D. Arkin, Note, "Discrimination and Arbitrariness in Capital Punishment: An Analysis of Post-*Furman* Murder Cases in Dade County, Florida, 1973–1976," 33 *Stan. L. Rev.* 75 (1980); Arnold Barnett, "Some Distribution Patterns for the Georgia Death Sentence," 18 *U.C. Davis L. Rev.* 1327 (1985); William J. Bowers, "The Pervasiveness and Arbitrariness of Post-*Furman* Capital Statutes," 74 *J. Crim. L. & Criminology* 1067 (1983) (Florida and Georgia); William J. Bowers and Glenn L. Pierce, "Arbitrariness and Discrimination Under Post-*Furman* Capital Statutes," 26 *Crime & Delinquency* 563 (1980) (Florida, Georgia, Texas, and Ohio); Sheldon Ekland-Olson, "Structural Discretion, Racial Bias, and the Death Penalty: The First Decade After *Furman* in Texas," 60 *Social Science Quarterly* 853 (1988); Linda A. Foley, "Florida After the *Furman* Decision: The Effect of Extralegal Factors on the Processing of Capital Offense Cases," 5 *Behav. Sci. & L.* 457 (1987); Samuel R. Gross and Robert Mauro, "Patterns of Death: An Analysis of Racial Disparities in Capital Sentencing and Homicide Victimization," 37 *Stan. L. Rev.* 27 (1984) (Florida, Georgia, and Illinois); Elizabeth Lynch Murphy, "Application of the Death Penalty in Cook County," 73 *Ill. B.J.* 90 (1984) (Illinois); Raymond Paternoseter, "Prosecutorial Discretion in Requesting the Death Penalty: A Case of Victim-Biased Racial Discrimination," 18 *L. & Soc'y Rev.* 437 (1984) (South Carolina); Michael L. Radelet, "Racial Characteristics and the Imposition of the Death Penalty," 46 *American Sociological Review* 918 (1981) (Florida); M. Dwayne Smith, "Patterns of Discrimination in Assessments of the Death Penalty: The Case of Louisiana," 15 *Journal of Criminal Justice* 279 (1987); Gennaro F. Vito and Thomas J. Keil, "Capital Sentencing in Kentucky: An Analysis of the Factors Influencing Decision Making in the Post-*Gregg* Period," 79 *J. Crim. L. & Criminology* 483 (1988); Hans Zeisel, "Race Bias in the Administration of the Death Penalty: The Florida Experience," 95 *Harv. L. Rev.* 456 (1981); Margaret Fae Klemm, "The Determinants of Capital Sentencing in Louisiana: 1979–84" (1986) (unpublished Ph.D. diss., University of New Orleans) (on file with the University of New Orleans library). A review of the research literature concludes that pervasive race discrimination effects are amply documented in reliable empirical studies. See 1990 GAO Report, *supra* note 37, at 5.

68. Throughout the 1980s, and especially before *McCleskey,* numerous state supreme courts considered proportionality review to be the appropriate mechanism for reviewing the fundamental fairness of a state capital case processing system, including the assessment of racial and geographical disparities introduced by plea bargaining practices and prosecutorial discretion in the selection of cases for capital prosecution. See, e.g., *Tichnell v. State,* 468 A.2d 1 (Md. 1983), discussed in online appendix A.

69. 481 U.S. 279 (1987).

70. 465 U.S. 37 (1984).

71. Only the New Jersey Supreme Court has taken upon itself the responsibility for collecting and maintaining a comprehensive database on capital case processing. The New Jersey Supreme Court has initiated the development of a scientific methodology capable of producing a reliable factual basis documenting the presence of race effects and other systemwide biases similar to those presented to the U.S. Supreme Court in *McCleskey v. Kemp,* 481 U.S. 279 (1987). See David C. Baldus et al., "Arbitrariness and Discrimination in the Administration of the Death Penalty: A Challenge to State Supreme Courts," 15 *Stetson L. Rev.* 133 (1986).

72. See Baldus et al., *supra* note 36, at 375 ("State courts, by contrast, are not bound by *McCleskey* and are free to entertain claims of racial discrimination under their state constitutions. Even so state courts routinely invoke *McCleskey* as a justification for dismissing such claims with or without a hearing") (footnote citing to cases omitted).

73. Given that there is little disagreement about the demonstrated effects themselves, the sharp disagreements in the legal community, and within the state high courts themselves, occur over the responsibility of the judiciary to address the issue. See, e.g., "The Proportionality Review of Capital Cases by State High Courts After *Gregg:* Only 'the Appearance of Justice.' " 87 *J. Crim. L. & Criminology* (1996): 130–314 appendix omitted.

74. See, e.g., *Whitmore v. Arkansas,* 495 U.S. 149 (1990) (holding that a third party does not have the standing to challenge the validity of a death sentence imposed on a capital defendant who elected to forgo his right to appeal); *Clemons v. Mississippi,* 494 U.S. 738 (1990) (holding that it is constitutionally permissible for an appellate court to reweigh aggravating and mitigating evidence in order to uphold a jury-imposed death sentence that is based in part on an invalid or improperly defined aggravating factor); *Butler v. McKellar,* 494 U.S. 407 (1990) (holding that a recently decided rule concerning police-initiated interrogation following a suspect's request for counsel is not retroactively available to support a federal habeas corpus petition under *Teague v. Lane,* 489 U.S. 288 (1989)); *Boyde v. California,* 494 U.S. 370 (1990) (holding that California capital sentencing instructions to juries on mitigation do not violate the Eighth and Fourteenth Amendments as to a defendant who presented mitigating evidence of background and character); *Blystone v. Pennsylvania,* 494 U.S. 299 (1990) (holding that a Pennsylvania death penalty statute mandating a death sentence if the jury finds at least one aggravating circumstance and no mitigating circumstances does not violate the Eighth Amendment). But see *McKoy v. North Carolina,* 494 U.S. 433 (1990) (holding that instructions which prevent the sentencing jury from considering any mitigating factor that the jury does not unanimously find violate the Eighth Amendment under *Mills v. Maryland,* 486 U.S. 279 (1987)).

75. *McCleskey* held that demonstrated racial disparities in the imposition of the death sentence were not sufficient grounds to overturn an individual death sentence or declare a state

system unconstitutional. *McCleskey v. Kemp*, 481 U.S. 279, 297–99, 319 (1987). The majority opinion in *McCleskey* did not deny or dispute the accuracy of the finding of racial disparities.

76. After *McCleskey*, it became increasingly apparent that a majority of the Court was more interested in speeding up executions than in overturning state-imposed death sentences. William H. Rehnquist, "Text of Chief Justice Rehnquist's Remarks to ABA," *Chi. Daily L. Bull.*, Feb. 14, 1989, at 2. Recently, constitutional challenges to capital punishment have been addressed to methods of execution. See, e.g., Deborah W. Denno, "Getting to Death: Are Executions Constitutional?" 87 *Iowa L. Rev.* (1997).

77. See online appendix A; James R. Acker and Charles S. Lanier, "Statutory Measures for More Effective Appellate Review of Capital Cases," *Crim. L. Bull.* 211, 237 n.102 (1995). The states which require proportionality review by statute include Alabama, Delaware, Georgia, Kentucky, Louisiana, Mississippi, Missouri, Montana, Nebraska, New Hampshire, New Mexico, New York, North Carolina, Ohio, Pennsylvania, South Carolina, South Dakota, Tennessee, Virginia, and Washington.

78. See Baldus et al., *supra* note 36, at 386 n.115, 410. See also 1990 GAO Report, *supra* note 37, at 5. Empirical studies of the application of the death penalty since *Furman* have repeatedly found evidence of discrimination by prosecutorial jurisdiction and by race of the victim and defendant. Bienen et al., *supra* note 44, at 737 n.112 (listing and annotating studies).

79. Many find *Furman* a difficult source of precedent:

> The [*Furman*] opinions presented a staggering array of arguments for and against the constitutionality of the death penalty and offered little means, aside from shrewd political prediction, of determining which arguments would dominate in the decision of any future cases.
>
> . . .
>
> . . . The Gregg, Proffitt, and Jurek opinions did not attempt to list in any definitive fashion the prerequisites for a valid capital punishment regime; rather, they simply upheld each particular scheme presented on the basis of its own peculiar mix of procedural protections. Hence, the 1976 opinions established the essentially "provisional" nature of the Supreme Court's capital punishment jurisprudence and thus marked the clear commencement of the Court's ongoing regulatory role. (Carol S. Steiker and Jordan M. Steiker, "Sober Second Thoughts: Reflections on Two Decades of Constitutional Regulation of Capital Punishment," 109 *Harv. L. Rev.* 357, 362–63 (1995) (footnotes omitted))

80. California has the largest death row of any state in the nation. In 1986, Governor George Deukmejian publicly warned two justices of the state's Supreme Court that he would oppose them in their retention elections unless they voted to uphold more death sentences. He had already announced his opposition to Chief Justice Rose Bird because of her votes in capital cases. Apparently unsatisfied with the subsequent votes of the other two justices, the governor carried out his threat. He opposed the retention of all three justices and all lost their seats after a campaign dominated by the death penalty. Deukmejian appointed their replacements in 1987. The removal and replacement of the three justices has affected every capital case the court has subsequently reviewed, resulting in a dramatic change. In the last five years, the Court has affirmed neatly 97% of the capital cases it has reviewed, one of the highest rates in the nation. (Stephen Bright and Patrick Keenan, "Judges and the Politics of Death: Deciding Between the Bill of Rights and the Next Election in Capital Cases," 75 *B.U. L. Rev.* 759, 760–61 (1995) (footnotes omitted))

Even before Chief Justice Bird's removal, justices in other states were influenced by perceived public reaction. A rare in-depth study of the voting behavior of Louisiana Supreme Court justices examined how "liberal" justices were inclined not to dissent from affirmances in capital cases:

> Justice "A" stated that he does not dissent in death penalty cases against the opinion of the court to affirm a defendant's conviction and sentence, expressly because of a perceived voter sanction, in spite of his deeply felt personal preferences to the contrary . . .
>
> . . .
>
> The other liberal justices, Justice "B" and Justice "C," when asked about voters, argued that they were relatively unconcerned with winning or losing their next elections. (Melinda Gann Hall, "Constituent Influence in State Supreme Courts: Conceptual Notes and a Case Study," 49 *Journal of Politics* 1116, 1120–21 (1987))

81. The timing of reenactment often played a role in whether the state enacted proportionality review. See *infra* tbl. 1. State legislatures and high courts eager to reinstate capital punishment after *Gregg* were very likely to include proportionality review provisions and/or institute procedures. The amount of time between reenactment, the court's first affirmance under the new statute, and the state's first execution may give some indication of a state's willingness to entertain constitutional challenges to the death penalty. Compare, e.g., the New Jersey, Alabama, and Colorado timing data in tbl. 1.

82. Six states have repealed their proportionality review statutes. They are Connecticut, Idaho, Maryland, Nevada, Oklahoma, and Wyoming. See online appendix A.

83. For example, the Pennsylvania Supreme Court set out the principles for proportionality review and authorized the Administrative Office of the Pennsylvania Courts to collect data on all homicides, but it has not been clear from subsequent opinions exactly how the court uses the information for proportionality review, or if it does use the database created for the purpose. See online appendix A.

84. Intracase proportionality is a comparison between the death sentence under review and the sentences received by codefendants in the same case. California and Illinois are two states that perform only intracase proportionality review. See online appendix A.

85. *McCleskey v. Zant,* 499 U.S. 467 (1991). Warren McCleskey was executed shortly after the Supreme Court rejected his second habeas corpus petition. The hope that the U.S. Supreme Court would again declare a state system unconstitutional died with Warren McCleskey.

86. See, e.g., *State v. Ross,* 646 A.2d. 1318, 1373–75 (Conn.) (Berdon, J., dissenting in part) (reviewing constitutional analysis in Connecticut state court decisions), cert. denied, 115 S. Ct. 1133 (1995).

87. "Justice Transcript," *supra* note 10, at 1101–2. See also Bright and Keenan, *supra* note 80, at 785; Phoebe C. Ellsworth and Samuel R. Gross, "Hardening of the Attitudes: Americans' Views of the Death Penalty," 50 *Journal of Social Issues* 19, 40–42 (1994).

88. See *infra* tbl. 1, tbl. 2.

89. "If the purpose of *McCleskey* was to provide closure, it certainly was successful in the federal courts. The decision has eliminated the federal courts as a forum for the consideration of statistically based claims of racial discrimination in capital sentencing." Baldus et al., *supra* note 36, at 374.

90. The capital punishment decisions of the New Jersey Supreme Court in the 1980s were preceded by controversial decisions on zoning and school financing.

Chief Justice Wilentz's landmark zoning opinion in 1983, which came to be known as Mt. Laurel II [*South Burlington County NAACP v. Mount Laurel Township,* 456 A. 2d 390 (N.J. 1983)] because it was the second involving that mostly white Burlington County suburb, set off a firestorm . . . The other major decision that is still roiling New Jersey is *Abbott v. Burke* (1990) . . . again written by Chief Justice Wilentz, in which the court ruled that the state's poorest school districts must be given enough state aid to bring their level of spending spend [*sic*] per pupil to that of the richest ones.

. . .

. . . In the summer of 1986, Robert N. Wilentz was very nearly fired. By then he had been Chief Justice for seven years, the point at which the Senate considers whether to give a judge a lifetime appointment. Some of his rulings, especially the Mount Laurel decision, made him enemies . . . (Jan Hoffman, "His Court, His Legacy," *New York Times* (New Jersey Section), June 30, 1996, at 13NJ6–7)

91. *Gregg v. Georgia,* 428 U.S. 153 (1976).

92. In some jurisdictions it took several years for post-*Gregg* statutes and procedures to be affirmed, even if the state reenacted immediately. Then it took some time for capital convictions to come to the state supreme court for proportionality review on appeal. The first proportionality review in the jurisdiction usually was incorporated in the first direct appeal of a death sentence. This was usually, but not always, the case holding the reenacted capital statute constitutional. See *infra* tbl.1 for the different time periods between reenactment, affirmance of the first death sentence, and the first execution, by individual state.

93. *Pulley v. Harris,* 465 U.S. 37 (1984).

94. See *supra* "Taking the Supreme Court at Its Word."

95. The state high court could say, after *Pulley,* "The United States Supreme Court does not require this, so we are not doing it." Or the court could just no longer conduct proportionality review or could just be very perfunctory. See online appendix A.

96. *State v. Koedatich,* 548 A.2d 939, 946 (N.J. 1988), cert. denied, 488 U.S. 1017 (1989). The factual parameters of such arguments are set out in appendix B (online).

97. See, e.g., *State v. Williams,* 301 S.E.2d. 335, 353 (N.C. 1983) (rejecting a statistical analysis of capital case processing).

98. State high courts have been unwilling to rule on behalf of capital defendants on the basis of statistical evidence of racial disparities in capital case processing, irrespective of the alleged cause. A weaker scientific showing in the context of employment discrimination, or racial discrimination in jury selection, has resulted in findings of racial discrimination. See Baldus et al., *supra* note 36, at 375–76.

99. Justice Powell's comment that "racial . . . discrimination still remains a fact of life" in the criminal justice system may have accurately expressed the view of many state supreme court justices, many of whom had trial court experience. *Rose v. Mitchell,* 443 U.S. 545, 558 (1979).

100. The Supreme Court of New Jersey confronted this issue when the Public Defender presented a series of reports titled "The Reimposition of Capital Punishment in New Jersey," which included the quantitative analysis of data on homicides and capital case processing in the jurisdiction as a whole. See Order, reprinted in Bienen et al., *supra* note 20, at 371–72 (requesting the special master to assess this data as one of his first tasks).

101. Increasingly, state supreme court chief justices have the administrative responsibility of overseeing the operation of the entire court system:

> Chief Justice Wilentz spent perhaps two-thirds of his time overseeing the state court system, which now includes 10,000 employees. More than a million cases were filed last year in trial level Superior Courts.
>
> . . .
>
> . . . [T]he Chief Justice strove to make the courts more efficient, accessible and credible.
>
> . . .
>
> . . . Toward the end of his tenure, he managed to centralize control of the budgets of the disparate judicial districts in an effort to erase distinctions in the services offered in poorer and wealthier counties—and, by extension, the quality of justice . . . (Hoffman, *supra* note 90, at 13NJ7)

102. Minorities are in some cases "benefiting" from the discrimination, and this may additionally disturb political alliances on these issues. See Leigh B. Bienen, "A Good Murder," 20 *Fordham Urb. L.J.* 585 (1993).

103. The "Guidelines for Prosecutorial Discretion" adopted by the County Prosecutors Association in response to the Supreme Court of New Jersey's opinion in *State v. Koedatich,* 548 A.2d 939 (N.J. 1988), declare that factors such as race, socioeconomic status, and the resources of the county prosecutor will not be a factor in the decision to declare a case capital. See Bienen et al., *supra* note 44, at 791–93. Nonetheless, patterns of urban/rural disparity persist. See appendix B, tbl. B8.

104. The district court and circuit court opinions in *McCleskey v. Kemp* were mired in detail and demonstrated that both courts did not understand the analytical finding. See Baldus et al., *supra* note 67, at 340–45.

105. The situation in New Jersey was unusual. The New Jersey Office of the Public Defender supported the collection and analysis of data during the entire proportionality review project, including the hiring of statistical experts from the University of Pennsylvania and Princeton University. See online appendix B, text accompanying notes 549–552. In most states public defenders have few financial resources and are unable to support any systematic, empirical research. The typical pattern is for the research to be conducted by academics whose research agenda is not designed for the litigation strategy of the defense. The completed academic research is then translated into legal arguments. See, e.g., Nakell and Hardy, *supra* note 67, at 93. The New Jersey Public Defender never set a limit on expenditures for capital appeals, and the New Jersey legislature consistently appropriated funds for capital defense during this period.

106. The New York Court of Appeals has implemented procedures to institutionalize systematic data collection and analysis by issuing a form for capital case data reports and by drawing upon the experience of other states. See *infra* "Statutory Provisions for Appellate Review and Proportionality Review."

107. See *infra* "Proportionality Review in Practice: Three States, Three Approaches"; appendix A.

108. *State v. Marshall,* 613 A.2d 1059 (N.J. 1992), shows a court struggling to maintain consensus while coming to terms with an expert analysis of comprehensive data concerning racial disparities in capital case processing. Proportionality review in New Jersey was an ongoing study of the development of social science data and methodology by a court. The court was criticized, often inaccurately, for attempting to be as precise as possible in its reference to facts and quantitative relationships. The court's commitment is especially noteworthy because it was exceptional.

> "It might be the best Supreme Court in the Country—state or federal," said Harvard law Prof. Laurence H. Tribe.

. . .

> "[A] fair amount of the credit for the Court's achievements belongs to Chief Justice Wilentz," said Professor Tribe, "but it's certainly not a one-man accolade." Professor Kamisar's [Professor Yale Kamisar, University of Michigan School of Law] personal applause is reserved for Stewart G. Pollock, 51, a liberal Republican who has, in speeches and articles, picked up a recurring theme of the court: the importance of the state constitution in protecting fundamental rights . . . (Bruce S. Rosen, "A Bold Court Forges Ahead," *National Law Journal,* Nov. 5, 1984, at 1)

109. Chief Justice Wilentz not only authored several important opinions building the jurisprudence concerning proportionality in capital cases, but he also had a commitment to the principled application of social science methods which the court needed to maintain its commitment. During this period the chief justice was personally attacked when the court reversed death sentences. The chief justice died shortly after he announced his early retirement for reasons of ill health. See Hoffman, *supra* note 90, at 13NJ1; David Stout, "Robert Wilentz, 69, Dies; Court Aided Women and Poor," *New York Times,* July 24, 1996, at D20.

110. See *infra* notes 216–17 and accompanying text.

111. The New York Court of Appeals may now be in a favorable position to demonstrate similar judicial leadership. See *infra* "The 1995 Reenactment in New York: New Rules for the Reimposition of Capital Punishment in the 1990s." Recently, the state high courts of Pennsylvania and Connecticut have expressed a willingness to take the responsibility of maintaining an adequate factual record in order to conduct systematic proportionality review. See *State v. Cobb,* 663 A.2d 948, 961–62 (Conn. 1995); *Commonwealth v. Banks,* 656 A.2d 467, 474 (Pa.), cert. denied, 116 S. Ct. 113 (1995).

112. See *Commonwealth v. Frey,* 475 A.2d 700, 712–13 (Pa. 1984) (proportionality review data collection instrument "Review Form: Murder of the First Degree"). The Pennsylvania Supreme Court database is described in John F. Kairns and Lee S. Weinberg, "The Death Sentence in Pennsylvania, 1978–1990: A Preliminary Analysis of the Effects of Statutory and Nonstatutory Factors," 95 *Dick. L. Rev.* 691 (1991).

113. See *Commonwealth v. DeHart,* 516 A.2d 656, 671 (Pa. 1986). Researchers have encountered problems in attempting to analyze the Pennsylvania database. Data are provided on a form by the trial court judge. Data are collected on the race, sex, and age of the defendant and the victim; the dates and disposition of the offense; and whether or not the death penalty was sought. The form also asks whether there was a factual basis for any statutory aggravating factor submitted or found, whether there were aggravating circumstances which were not pursued by the state, and the court's opinion as to why the commonwealth did not seek the death penalty or failed to pursue aggravating circumstances if there was a factual basis for seeking the death penalty. Information is sought on the statutory mitigating circumstances submitted and found, the statutory mitigating circumstances which were not pursued, and the court's assessment of why defense counsel may have failed to pursue any mitigating circumstances. Finally, both the prosecutor and the defense attorney, in theory, certify the accuracy of the data and provide additional information. See *Frey,* 475 A.2d at 712–13. The open-ended database is intended to be maintained on a standardized statistical file. The absence of a narrative summary for each case is a serious methodological problem. Without case narratives it is impossible to verify facts or procedural decisions to ensure a reliable analysis.

114. For example:

> In most jurisdictions, prosecutors file such notice [to seek the death

> penalty] in a small percentage of eligible homicides: in Pittsburgh, for example, W. Christopher Conrad, Allegheny County's deputy district attorney for homicide, estimates that his office files a Rule 352 [a notice of intention to seek the death penalty] in about a quarter of the cases in which aggravators are present. Philadelphia files one in virtually every case . . .
>
> . . .
>
> . . . In 1991, the last year for which figures are available for comparison, Houston's prosecutors sought death in seven cases at trial and won it in six. That year, Philadelphia sought it at trial in at least 59 cases, and probably many more . . . and won it 12 times. (Tina Rosenberg, "The Deadliest D.A.," *New York Times Magazine,* July 16, 1995, at 42, 46)

115. The Philadelphia Public Defender's Office is updating and verifying a segment of this database as part of its challenge to racial and geographic disparities in the application of the death penalty in Philadelphia. The Defender Association of Philadelphia is in the process of creating a database for a statewide study of proportionality in the imposition of death sentences in Pennsylvania. The sample includes all death sentences, a sample of penalty-phase life cases and death-possible non-penalty phase cases, including trials and pleas. The Administrative Offices of Pennsylvania Courts have provided this project with its own data and research going back to 1978. Professor David C. Baldus is a consultant to the Defender Association. The project is modeled after the Proportionality Review Project of the Supreme Court of New Jersey. Telephone interview with David Zuckerman, assistant defender, Appellate Division, Defender Association of Philadelphia, Nov. 19, 1996.

116. When the court engages in independent data verification and maintains a factual record of potentially capital homicides, that record is usually a public record, available to any interested party, including those challenging the imposition of the death sentence. The Pennsylvania Supreme Court, for example, routinely gives its data files to capital defense attorneys. But see *Skaggs v. Commonwealth,* 694 S.W.2d 672, 681–82 (Ky. 1985) (holding that the public advocate is not entitled to data compiled for the Supreme Court pursuant to the court's authority to review death sentences). Some state high courts have created permanent data files on all capital appeals. The court typically appoints a special clerk or administrative agency to collect the data and ensure its reliability. In other states, the court will cooperate with independent researchers to prepare a database on capital cases. See the description of the data collection methods in Nakell and Hardy, *supra* note 67, at 93.

117. See *infra* tbl. 1.

118. The date of the first death sentence affirmed should not be confused with the date the statute was held constitutional. In New Jersey, for example, the statute as a whole was held to be constitutional in *State v. Ramseur,* 524 A.2d 188 (N.J. 1987). However, the first capital conviction was not affirmed until *Marshall I* in 1991. *State v. Marshall,* 586 A.2d 85 (N.J. 1991). The death sentence of Robert Marshall was affirmed in 1992 after proportionality review in *Marshall II. State v. Marshall,* 613 A.2d 1059 (N.J. 1992). Although federal and state habeas actions are pending in Marshall's case, the New Jersey Supreme Court has issued a ruling on the direct appeal and upheld the death sentence after proportionality review—the final appellate action in a capital appeal. Similarly, in Connecticut, the state high court has upheld the statute's constitutionality as a whole, but the court has not yet upheld an individual death sentence after proportionality review.

119. The subtractions and the rankings within each column were done using Microsoft Excel.

120. If *Gregg* had declared the Georgia statute unconstitutional, it would have sent all of those states back to square one. The political cost might have been very high indeed.

121. No states reenacted in 1980, 1981, 1983–1990, 1992, or 1993.

122. The states which have not affirmed their first death sentence as of 1996 include Connecticut (reenacted in 1973), Kansas (1994), New Hampshire (1991), New York (1995), and South Dakota (1979).

123. See Baldus et al., *supra* note 36, at 413–17 (discussing Florida's capital jurisprudence).

124. And, of course, a state will have a death row population as soon as the first defendant is sentenced to death at the trial level. The state need not have affirmed its first death sentence for a death row population to exist.

125. Changes in the number of people on death row reflect not only executions but also defendants removed from death row because their death sentences were overturned by courts—either on direct appeal, or by a state or federal court on post-conviction relief. To date no one has compiled an accurate account of the affirmance rate for each individual state supreme court, and defining such a rate has many methodological difficulties. For example, are reversals on direct appeal the only reversals counted? What about the reversal rate for federal district courts and federal circuit courts? Additionally, some circuits are much more likely to reverse death sentences than other circuits. Defining categories, as well as counting and tabulating, present difficult questions which must be resolved consistently if comparative figures are to have any meaning. For this reason, tbls. 1 and 2 only contain numbers as of a specific date which could in theory be established with certainty.

126. In the entire history of capital punishment in America, Virginia has executed more women than any other state, and more than twice as many as the next state (112 executions of women in Virginia, as opposed to 49 in Maryland). Victor L. Streb, "Death Penalty for Battered Women," 20 *Fla. St. U. L. Rev.* 163, 172 (1992).

127. These states have had a great deal of interplay between the state high court and federal courts on capital punishment issues. See, e.g., Deborah W. Denno, "Testing Penry and Its Progeny," 22 *Am. J. Crim. L.* 1 (1994) (chronicling the interplay between the federal courts, the state appellate courts, and the Texas legislature on the question of statutory mental mitigating factors).

128. See Bright and Keenan, *supra* note 80, at 766. Bright and Keenan discuss the replacement of Chief Justice Rose Bird and three other justices on the California Supreme Court, after a campaign in which the chief justice's prior reversal of death sentences played a prominent part. The affirmance rate for capital cases went up dramatically after that election.

129. See *infra* tbl.1.

130. Frequently a court will reverse on proportionality and on other grounds. But see *Sinclair v. State,* 657 So. 2d 1138, 1142 (Fla. 1995) (death sentence was not proportionate); see also *State v. Pratt,* 873 P.2d 800, 824 (Idaho 1993) ("We hold that the death penalty in this case is disproportionate").

131. See, e.g., Conference: "The Death Penalty in the Twenty-First Century," 45 *Am. U. L. Rev.* 239, 327–31 (1995) (comments of Paul D. Kamenar). The chief justice of the Supreme Court went on record endorsing the speeding up of executions—a view that was shared by many in the judiciary. See Rehnquist, *supra* note 76, at 2.

132. If the administrative unit for the public defender is the county, then the typical pattern is that the Office of the Public Defender will be effective in the large cities, where there is a large volume of serious criminal cases and a professionalized staff. Even those attorneys, however, cannot undertake systematic data collection on homicides throughout the state. The New York

statute enacted in 1995, N.Y. Jud. Law 35-b(3) (McKinney Supp. 1996), creates a central Capital Defenders Office for this purpose. In many states public defenders are appointed by local authorities, and there are vast differences in the quality of defense counsel in different parts of the same state.

133. In many jurisdictions, limits on defense spending limit the capability of the defense:

> In [capital] cases, Philadelphia pays a $1,700 flat fee for preparation and $400 for each day in court. This averages $3,519 a case, according to Geoff Gallas, the executive administrator of Philadelphia's courts . . . Since the public defenders began taking murder cases in April 1993 [in Philadelphia], their clients have not been given a single death sentence, while 33 of those privately represented—most, if not all, court appointed—have been given one. (Rosenberg, *supra* note 114, at 50 (citations omitted))

In Alabama, a court-appointed lawyer in a death penalty case is awarded $20 an hour and limited to $2,000 for out-of-court time. In Mississippi, the limit is $1,000. See "The O.J. Simpson Case and Capital Punishment," 38 *How. L.J.* 247, 265 (1995) (panel discussion) (comments of Stephen Bright).

134. See Bright and Keenan, *supra* note 80, at 781.

135. Those states were Connecticut, Idaho, Maryland, Nevada, Oklahoma, and Wyoming. See *infra* appendix A.

136. See *infra* appendix A.

137. California was engaged in a systematic data analysis project prior to *McCleskey.* It was abandoned after *McCleskey* was decided.

138. See online appendix A.

139. See online appendix A.

140. Courts and legislatures define the relevant terms differently. The important analytic point is that a "pool" or "universe" of cases is the group of cases to which the death case under review is being compared, however that group is defined. Courts also use terms such as "death-eligible" and "capital" to mean different things.

141. This is the "precedent-seeking" approach in the typology of the National Center for State Courts. See *Equal Justice and the Death Penalty: A Legal and Empirical Analysis, supra* note 53, at 281. The death sentence under review is not disproportionate if the court can find at least one other similar case in which the death sentence has been upheld.

142. See online appendix A. The states which limit the pool of comparison cases to other death sentences imposed, either by statutory provision or by an explicit holding in the case law, are Alabama, Kentucky, Louisiana, Mississippi, Nebraska, New Jersey, Ohio, South Carolina, and Virginia. Even in these states, however, the court will occasionally depart from its own procedures and consider other non-death cases.

143. This type of proportionality review, however, makes no sense. Assume for the moment that it was demonstrated that the jurisdiction in question was found to only impose death in cases involving black defendants and white victims. Under the logic of this approach, it would be irrelevant that there were five, ten, or one hundred allegedly similar cases involving white defendants and white victims in which the defendant was not sentenced to death. As long as the class of people sentenced to death was internally consistent, the standard is satisfied. The attorney general of New Jersey conceded this point in the oral argument in *Marshall.*

144. See Steven M. Sprenger, Note, "A Critical Evaluation of State Supreme Court Proportionality Review in Death Sentence Cases," 73 *Iowa L. Rev.* 719, 738 n.154 (1988) ("A reasonably diligent review of proportionality review opinions of state supreme courts that limit

their universe to death sentence cases reveals that within all those states, courts have identified a death sentence as comparatively excessive in only one case") (citing *Coleman v. State,* 378 So. 2d 640 (Miss. 1979)).

> In *Coleman v. State,* the defendant was convicted and sentenced to death for committing a murder while engaged in the commission of a burglary. In conducting its proportionality review, the Mississippi Supreme Court refused to include similar life sentence cases in its universe even though it failed to identify any similar death sentence cases. Lacking such cases, the court vacated the death sentence as excessive. (Id. at 738 (footnotes omitted))

A search of post-1987 proportionality review cases did not reveal another such case.

145. See, e.g., *Turner v. Commonwealth,* 364 S.E.2d 483, 490 (Va. 1988).

> "[The defendant] cites prior cases where the "vileness" involved was admittedly greater than the "vileness" present here. But no concept of proportionality requires that each new capital murder case equal in horror the worst possible scenario yet encountered, else the death penalty may not be imposed . . . While the atrociousness involved in Turner's murder does not rise to the level evidenced in Stamper, James Dyral Briley, or Coppola, Turner's murder is just as brutal as the murders in Linwood Earl Briley and Clark . . ." (Id. (citation and footnotes omitted) (second ellipses in original))

146. Even in this circumstance, however, state high courts will not always set aside the death sentence as disproportionate. See, e.g., *Coppola v. Commonwealth,* 257 S.E.2d 797, 807 (Va. 1979).

147. See online appendix A. The states which define their pool of comparison cases as all other penalty phase cases, either by statute or by an explicit holding to that effect by the state high court, are Delaware, Georgia, Idaho, Maryland, Missouri, Montana, New Mexico, North Carolina, and Washington.

148. See *Marshall II,* 613 A.2d 1059, 1070–72 (N.J. 1992).

149. This is due to the fact that some states do not include death sentences which have been reversed at guilt phase or penalty phase. Some states do not include death sentences which have not yet been upheld on appeal. This pool, therefore, is not in every instance all penalty phase cases, nor does it result in the same universe in every state. As the New Jersey Supreme Court explained:

> We realize that other courts throughout the country have used different measures of comparison . . . the Georgia Supreme Court uses all capital felony cases which have been appealed for comparison . . . Delaware's universe consists of a comparison between the subject case and "the penalties in all first degree murder cases which have gone to trial and a penalty hearing." (*State v. Marshall,* 613 A.2d 1059, 1073 (N.J. 1992) (citations omitted))

150. There may also be convictions for capital murder imposed by a judge. In some rare cases the conviction may be imposed pursuant to a plea bargain. See Bienen et al., *supra* note 20, at 94 n. 337 (discussing the conditional plea to capital murder in New Jersey); see also *State v. Wright,* 483 A.2d 436 (N.J. Super. Ct. Law Div. 1984) (involving a plea to capital murder in exchange for a sentence recommendation of four life sentences, where a mother killed her four children under circumstances similar to those in the highly publicized Susan Smith case).

151. For example, in Florida and Indiana the judge can override a jury's verdict at penalty phase. See online appendix A.

152. The inclusion of reversed death sentences is especially problematic. See *State v. Marshall,* 613 A.2d 1059, 1129 (N.J. 1992) (Handler, J., dissenting).

153. In the terminology of stage analysis, these jurisdictions look at one stage prior to the decision-making stage examined by courts that limit their universe solely to other death sentences. See online appendix B, fig.1 (outlining the stages of capital case processing). They stop short, however, of analyzing the two previous stages: all cases where there was a factual basis for capital murder, although the case never resulted in a prosecution for capital murder or a capital conviction. Not surprisingly, jurisdictions following this method have accounted for almost all of the reversals of death sentences on grounds of disproportionality.

154. 646 A.2d 1318 (Conn. 1994), cert. denied, 115 S. Ct. 1133 (1995). The principal constitutional issues involved the structure of jury decision-making and the standards and procedures for evaluating mitigating factors, as well as Eighth Amendment questions and other issues. See id. at 1353–58 (citing *State v. Ramseur,* 524 A.2d 188 (N.J. 1987)). For a detailed history of Connecticut constitutional history, see id. at 1373–95 (Berdon, J., dissenting). See also appendix B (online).

155. Dissenting Justice Berdon, however, noted that the defendant in *Ross,* who was convicted of six murders, was allowed to plead guilty and avoid the death penalty by a prosecuting attorney who had full knowledge of the convictions. In contrast, a prosecutor in another judicial district did seek the death penalty: "This life-and-death difference between the sentences received by the defendant for identical crimes proves that an unacceptable level of arbitrariness exists due to prosecutorial discretion, even if the jury is adequately guided by the statute." Id. at 1382 (Berdon, J., dissenting). Justice Berdon went on to say that in his opinion the death penalty was discriminatory on the basis of the race of the victim. He cited studies from other jurisdictions and noted that all of the five defendants on death row in Connecticut had killed white victims, and that two of the defendants were African American. Id. at 1384–85 (Berdon, J., dissenting). The dissent noted that the court was divided: "Two justices of this court believe the death penalty is constitutional, one does not, and four are silent." Id. at 1387 (Berdon, J., dissenting). In a subsequent case, *State v. Breton,* 663 A.2d 1026, 1054 n.2 (Conn. 1995) (Berdon, J., dissenting), Justice Berdon noted that only three supreme court justices were qualified to sit in *Ross,* and in *Breton* three justices still had not yet addressed the state constitutionality of the death penalty. Justice Berdon continued to express his view that the death penalty was applied in a discriminatory manner due to different prosecutorial charging practices. Id. at 1055, nn.5–6 (Berdon, J., dissenting). The court's opinion in *Breton* did not address proportionality since the death sentence was reversed for other reasons.

156. "The legislature recently eliminated proportionality review altogether on a prospective basis." *State v. Cobb,* 663 A.2d 948, 950 n.2 (Conn. 1995) (citing Conn. Gen. Stat. Ann. 53a-46(b) (West Supp. 1996)). Connecticut previously had a standard proportionality review provision, using a slight variant of the language in *Gregg.* Conn. Gen. Stat. Ann. 53a-46(b)(3) (West 1994) (repealed) ("The sentence is excessive or disproportionate to the penalty imposed in similar cases, considering both the circumstances of the crime and the character and record of the defendant").

157. 663 A.2d 948 (Conn. 1995).

158. One issue in *Cobb* was whether the proportionality question had been addressed and decided in *Ross.* See id. at 952. In *Cobb,* the court declined to rely upon its decision in *Ross.* Id.

159. The dissent discussed the issue of racial bias in terms of the state constitution. *Cobb,* 663 A.2d at 965 (Berdon, J., dissenting).

160. As the court described its process:

> We emphasize that we do not decide whether a statistical study

> comparable to that offered in *McCleskey v. Zant* would establish a violation of [the appellate review provision] in any particular case. Nor do we suggest that only such a broad scale attack could establish such a violation. Obviously, if the record in any given case indicated that, irrespective of any statistics, the death sentence was the product of passion, prejudice or any other arbitrary factor incident to that particular trial, there would be a violation of [the appellate review provision]. We conclude only that, subject to the requirement that the defendant make his statistical challenge at trial, [the appellate review provision] provides an appropriate statutory vehicle for his statistical claim on appeal. (Id. at 961 n. 20 (citation omitted))

161. The universe of cases for proportionality review was governed by Practice Book 4066A(b), authorized by the court under its rule-making authority. This rule provides that the universe of cases shall be "only those capital felony cases that have been prosecuted in this state after October 1, 1973, and in which hearings on the imposition of the death penalty have taken place . . . unless the court . . . shall modify this limitation in a particular case." Id. at 952 n. 6 (emphasis omitted).

162. Id.

163. Id. at 952 n. 7. The court denied Ross's application, but granted a more limited request. Id. Prior to *Ross,* the court had granted two other enlargements to the proportionality universe. Id.

164. See id. at 955. The state argued that an expanded proportionality review would require the court to inquire into "the nature and circumstances of every case since 1973 that ended in a homicide conviction in order to determine whether that case could have been charged as a capital felony." Id. at 956. The court inaccurately noted that only Pennsylvania now conducts such fact-finding. Id. at 957. New Jersey, Tennessee, Washington, and Georgia review homicide cases to determine which could have resulted in a capital prosecution. See online appendix A.

165. 613 A.2d 1059 (N.J. 1992).

166. *Cobb,* 663 A.2d at 962 ("The nature of the defendant's claim of systematic racial bias, and the seriousness and finality of the death penalty, counsel against raising any undue procedural barriers to review of such a claim"). The dissent, which now included three justices of the court, believed that the statistical showing put forward by the defense in *Cobb* was sufficient to show that the death penalty was more likely to be imposed if the victim was white or otherwise not African American. The data presented were preliminary. The dissenters believed that proportionality review was the appropriate rubric for these arguments and that the Supreme Court of Connecticut, not the trial court, was the appropriate forum in which to conduct a factual inquiry. Id. at 965 (Berdon, J. dissenting, joined by Norcott, J., and Katz, J.).

167. The Nebraska legislature enacted a statute requiring proportionality review which read as follows:

> (3) State law should be applied uniformly throughout the state and *since the death penalty is a statewide law an offense which would not result in a death sentence in one portion of the state should not result in death in a different portion; . . .*
>
> The Supreme Court shall within a reasonable time after July 22, 1978, review and analyze all cases involving criminal homicide committed on or after April 20, 1973. [The date of reenactment.] Such review and analysis shall examine (1) the facts including mitigating and aggravating circumstances, (2) the charges filed, (3) the crime for which defendant was

convicted, and (4) the sentence imposed. Such review shall be updated as new criminal homicide cases occur. (Neb. Rev. Stat. 29-2521.01(3), 29-2521.02 (Reissue 1995) (emphasis added))

This statute is also referred to as L.B. 711, Laws 1978.

168. *State v. Williams,* 287 N.W.2d 18, 28 (Neb. 1979). This ruling contradicted the specific statutory mandate to "review and analyze all cases involving criminal homicide." Neb. Rev. Stat. 29-2521.02.

169. *State v. Welsh,* 275 N.W.2d 54, 57 (Neb. 1979). This holding was reaffirmed in *State v. Reeves,* 453 N.W.2d 359, 386 (Neb. 1990).

170. The statute reads:

> In order to compensate for the lack of uniformity in charges which are filed as a result of similar circumstances it is necessary for the Supreme Court to review and analyze *all criminal homicides committed under the existing law* in order to insure that each case produces a result similar to that arrived at in other cases with the same or similar circumstances. Neb. Rev. Stat. 29-2521.01(4) (Reissue 1995) (emphasis added)

The court trumped this legislative directive. "In a series of cases this court determined that if read literally, L.B. 711 would unconstitutionally encroach upon the judicial function . . . we held that the proportionality review under L.B. 711 should include only those cases in which the death penalty was imposed." *State v. Reeves,* 453 N.W.2d 359, 386 (Neb. 1990) (citations omitted).

171. As the court noted:

> There is language in at least two sections of L.B. 711, Laws of 1978, directing the Supreme Court to review and analyze "all criminal homicides." If the language [*sic*] be interpreted to extend beyond first degree murder convictions, *problems relating to the exercise of prosecutorial discretion in homicide cases* and the exercise by juries of the decisional power of determining guilt or innocence or fixing degrees of culpability in homicide cases are all involved. To interpret that language of L.B. 711 literally would create insurmountable constitutional problems. In view of the disposition made here, it is unnecessary to discuss constitutional issues. (*Williams,* 287 N.W.2d at 29 (emphasis added))

172. Id.

173. In *Williams,* the court first considered cases which did not result in a death sentence. It reviewed thirty-two cases which resulted in a conviction for first-degree murder, including eight cases which were not appealed and seven death sentences which were on appeal. The remaining twenty-five cases it considered were life sentences. Id. The court began with a consideration of the aggravating and mitigating circumstances.

> In all of the death penalty cases previously affirmed or now pending in this court, each has involved at least three separate and distinct statutory aggravating factors and only one or no statutory mitigating factors . . . Any objective weighing and balancing of aggravating and mitigating circumstances and comparison to the other death penalty cases now pending establishes that the death sentence in the case now before us is not excessive or disproportionate to the death penalties imposed in the other death penalty cases. (Id. at 29–30)

174. The chief justice of the Nebraska Supreme Court, in dissent, described his concerns as follows:

I am more concerned, as I believe L.B. 711, Laws 1978, requires me to be concerned, as to how this case squares with the remaining 25 cases where the death penalty was not imposed. [The chief justice then reviewed the statute and its relationship to an earlier provision.] All of that makes it seem clear to me that not only is this court required to examine aggravating and mitigating circumstances, but in addition to that we are supposed to in some manner place each first degree murder case one on top of the other to see whether or not they all conform. While I may be the first to concede that imposing such a duty upon the court is at best difficult and perhaps impossible, nevertheless, I cannot find how I can ignore that requirement. [The chief justice's opinion then goes on to enumerate a number of cases "similar" to the case under review in which the defendant was not sentenced to death, either because the defendant pled guilty or the defendant was sentenced to life imprisonment . . . The chief justice then concludes that the legislative intent of L.B. 711 must have been to further restrict the imposition of the death penalty] by directing us not to impose the death penalty if on previous occasions of cruel and senseless killings we have not imposed the death penalty. (Id. at 32–35 (Krivosha, C.J., concurring in part and dissenting in part))

175. 399 N.W.2d 706 (Neb. 1986).

176. The majority opinion commented:

It would be possible to construe the statute so that cases in which the death penalty was not imposed, although upon reflection it could be said that the death penalty might have been imposed, would be the standard against which all future death penalty cases would be compared. By a process of "attrition" this would result in a substantial narrowing of the group of cases in which the death penalty would be a possible sentence and, eventually, for all practical purposes, could amount to a repeal of the death penalty. We do not understand that the Legislature intended the statute to effect a repeal of the death penalty. (*State v. Palmer,* 399 N.W.2d 706, 735–36 (Neb. 1986) (citing *State v. Copeland,* 300 S.E.2d 63, 71–72 (S.C. 1982))

177. Once again, the court's intention was clear:

The plain language of the act seems to make it clear that *all criminal homicide cases* are to be reported to the Supreme Court and that the Supreme Court, in conducting its review, is to look at *all of these cases and to then compare the case on appeal with those other cases having same or similar circumstances,* not penalties, to determine whether the imposition of the death penalty in the case on appeal is more severe than that imposed in other cases having same or similar circumstances . . . Limiting the review to be conducted by this court to those cases in which the death penalty has been imposed is to rewrite the statute . . . The language of the act simply will not, absent painful distortion, permit a finding that the review is to be limited to only cases in which the death penalty had been imposed. (*Palmer,* 399 N.W.2d at 747–48 (Krivosha, C.J., concurring in part and dissenting in part) (emphasis added))

Chief Justice Krivosha cited voluminous legislative history supporting this interpretation of the act. See id. at 751–52.

178. Id. at 752 (Krivosha, C.J., concurring in part and dissenting in part). Justice Handler, in *Marshall II,* used the same analogy. See *State v. Marshall,* 613 A.2d 1059, 1130 (N.J. 1992) (Handler, J., dissenting).

179. This discussion, including the annotations to allegedly similar cases in the concurring and dissenting opinion of Chief Justice Krivosha, comprises fifty pages. See *Palmer,* 399 N.W.2d at 733–83.

180. Id. at 753 (Krivosha, C.J., concurring in part and dissenting in part).

181. Id. (Krivosha, C.J., concurring in part and dissenting in part).

182. Id. at 753 (Krivosha, C.J., concurring in part and dissenting in part).

183. Id. at 753 (Krivosha, C.J., concurring in part and dissenting in part). The chief justice concluded that analysis of similar cases supported the conclusion that the death penalty for a killing during a robbery, absent other circumstances, was by definition disproportionate: "The death penalty for murdering an individual while attempting to or in fact robbing the individual was imposed in only 12.8 percent of the cases, while life imprisonment or less was imposed in 87.2 percent of the cases." Id. at 754 (Krivosha, C.J., concurring in part and dissenting in part).

184. Id. at 754–55 (Krivosha, C.J., concurring in part and dissenting in part).

185. 524 A.2d 188 (N.J. 1987).

186. 613 A.2d 1059 (N.J. 1992) (*Marshall II*).

187. *Marshall II* was the first case to implement proportionality review in New Jersey. The entire opinion, exceeding one hundred pages, is devoted to proportionality review. The opinion summarizes the history of proportionality review litigation in New Jersey and applies the analysis and data of the Proportionality Review Project's "Final Report" to the facts and circumstances of the imposition of Robert Marshall's death sentence, which had been upheld on direct appeal a year earlier in *State v. Marshall,* 586 A.2d 85 (N.J. 1991) *(Marshall I)*.

188. The Supreme Court of New Jersey continues to analyze racial and geographic disparities in capital processing as new capital cases come before the court. Unfortunately, the race effects persist. See online appendix C. For example, the data in the court's most recent proportionality review, *State v. Harris,* 660 A.2d 539 (N.J. Super. Ct. App. Div. 1995), involved a black defendant and a white victim and showed evidence that the victim's race had a significant effect. However, the New Jersey Supreme Court did not address the proportionality data in that case because Harris died prior to the proportionality hearing.

189. See online appendix A.

190. Appendix B (online) sets out some of the basic parameters from the *Marshall II* data set and presents a summary analysis of the proportionality review issues, such as racial and geographic disparities in capital case processing, that arise in death penalty jurisdictions.

191. The work of the Proportionality Review Project has been described and compared with the analogous data collection and analyses that were presented to the U.S. Supreme Court in *McCleskey v. Kemp,* 481 U.S. 279 (1987). Baldus et al., *supra* note 36, at 405–13.

192. See *State v. Marshall,* 613 A.2d 1059 (N.J. 1992) (*Marshall II*). The court stated, "we have but little knowledge of the science of statistical probabilities." Id. at 1111. This somewhat wistful comment in the court's opinion followed an extensive discussion of technical methodological issues. "If a court concludes that the statistical evidence is so deviant as to compel a conclusion of substantial significance, the court must then look to the circumstances surrounding that statistical showing to determine its full constitutional import." Id. at 1111.

193. The implementation of concepts based upon equity and principles of proportionality has been difficult in other areas of the law as well. For example, the principle of proportionality has been the doctrinal foundation of recent cases involving challenges to inequalities and

disparities in a university's allocation of resources for men's and women's athletic teams. See *Cohen v. Brown University,* 879 F. Supp. 185 (D. R.I. 1995); "Judge Says Brown Plan Won't Work," *Plain Dealer,* Aug. 18, 1995, at 3D.

194. These methodological refinements are transferable to research on other forms of criminal conduct. The Proportionality Review Project sets out a graduated standard for evaluating the strength of evidence of guilt which is applicable to cases other than murder cases. The model carefully distinguished between circumstantial aspects of a case, aspects of the defendant's conduct, and facts relevant to criminal intent and is generalizable to other jurisdictions and crimes.

195. Justice Garibaldi, in her concurring and dissenting opinion, disagreed with several key points made by the *Marshall II* majority. See *Marshall II,* 613 A.2d at 1115 (Garibaldi, J., concurring in part and dissenting in part). See *infra* footnotes 221–23, 229–30 and accompanying text. Justice Handler took a position similar to that of former justices Brennan and Marshall of the U.S. Supreme Court. Justice Handler believed that "our experience over the last ten years with capital punishment, capped by the lessons wrought from our gargantuan effort to attain proportionate sentencing, confirms the constitutional impossibility of capital punishment." *Marshall II,* 613 A.2d at 1144 (Handler, J., dissenting).

196. Reenactment was delayed in New Jersey because the then governor, Brendan Byrne, refused to sign legislation reenacting capital punishment during his two terms in office. However, in 1982 the New Jersey legislature passed a capital punishment statute that was drafted to comport with the federal constitutional requirements specified in *Gregg v. Georgia,* 428 U.S. 153 (1976). See 1982 N.J. Laws 555. For a discussion of the legislative history of reenactment in New Jersey, see Bienen et al., *supra* note 20, at 66–70; Connie Chen, "A Review and Analysis of the 1982 Legislative Decision Making Process Reenacting Capital Punishment in New Jersey (1992)" (unpublished); the Woodrow Wilson School Policy Conference Final Report, "A Decade of Capital Punishment in New Jersey" (1992) (unpublished) (presented to the New Jersey Assembly Judiciary Committee and the New Jersey Senate Judiciary Committee in 1992 and included in the legislative history of A.C.R. 20, a pending amendment to the New Jersey Constitution) (on file with State Documents Section, Northwestern University School of Law Library) [hereinafter 1992 WWS Final Report]; and Tanya Minhas, "Newspapers, Crime and the Public: The Role of the Media in the Reinstatement of the Death Penalty in New Jersey (1992)" (unpublished), in 1992 WWS Final Report.

For a description and statistical analysis of the structure of the New Jersey statute, see Bienen et al., *supra* note 20, at 242–62; Bienen et al., *supra* note 44, at 715–35.

197. A constitutional amendment ratified in 1992, N.J. Const. art. I, par. 12 (West Supp. 1996), reduced the intent requirement for a conviction of capital murder, reversing the Supreme Court of New Jersey's opinion in *State v. Gerald,* 549 A.2d 792, 819 (N.J. 1988) (holding that a conviction for capital murder must include a finding of specific intent to commit capital murder). None of the cases prior to *Marshall II* or included in appendix B online are affected by the 1992 amendment.

198. N.J. Stat. Ann. 2C:11-3e (West 1995). Compare *Gregg v. Georgia,* 428 U.S. 153, 212 (1976) (White, J., concurring).

199. Most states institutionalized proportionality review in this manner. In New Jersey, the Proportionality Review Project was located within the Administrative Office of the Courts. In *Gregg* the court cited with approval the fact that "in order that information regarding 'similar cases' may be before the court, the post of Assistant to the Supreme Court [of Georgia] was created. The Assistant must 'accumulate the records of all capital felony cases in which the sentence was imposed after January 1, 1970, or such earlier date as the court

may deem appropriate.'" *Gregg v. Georgia,* 428 U.S. 153, 212 (1976) (White, J., concurring) (citation omitted). The language of *Gregg* was both very simple and very general: "similar cases considering both the crime and the defendant." Id. The Georgia Supreme Court had not implemented any procedures or conducted a proportionality review at the time the U.S. Supreme Court endorsed the Georgia statute and rules.

200. Arguments concerning disproportionality based on preliminary results from the Public Defender Homicide Study have been raised by defendants since *State v. Ramseur,* 524 A.2d 188 (N.J. 1987) and *State v. Koedatich,* 548 A.2d 939 (N.J. 1988). The arguments have taken different forms. See, e.g., Brief for Defendant at 28–56, *State v. Koedatich,* 548 A.2d 939 (N.J. 1988) (arguing abuse of prosecutorial discretion in the decision to charge capital murder); *Ramseur,* 524 A.2d at 178–80 (systemwide disproportionality and race- and county-based disparities documented in the then available findings of the Public Defender Homicide Study). Earlier briefs relied upon data from the "Preliminary Report" (1986) of the Public Defender Homicide Study. Later briefs relied upon the "Interim Report" (1987) of the Public Defender Homicide Study or the statistical findings published in Bienen et al., *supra* note 20.

201. The work of the Public Defender Homicide Study was included in an annotation of major studies in the 1990 GAO Report, *supra* note 37. The GAO report stated:

> It is important to evaluate research quality . . . By quality we mean the strength of the design and the rigor of the analytic technique that leads to a level of confidence we have in the study findings. We judged a study to be of high quality if it [1] was characterized by a sound design that analyzed homicide cases throughout the sentencing process; [2] included legally relevant variables (aggravating and mitigating circumstances); and [3] used statistical analysis techniques to control for variables that correlate with race and/or capital sentencing. (Id. at 3)

See Bienen et al., *supra* note 20, at 330 fig.1 (indicating the stages of capital case processing in New Jersey).

202. 524 A.2d 188 (N.J. 1987). *Ramseur* has been influential outside of New Jersey as well. See *State v. Black,* 815 S.W.2d 166, 189 (Tenn. 1991) ("We adhere to the analysis in *Gregg v. Georgia* . . . particularly as followed by the New Jersey Supreme Court in *State v. Ramseur* . . . and find persuasive the reasoning of both decisions") (citations omitted).

203. 613 A.2d 1059 (N.J. 1992).

204. The post-reenactment capital cases prior to *Ramseur* address specialized constitutional issues, such as the access of the press and the public to pretrial proceedings in a capital trial. See, e.g., *State v. Williams,* 459 A.2d 641 (N.J. 1983); Bienen et al., *supra* note 20, at 70–100 (summarizing the early case law interpreting the statute).

205. 465 U.S. 37 (1984).

206. 1985 N.J. Laws 536, 541 (amending N.J. Stat. Ann. 2C:11-3e).

207. *State v. Ramseur,* 524 A.2d 188, 291–92 (N.J. 1987) (citation omitted). Proportionality review, said the court in *Ramseur,* is required because the death sentence is "profoundly different from all other penalties" and consequently there is a heightened need for reliability in the imposition of that sentence. Id. at 292 (citing *Lockett v. Ohio,* 438 U.S. 586, 605 (1978)). Proportionality review acts "as a check against the random and arbitrary imposition of the death penalty." *Ramseur,* 524 A.2d at 292.

208. *Ramseur,* 524 A.2d at 291 ("In doing so, we intend only to guide future parties in their exploration of some of the issues that appear essential to the development of a proportionality review process that would satisfy the requirements of the statute and any applicable constitutional obligations").

209. *State v. McCrary,* 478 A.2d 339, 343–45 (N.J. 1984) (permitting limited judicial review of the prosecutorial decision to charge capital murder under the Act).

210. *Ramseur,* 524 A.2d at 293–94.

211. Id. at 293.

212. Id. at 293. The court then cited Joseph H. Rodriguez et al., "Proportionality Review in New Jersey: An Indispensable Safeguard in the Capital Sentencing Process," 15 *Rutgers L.J.* 399, 437 (1984).

213. "First, we must determine what will be the 'universe of cases' . . . against which a comparison of the imposed death sentence will be made . . ." *Ramseur,* 524 A.2d at 293 (citation omitted). In comparison to the practice in some other states, the court said it believed that

> statewide uniformity is the more appropriate measure, and therefore [we] anticipate that comparisons will be made to "similar" cases throughout the state.
>
> But a decision to adopt statewide comparisons does not end the analysis. We must also decide whether to include in the statewide universe of cases only those in which a death penalty was actually imposed, or to expand the potential cases for comparison to include all those in which the death penalty could have been requested by the State. (Id. at 293 (citation omitted))

214. Determining the universe of cases was a source of conflict in other states as well. See, e.g., *supra* "Proportionality Review in Practice: Three States, Three Approaches"; and online appendix B (discussing Nebraska).

215. The Supreme Court of New Jersey's Order of July 29, 1988, creating the Proportionality Review Project and appointing Professor David Baldus as the special master is reprinted in Bienen et al., *supra* note 20, at 371. The duration of the first phase of the Proportionality Review Project was approximately four years, from July 1988, the date of the appointment of Professor Baldus as special master, until July 1992, when the court decided *Marshall II.*

216. David C. Baldus is the Joseph B. Tye Professor of Law at the University of Iowa College of Law. With George Woodworth and Charles Pulaski he conducted two empirical studies of the Georgia capital punishment system after *Furman.* See David C. Baldus et al., "Arbitrariness and Discrimination in the Administration of the Death Penalty: A Challenge to State Supreme Courts," 15 *Stetson L. Rev.* 133 (1986); David C. Baldus et al., "Comparative Review of Death Sentences: An Empirical Study of the Georgia Experience," 74 *J. Crim. L. & Criminology* 661 (1983). The Georgia studies formed the factual basis for the statistical arguments presented to the U.S. Supreme Court in *McCleskey v. Kemp,* 481 U.S. 279 (1987). The Georgia studies and that litigation are described in detail in David Baldus et al., *Equal Justice and the Death Penalty: A Legal and Empirical Analysis* (Boston: Northwestern University Press, 1990). See also Bienen et al., *supra* note 20, at 147–58 (discussing "the Baldus Studies").

Professor Baldus has also served as a consultant to the supreme courts of South Dakota and Delaware and to the National Center for State Courts' Project on Comparative Proportionality Review of Death Sentences by State Supreme Courts. See Baldus et al., *supra* note 36.

217. "We authorized the consideration of the data base that formed the basis of the report of the New Jersey Public Defender entitled 'The Re-Imposition of Capital Punishment in New Jersey' . . ." *Marshall II,* 613 A.2d at 1062. This reference is to parts I and II of the "Interim Report" of the Public Defender Homicide Study (on file along with the "Preliminary Report" of the Public Defender Homicide Study in the State Documents Collection of Northwestern

University School of Law). The "Interim Report" of the Public Defender Study was submitted to the New Jersey Supreme Court in *State v. Koedatich,* 548 A.2d 939 (N.J. 1988) before its findings were published in Bienen et al., *supra* note 20, at 27, 36–37. The "Interim Report" of the Public Defender Study included data on 703 cases. A "Preliminary Report" of the Public Defender Study was submitted to the New Jersey Supreme Court in 1987 during the appeal in *Ramseur.* It contained data on 568 homicide cases. The majority opinion in *Koedatich* cites to data from the "Preliminary Report" of the Public Defender Study (1988). *Koedatich,* 548 A.2d at 955. In contrast, Justice Handler's dissent cites to the "Interim Report" of the Public Defender Study (1988). Id. at 1018–19 (Handler, J., dissenting). The research reports of the Public Defender Homicide Study are detailed in Bienen et al., *supra* note 20, at 27 n. 3, 36–37; Bienen et al., *supra* note 44, at 744.

218. The work of the Proportionality Review Project, with particular emphasis upon the methodological issues, is described in David Baldus and George Woodworth, "Proportionality: The View of the Special Master," 6 *Chance: New Directions for Statistics and Computing* 9–17 (1993). The attorney general's position on these issues is described in Herbert I. Weisberg, "Proportionality: An Alternative View." 6 *Chance: New Directions for Statistics and Computing* 18–24 (1993).

219. The Court noted:

> We must take steps to assure that it [the database] is kept current and accessible to the parties and the Court . . . the data base is relevant to evaluate the systemwide claims of constitutional dimension, . . . We have no way of knowing how long the Master will continue to assist the Court in the data-gathering process. Any system we maintain should be able to operate efficiently even after his departure, and, indeed, after our departure . . . Hence . . . we shall appoint a Superior Court judge familiar with the relevant statistical and data-assembly concepts to oversee development of a recommended plan for future maintenance of the Court's records . . . (*Marshall II,* 613 A.2d at 1113)

See online appendix C for developments subsequent to *Marshall II.*

220. The Proportionality Review Project under the administrative supervision of John P. McCarthy, Jr., of the Administrative Office of the Courts, and with the assistance of other staff, including Nina Rossi, staff attorney, screened over three thousand New Jersey homicide cases arising between 1982 and 1990. In the first proportionality review, the special master presented the Supreme Court of New Jersey with a detailed and accurate quantitative and qualitative analysis of 246 death-eligible cases, including all cases in which the death sentence had been imposed or considered during the period. Staff at the Administrative Office of the Courts tracked cases, collected and verified official records, and contacted prosecutors and defense attorneys to clarify ambiguities, in addition to performing the ordinary tasks of any research team, such as data entry, systematic error-checking, and the mechanics of generating computer runs. Important and fundamental factual errors were identified in official documents and court records at every stage—documents routinely relied upon by sentencing and parole authorities, courts, prosecutors, and other decision makers. The accuracy of record-keeping varied widely among counties.

221. This was the first and only time that the attorney general complied with the court's suggestion that all parties collect data on capital case processing. The Proportionality Review data set, augmented by the cases added by the attorney general, became the *Marshall II* data set. This is the data set analyzed in online appendix B. It is a data set unique to the *Marshall II* case, which is unlikely to be used again by the court. See Herbert I. Weisberg, "Proportionality

Review of Death Sentences in New Jersey: An Independent Analysis of Data on Capital Charging and Sentencing" (Nov. 26, 1991) (on file with the State Documents Collection of the Northwestern University School of Law) [hereinafter 1991 Weisberg Report]. The attorney general's report is also part of the record on appeal in *Marshall I* and can be requested from the Administrative Office of the Courts or the New Jersey Supreme Court.

222. The 1991 "Final Report" of the New Jersey Proportionality Review Project, including a summary of its data and analyses in appendices and the technical commentary, is part of the record on appeal in *State v. Marshall,* 586 A.2d 85 (N.J. 1991) (*Marshall I*). In *Marshall I* the court upheld the death sentence but reserved the issue of proportionality review. See David C. Baldus, "Death Penalty Proportionality Review Project Final Report to the New Jersey Supreme Court" (Sept. 24, 1991) (unpublished) (on file with the State Documents Collection of the Northwestern University School of Law) [hereinafter "Final Report"]. The "Final Report," including its technical appendices, annotations to the data set and data collection process, a detailed description of the methodology, and a discussion of the legal issues raised, can be obtained upon written request from John P. McCarthy, Jr., Assistant Director, Administrative Office of the Courts, CN 982, Justice Complex, Trenton, NJ 08625.

223. See *State v. Marshall,* 613 A.2d 1059, 1117 (N.J. 1992) (*Marshall II*) (Garibaldi, J., concurring in part and dissenting in part). She believed the Proportionality Review Project could not accurately determine the facts of cases which did not go to a penalty phase trial.

> The validity of the entire system depends on the correctness of the subjective evaluations made by personnel of the Administrative Office of the Court concerning the "deathworthiness of a case" as contrasted with the evidentiary concerns and other hazards of litigation that a case presents. Such evaluations made on a cold record are extremely difficult, even if undertaken by experienced prosecutors and defense counsel. To replace the reasoned determination of prosecutors, trial judges, and, in some cases, juries, and to rely instead on the subjective evaluations of persons who have never faced the realistic difficulties of trying a criminal case creates an unreliable data base and misleading conclusions. (Id. (Garibaldi, J., concurring in part and dissenting in part))

224. See *In re Proportionality Review Project,* 585 A.2d 358 (N.J. 1990).

225. Id. See also *Marshall II:*

> In an earlier proceeding we declined to determine in advance the appropriate "universe" of cases against which to compare challenged death sentences in order to assure proportionality. The Attorney General had contended that the only appropriate universe is one comprised exclusively of cases in which a death sentence has been imposed under our Capital Punishment Act. (613 A.2d at 1063 (citation omitted))

226. The court continued:

> Following oral argument, the Legislature amended the Capital Punishment Act to provide that "proportionality review . . . shall be limited to a comparison of similar cases in which a sentence of death has been imposed." L. 1992, c. 5 (eff. May 12, 1992) . . . Because there are several capital appeals pending under the prior law, we address the issues in sufficient detail to deal with those appeals as well as this, depending on the ultimate effect of L. 1992, c.5. (Id. at 1063–64)

227. *State v. Ramseur,* 524 A.2d 188, 292 (N.J. 1987).

228. See *Marshall II,* 613 A.2d at 1110. *Marshall II* also states: "To countenance

racial discrimination in capital sentencing would mock that tradition [to eliminate racial discrimination] and our own constitutional guarantee of equal protection of the laws under New Jersey Constitution Article I, paragraph 1." Id. at 1109. Recognizing that a white defendant could argue that the capital punishment system in New Jersey was unconstitutional because it discriminated against nonwhites, id., *Marshall II* stated that were it presented with a statistical showing analogous to that before the U.S. Supreme Court in *McCleskey,* "we would not hesitate to invalidate the sentence of death." Id. at 1112.

229. *Ramseur,* 524 A.2d at 292.

230. As the court stated:

> Proportionality review is not a second appellate review nor a broad review of due-process concerns or other constitutional issues . . . It is not a vehicle for determining whether prosecutors abused their discretion. Nor is proportionality review a means of addressing individual instances of racial discrimination or other denials of due process. Of course, this Court will not tolerate such impermissible influences, and any sentence of death that results therefrom will be fatally infected. However, the proper avenue for addressing those issues is the capital defendant's direct appeal, not on proportionality review. (*Marshall II,* 613 A.2d at 1116–17 (Garibaldi, J., concurring in part and dissenting in part))

Meanwhile, Justice Handler again expressed his view that the New Jersey capital punishment scheme violated the state constitution's cruel and unusual punishment clause:

> The unequal treatment of capital defendants also implicates Article I, paragraph 5 of the [New Jersey] Constitution, which bars the denial of civil rights or discrimination against persons in the exercise of any right because of religion, race, or national origin. When inequality arises from improper considerations such as race, those concerns are most acute. The Special Master's study preliminarily shows the race of the victim to be a factor in many decisions to impose the death penalty, and seems to confirm many long-held suspicions . . . The doctrine of evenhandedness and the accordant requirement of comprehensive proportionality review implicates, perhaps most directly, the protections secured by the cruel and unusual punishment clause. (Id. at 1126 (Handler, J., dissenting) (citations omitted))

231. Here, a critical part of the analysis is defined:

> Second, we must determine what are "similar crimes" . . . in order to narrow the scope of the similar crimes to be used in the proportionality review, such categories as "torture," "sexual mutilation," or "multiple victim" crimes have been suggested. But beyond these, there is a difficult question whether there are subcategories of "murder" that can be appropriately identified and considered. "Domestic," "depravity of mind," and "execution style" crimes, for example, may be too broad or ambiguous to allow any real comparison for proportionality. We anticipate and welcome suggestions regarding which criminological, sociological, and statistical models are appropriate for analyzing the similarity of crimes and sentencing. (*Ramseur,* 524 A.2d at 293 (citation omitted))

232. The Court spelled out what was expected:

> Third, after the crimes similar to the case on review are identified, we must compare those defendants with the one before the court . . . The aggravating and mitigating factors set forth in Section c(4) and Section c(5)

are a beginning. But other factors such as race, sex, and socioeconomic status might also be appropriate considerations for reviewing proportionality. Moreover, the relationship between the defendant and victim, whether defendant pleaded guilty or not guilty, and the race and sex of the victim might also be appropriate factors. This list is only a beginning and still other factors could be relevant to proportionality review of the defendants. Our task in this process will be to sift through these factors to determine those that have an effect on the capital sentencing decision. We must ensure that discriminatory factors are not shifting the balance between life and death. (*Ramseur,* 524 A.2d at 293–94 (citations omitted))

233. The majority opinion in *Marshall II* compared the death sentence under review according to the following categories: (1) similar cases as defined by the same aggravating factor, and/or a similar constellation of aggravating and mitigating factors, *Marshall II,* 613 A.2d at 1085, 1090; (2) contract killers, both principals and hit men, id. at 1089, 1095–96; (3) spousal murders involving a high level of blameworthiness and a defenseless victim, id. at 1090; (4) premeditated robbery/kidnap murder cases involving extensive premeditation, a pecuniary motive, deception/entrapment of the victim, and a defenseless victim, id. at 1090, 1097–98; (5) first-time murderers of spouses, id. at 1092; and (6) "other cases" offered as similar by the public defender, id. at 1098. The court also applied frequency analysis, the precedent-seeking approach, Dr. Weisberg's approach, the salient-factors approach, arguments based upon the infrequency with which juries return the death penalty in New Jersey, id. at 1099, and arguments based upon geographical and racial patterns in charging and sentencing. Id. at 1102. The court carefully explained each approach prior to its analysis.

234. "Here we may anticipate considering whether to address concerns about possible misuse of prosecutorial discretion presented to the courts of this state, including in the review all cases in which a prosecutor had the discretion to seek the death penalty." *Ramseur,* 524 A.2d at 293 (citations omitted).

235. The role of prosecutorial discretion as one possible source of racial bias or arbitrariness in capital charging was at issue in *McCleskey v. Kemp,* 481 U.S. 279, 357 (1987) (Blackmun, J., dissenting). The Fulton County, Georgia, district attorney, who had served in that office for eighteen years, testified that there were no standards for the assistant district attorneys regarding plea bargaining in death-eligible cases or to guide them in when to seek the death penalty. See the discussion concerning the identification of prosecutorial discretion as a source of bias in Baldus et al., *supra* note 36, at 414–15. See also *U.S. ex rel. Silagy v. Peters,* 713 F. Supp. 1246 (C.D. Ill. 1989) (holding the Illinois capital case processing system in violation of the Eighth Amendment because of a lack of guidelines for the exercise of prosecutorial discretion in the selection of cases for capital prosecution), rev'd, 905 F.2d 986 (7th Cir. 1990).

236. Citing data from the Public Defender Homicide Study, the court noted that

> while prosecutorial decision-making is normally beyond its purview, fundamental fairness required that this Court review the basis for the State's notice of aggravating factors in a capital case to ensure that prosecutors have cause to designate defendants as death-eligible. To be sure, we stated that our goal was to "effect on a minimal intrusion into this area of prosecutorial discretion." Nevertheless, we believe there is a need to promote uniformity in the administration of the death penalty, which will be an additional safeguard against arbitrariness and an assistance to the Court in its developing proportionality review. Accordingly, we strongly recommend that the Attorney General, and the various County Prosecutors, in

> consultation with the Public Defender, adopt guidelines for use throughout the state by prosecutors in determining the selection of capital cases. (*State v. Koedatich,* 548 A.2d 939, 955 (N.J. 1988), citing *State v. McCrary,* 478 A.2d 339, 340 (N.J. 1984))

In December 1995, using the analytic framework established by the Proportionality Review Project, the Administrative Office of the Courts reported a statistically significant race effect. See also online appendixes B and C.

The majority opinion in *Marshall II* reasserted the court's willingness to review the charging decisions of prosecutors. *Marshall II,* 613 A.2d at 1071. The court suggested that the attorney general set up a statewide panel to review the charging decisions of county prosecutors.

> We have encouraged the Attorney General, as the chief law-enforcement officer of the State of New Jersey, to exercise his undoubted authority to instill uniformity in the charging and prosecuting practices throughout the state. We realize the differing attitudes in counties and the jurisdictional concerns. If the system fails to eliminate unconstitutional disparities, that failure should not be because of hesitancy to invoke authority currently conferred on the Attorney General. A statewide review panel, appointed by the Attorney General in consultation with prosecutors, would be able to screen out any possible effects of race or socioeconomic status in the charging and selection process. (Id. at 1112)

Not all members of the court subscribed to the majority's view, however, that the review of prosecutorial discretion in charging was an appropriate consideration in performing proportionality review.

> Second-guessing prosecutorial decisions to pursue capital sentences will riddle the proportionality review with uncertainty . . . The Special Master's classification of death-eligibility cases is an extremely subjective process carried out in the absence of factual findings or jury determinations . . . Such determinations [as to why a case was not prosecuted as a capital offense] are clearly outside the scope of a proper proportionality review. (Id. at 1118 (Garibaldi, J., concurring and dissenting))

But "proportionality review is the obvious antidote for the enduring arbitrariness of disparate sentencing . . . The legislative history to New Jersey's death-penalty statute evinces similar concerns: proportionality review ensures that death sentences 'are being meted out in a fair, even-handed way throughout the State.'" Id. at 1121–22 (Handler, J., dissenting) (citations omitted).

237. These guidelines are reprinted in Bienen et al., *supra* note 44, at 791–93 and discussed at 732–34. The guidelines were submitted on Feb. 22, 1989, to the chief justice of the Supreme Court and to the special master and have been in effect ever since.

238. Preamble to the "Guidelines for the Designation for Capital Prosecution" reprinted in Bienen et al., *supra* note 44, at 791–92.

239. Id. at 792. A communication subsequent to the original letter added that the words "or victim" were inadvertently left out of the preamble. The guidelines were formally amended on Jan. 23, 1990, by the county prosecutors to correct this oversight. Id. at 791 n. 2.

240. Id. at 792.

241. *Marshall II,* 613 A.2d at 1118 (Garibaldi, J., concurring and dissenting).

242. See online appendix B for the selected economic and demographic indicators of the New Jersey counties.

243. At the time of the Proportionality Review Project, all indigent capital cases were

represented by the public defender or by counsel appointed and assisted by the public defender. This is atypical. Also exceptional was that the Office of the Public Defender in New Jersey did not place an overall per-case limit on capital defense expenditures.

> For example, an audit established that New Jersey spent nearly $3 million extra in 1984 to defend indigent defendants charged with capital crimes . . . Specifically, of the $296,449.41 the Public Defender's Office spent to defend Thomas Ramseur at trial, the largest portion, $191,881, was spent on psychiatrists. The Public Defender spent more than $75,000 successfully attacking the makeup of grand and petit juries in Atlantic County. (*Marshall II,* 613 A.2d at 1144–45 (Handler, J., dissenting) (citations omitted))

244. The exceptionally high expenses for capital trials begin long before the trial itself. If a case is to proceed capitally, there will be special pretrial motions concerning the Notice of Aggravating Factors. Moreover, if a case is going to trial as a capital case, typically both sides will assign additional resources and an extra attorney to prepare the case. Also, prior to the trial, the special procedures for the selection of a death-qualified jury will consume considerably more resources than the selection of an ordinary jury. See id. at 1144–49 (Handler, J., dissenting) for the most complete annotation to date of sources on the differential cost of capital prosecutions.

245. At least one state, New Hampshire, has provided for centralized decision-making within the state for the prosecution of all homicide cases, including all capital cases, in order to insure uniformity in the application of prosecutorial standards. See N.H. Rev. Stat. Ann. 7:6 (West, WESTLAW, updated through 1996).

246. See online appendix B for statistics on selected demographic characteristics of New Jersey counties. See also *South Burlington County NAACP v. Township of Mt. Laurel,* 336 A.2d 713 (N.J. 1975) (discussing regional economic disparities in the context of a community's obligation to provide low-income housing).

247. See *supra* tbl. 2.

248. See *supra* tbl. 1.

249. Since reenactment, there have been years when the Essex County Prosecutor's Office had no cases or one to two cases that proceeded as capital trials. There were at least two dozen cases whose facts would have supported a prosecution for death-eligible murder during the period when the Essex County prosecutor brought no capital prosecutions. Prior to the Koedatich guidelines—see *supra* notes 237–39 and accompanying text—a New Jersey Superior Court ordered the Essex County prosecutor to come forward with guidelines for the selection of cases for capital prosecution because of the arbitrariness with which this defendant was singled out for capital prosecution. *State v. Smith,* 495 A.2d 507, 516 (N.J. Super. Ct. Law Div. 1985). The court noted that there were fifteen similar cases of felony murder which had not been designated capital offenses. Id. at 514. The Smith case eventually pled out to manslaughter.

250. The statute reads:

> a. Except as provided in N.J.S.2C:11-4 criminal homicide constitutes murder when:
>
> (1) The actor purposely causes death or serious bodily injury resulting in death; or
>
> (2) The actor knowingly causes death or serious bodily injury resulting in death; or
>
> (3) It is committed when the actor, acting either alone or with one or more other persons, is engaged in the commission of, or an attempt to commit, or flight after committing or attempting to commit robbery, sexual

assault, arson, burglary, kidnapping or criminal escape, and in the course of such crime or of immediate flight therefrom, any person causes the death of a person other than one of the participants; . . .

c. Any person convicted under subsection a.(1) or (2) who committed the homicidal act by his own conduct; or who as an accomplice procured the commission of the offense by payment or promise of payment of anything of pecuniary value; . . . (N.J. Stat. Ann. 2C:11-3a, c (West 1996))

251. In their Notice of Motion, the attorney general and the county prosecutors took the position that (1) the only appropriate universe of cases for proportionality review consists of other cases in the state in which the death sentence has been imposed; and (2) prosecutorial discretion in the selection of cases for capital prosecution should not be reviewable within the context of proportionality review. *In re Proportionality Review Project,* 585 A.2d 358 (N.J. 1990) (rejecting point 1 and not addressing point 2).

On Nov. 1, 1989, the New Jersey Supreme Court asked the special master to provide his

> analysis as to the advantages and disadvantages of each potential alternative "universe" of cases. Your analysis should consider the impact on the process of proportionality review if the universe were to include, for instance, on death-sentenced cases, or cases which advance to a capital sentencing proceeding, or broader universes such as all cases where a notice of aggravating factors was served. Your analysis should discuss the advantages and disadvantages of each alternative "universe" in terms of cost, the validity of the process, the utility of the final product, the ability to address broader issues related to proportionality, the criteria defining the universe, the standards used to determine whether individual cases should qualify to be ultimately considered in an actual proportionality review, the effect of recent decisions on the includability of prior death eligible cases, availability of data, the ability of county agencies to sustain and assist the research, and any other related issues which you care to raise. (Letter from Chief Justice Robert N. Wilentz to Professor David C. Baldus (Nov. 1, 1989) (on file at the State Documents Collection of the Northwestern University School of Law))

See, e.g., "Final Report," *supra* note 222; 1991 Weisberg Report, *supra* note 221, reprinted in Brief of Attorney General, *State v. Marshall,* 586 A.2d 85 (N.J. 1991).

252. On Sept. 11, 1989, at oral argument Justice O'Hern asked the attorney general if the court should be prevented from considering the possibility of racial imbalance in a situation where, for example, nine death sentences had been imposed and all of the defendants were Asian. The attorney general replied that under its proposed formulation of proportionality review, the court would be prevented from considering the possibility of racial disparity in the implementation of the death penalty in that circumstance. Oral Argument, *In re Proportionality Review Project,* 585 A.2d 358 (N.J. 1990).

253. "Although there were over 250 cases where the death penalty could have been sought, and over 120 cases which went to a capital penalty trial after a verdict of guilty of capital murder, less than a quarter of all aggravated murders and less than a third of the cases which reached the second stage of a penalty trial resulted in the jury imposing a death sentence." Bienen, *supra* note 102, at 593.

254. For example, Maryland:

> For the first time, this Court has before it data concerning the exercise of prosecutorial discretion in death penalty cases. This data dramatically

> demonstrates that the inventory of relevant cases for proportionality review must include all death-eligible murder cases—not only those in which the prosecutor sought the death penalty, but also those in which he did not.
>
> This data reveals that in Maryland prosecutors seek the death penalty in only 7.8% of the death-eligible cases, whereas in 92.2% of the death-eligible cases the death penalty is not sought. Consequently, this data establishes that Maryland prosecutors rarely seek the death penalty, a fact that is relevant, in and of itself, in determining whether the death penalty is disproportionate . . . In addition, the data concerning the exercise of prosecutorial discretion reveals that in cases in which the death penalty has been sought juries in Garrett County have imposed the death penalty in 50% of the cases, whereas juries in Baltimore City have imposed the death penalty in 33%. This data suggests that in these two jurisdictions the death penalty has been imposed in a somewhat consistent manner. The data further reveals, however, that in Maryland there is a substantial variation in the exercise of prosecutorial discretion. In Garrett County prosecutors seek the death penalty in 100% of the death-eligible cases, whereas in Baltimore City, they seek that penalty in only 1.8%. This data further shows that when prosecutorial discretion is taken into account, juries in Garrett County have imposed the death penalty in 50% of all the death-eligible cases, whereas juries in Baltimore City have imposed the death penalty in only .6%. Consequently, this data demonstrates that in these two jurisdictions the death penalty has been imposed in an inconsistent manner. (*Tichnell v. State,* 468 A.2d 1, 31–32 (Md. 1983) (Davidson, J., dissenting) (footnotes omitted))

255. *Marshall II,* 613 A.2d 1059, 1069 (N.J. 1992) (quoting *State v. Ramseur,* 524 A.2d 188, 292 (N.J. 1987)). "That" refers to an opinion offered by the dissent in *Pulley v. Harris* which "suggested only that discretion must be suitably directed and limited so as to minimize the risk of wholly arbitrary and capricious action. In their view, proportionality review, although clearly no panacea, often serves to identify the most extreme examples of disproportionality among similarly situated defendants." *Marshall II,* 613 A.2d at 1069 (citing *Pulley v. Harris,* 465 U.S. 37, 71 (1984) (Brennan, J., dissenting)) (quotations omitted).

256. "The focus in the *Marshall* case was on the constitutional legitimacy of the system as a whole, rather than on the risk that race might have adversely influenced the decision of the prosecutor or jury in an individual case." Baldus et al., *supra* note 36, at 406.

257. Justice Garibaldi noted:

> I would limit the universe of cases considered during proportionality review to those in which a prosecutor has served a notice of aggravating factor, thereby indicating an intention to seek a capital sentence . . . Most prosecutorial decisions concerning the pursuit of capital sentences rely on permissible considerations. Most prosecutors will seek the death penalty for homicides that objectively satisfy one or more of the aggravating factors and where the physical and testimonial evidence create a reasonable likelihood that the State will be able to meet its burden of proof. (*Marshall II,* 613 A.2d at 1116, 1118 (Garibaldi, J., concurring and dissenting))

258. The initial screening removed cases involving death by auto, cases in which the homicide charge was only for an attempt or conspiracy to commit homicide, cases that resulted in an acquittal or dismissal of homicide charges, and cases in which the defendant was a

juvenile. This reduced a database of over 3,000 cases to a screened data file of 1,372 murder cases. See online appendix B tbl. 1.

The project began with the State Police (SBI) list of 2,300 persons arrested for a homicide offense between 1982 and 1988. This list was supplemented by an additional 500 cases identified by the Administrative Office of the Courts and by yet an additional 200 cases which were identified by the Public Defender Homicide Study. In other words, the Administrative Office of the Courts and the Public Defender together identified an additional 700 cases which were not in the official files of the State Police. The State Police files, the source of data for the F.B.I. Uniform Crime Reports, were missing almost one-sixth of the cases. *These missing cases were all cases which were formally charged as homicide offenses, cases that went to final disposition at the trial court stage.* After removing the identifiers for some variables, the Public Defender turned over to the Proportionality Review Project its data tapes on the 703 cases. See Bienen et al., *supra* note 20 (analyzing the cases).

259. Ga. Code Ann. 17-10-35(c)(3) (WESTLAW, updated as of 1996) (statutory language endorsed by the Supreme Court in *Gregg v. Georgia,* 428 U.S. 325 (1976)) (formerly codified at 27-2537).

260. This methodology was refined to address the concerns of trial attorneys expressed in the proportionality review meetings held throughout the four years of data collection. Factual summaries of identified homicides were presented to prosecutors and defense attorneys who were then asked for their suggestions on ways to code ambiguous facts or classify problematic variables. See "Final Report," *supra* note 222.

261. "We have used scientific and statistical measures, when helpful, although we recognize that a value judgment is built into practically every measurement." *Marshall II,* 613 A.2d at 1064. This recognition was a hallmark of all of the opinions in *Marshall II.* The majority and the justices writing separately acknowledged that their opinion reflected their personal experiences and ultimately a value judgment. In some sense, statistics were the least of it.

262. The data analysis of death eligibility incorporated relevant changes in the legal definition of the intent requirement for capital murder as they occurred. See *State v. Gerald,* 549 A.2d 792 (N.J. 1988) (declaring the death penalty disproportionate under the New Jersey Constitution where the defendant acted without intent to kill and without knowledge that death would result).

263. An important distinction between New Jersey and other states lies in the fact that in New Jersey non-slayer participants in felony murders are not eligible for capital prosecution. As a result, the New Jersey Supreme Court has not yet been required to address the constitutional issues raised by the attribution of intent to kill to a person who did not commit the homicidal act. See Bienen et al., *supra* note 44, at 722–32 (describing the history of felony murder at British common law and in New Jersey law, and the distinction between death eligibility for principals and codefendants). These issues have been troublesome for many state supreme courts and have produced an opaque series of opinions from the U.S. Supreme Court. See, e.g., *Tison v. Arizona,* 481 U.S. 137 (1987); *Enmund v. Florida,* 458 U.S. 782 (1982). Moreover, the issues arise frequently in the context of proportionality review when courts are asked to consider the comparative proportionality of the death sentence of a relatively less culpable codefendant, when the principal was sentenced to life or less, or when two equally culpable codefendants receive disparate sentences. See *State v. Middlebrooks,* 840 S.W.2d 317 (Tenn. 1992) (discussing constitutionality of the death penalty as punishment for felony murder under state and federal constitutions, and the interplay between state and federal principles on that issue).

264. "The New Jersey court in *Marshall* expressed concern about the evidence of

discrimination in its capital sentencing system, especially in jury sentencing decisions." Baldus et al., *supra* note 36, at 412–13 (citing *Marshall II,* 613 A.2d at 1112). "As noted, the focus of Marshall was a 'structural challenge' to the system as a whole." Id. at 419 n.182 (citing *Marshall II,* 613 A.2d at 1112). See id. at 405–13 (comparing the race effects reported in the "Final Report" with the race effect found in the Georgia studies).

265. This was how the project was originally outlined:

> There were five main goals in this project. The first was to conduct a census of New Jersey homicide cases and to identify those defendants who were death-eligible under the New Jersey capital-sentencing statute. Our second task was to develop a machine-readable data base of these cases that could be used by us to develop and refine measures of defendant culpability and, by interested parties, to evaluate the evenhandedness and consistency of New Jersey's capital sentencing system. The third task was to develop measures of defendant culpability which will assist the Court in identifying death-eligible cases that are "similar . . . considering both the crime and the defendant" within the meaning of N.J.S.A. 2C:11-3e. Our fourth task was to recommend approaches to proportionality review, including the basic universe of cases that the Court should routinely consider in its reviews. Our final assignment was to recommend an ongoing system of (a) contemporaneous data collection at the trial court level, and (b) data management and analysis in the AOC. ("Final Report," *supra* note 222, at 1–2)

266. The research methodology was described as follows:

> Five capital case processing stages are analyzed in this study. Beginning with all homicides in the data base [N=703], the first stage is death-possible, cases identified as having a factual basis for serving a notice of factors [N=404]. The second stage is death-eligible, cases where the prosecutor actually serves a notice of factors, designating the case capital [N=131]. The third stage is capital trial, cases which progress to capital trial before a judge or a death qualified jury [N=94]. The fourth stage is penalty phase, cases which result in a conviction for death-eligible murder and consequently progress to a penalty phase decision before a judge or a death qualified jury [N=69]. The fifth or final stage is the imposition of the death penalty [N=25]. (Bienen et al., *supra* note 20, at 164 (footnotes omitted))

The analysis then continued:

> Our analysis of prosecutorial decision making in felony murder cases focuses on the early stages of capital case processing because it is there that key determinative decisions are made. Seemingly technical or procedural pretrial decisions concerning charging may well determine a case's outcome and have other far-reaching consequences for the defendant and all other participants in the criminal justice system. (Bienen et al., *supra* note 44, at 739)

267. One theme emerges again and again:

> One thing the most fervent district attorneys share is political ambition. For example, take the three recent Chicago prosecutors who have been avid users of the death penalty in Cook County, the only large county that rivals Philadelphia for aggressiveness . . . Richard M. Daley [former Cook County prosecutor] is now Mayor and the current prosecutor, Jack O'Malley, has openly been contemplating higher office. Harry Connick Sr., New Orleans's

District Attorney, ran for Louisiana Attorney General in 1987. (Rosenberg, *supra* note 114, at 46. See also Bright and Keenan, *supra* note 80.)

268. In only three states are prosecutors not elected: Connecticut, Delaware, and New Jersey. Connecticut, Delaware, Hawaii, Massachusetts, New Hampshire, New Jersey, New York, and Rhode Island do not elect judges, either initially or for retention. Bureau of Justice Statistics, U.S. Dept. of Justice, *Sourcebook of Criminal Justice Statistics* (1994).

269. *Marshall II,* 613 A.2d at 1110–12.

> [The court] concluded, however, that the data were less strong than the evidence presented in *McCleskey* and did not establish a constitutional violation. In terms of the overall race-of-victim effects . . . this conclusion seems correct because the disparity is smaller than the *McCleskey* disparity and is not statistically significant. As for the race-of-defendant effects in the jury penalty-trial data, the court was cautious because changes in the law that would be likely to reduce discrimination had occurred in 1987 and 1988 and because there were an inadequate number of post-1988 cases with which to estimate race-of-defendant effect. (Baldus et al., *supra* note 36, at 413 (footnotes omitted))

270. For example:

> There was stronger evidence of race effects in prosecutorial decision making. Nevertheless, the practical effect of these prosecutorial decisions has been ameliorated by the fact that according to the records of the Administrative Office of the New Jersey Courts, over 80% of all of New Jersey's death sentences imposed since 1982 have been vacated because of legal errors unrelated to racial issues. The data are disturbing nonetheless. To meet those concerns, the New Jersey court in *Marshall* urged the state's Attorney General and prosecutors to cooperate with the court and its staff in maintaining and improving the court's data base in order to enhance its capacity to detect signs of discrimination in the system. The court also suggested that its "unease" about racial issues would be ameliorated "if there were some type of inter-agency review to provide the most rudimentary monitoring of [prosecutorial] capital-charging decisions." (Id. at 413 (footnotes omitted) (discussing *Marshall II,* 613 A.2d at 1110–14))

271. 662 A.2d 333 (N.J. 1995). Joseph Harris died prior to the scheduled oral argument in his case before the Supreme Court of New Jersey. His appeal was then dismissed as moot. The proportionality issues and the question of possible race effects will be addressed in *State v. Loftin.* See online appendix C.

272. See online appendix C for the models and significant race effects found in *State v. Harris.* The court has appointed Judge Richard S. Cohen as the new special master for proportionality review. See online appendix C (*State v. Loftin,* No. A-86 (N.J. Oct. 22, 1986) (order appointing new special master)). The Oct. 22, 1996, order demonstrates that the newly constituted court will continue the court's prior commitment to a rigorous scientific analysis based upon a reliable factual foundation. The new chief justice, Deborah T. Poritz, formerly attorney general of New Jersey, announced that she would recuse herself from those pending capital appeals with which she had been directly involved. See Stephen W. Townsend, clerk of the Supreme Court, "Notice to the Bar, Recusal Policy of the Chief Justice," *New Jersey Law Journal,* Sept. 2, 1996, at 2.

273. 524 A.2d 188 (N.J. 1987).

274. 613 A.2d 1059 (N.J. 1992).

275. See Bright and Keenan, *supra* note 80, at 770–76. See also Rosenberg, *supra* note 114, at 46 ("[The death penalty's] political value is the unstated dark side to prosecutors' argument that they use the death penalty because their public demands it. One thing the most fervent district attorneys share is political ambition"); id. at 42 ("The 1994 campaign [for governor of Pennsylvania] was in itself a classic illustration of the political pressures on officials who deal with crime . . . There is only one way to be safe: Always take the most hard-line position possible"). See Bienen, *supra* note 102, at 585 for other arguments regarding the politics of the death penalty, with specific reference to the high-publicity circumstances surrounding Robert Marshall's trial.

276. Prior to reenactment, there was an unsuccessful attempt by Assembly Speaker Alan Karcher to attach a fiscal note to the bill reenacting capital punishment. See Untitled, UPI, May 19, 1982, available in LEXIS, NEWS Library, NEAST File. "In New Jersey, sentencing one person to death has been estimated to cost about $7.3 million . . . For example, the prosecution estimated that the *Ramseur* case cost $60,000 a year to litigate." *Marshall II,* 613 A.2d. at 1144 (Handler, J., dissenting). In New York, the 1995 reenactment legislation did appropriate additional funds for the reimposition.

277. For almost twenty years the question of the constitutionality of property-tax-based school funding in New Jersey has oscillated between the state legislature and the courts, with the Supreme Court of New Jersey as final arbiter. See, e.g., *Abbott v. Burke,* 477 A.2d 1278 (N.J. Super. Ct. App. Div. 1984), rev'd, 495 A.2d 376 (N.J. 1985); *Robinson v. Cahill,* 287 A.2d 187 (N.J. Super. Ct. Law Div. 1972), modified, 303 A.2d 273 (N.J. 1973). See also Peter Enrich, "Leaving Equality Behind: New Directions in School Finance Reform," 48 *Vand. L. Rev.* 101 (1995). The role of the Supreme Court of New Jersey in mandating affordable housing provoked similar conflict between that court and other branches of state government. See, e.g., *South Burlington County NAACP v. Township of Mt. Laurel,* 336 A.2d 713 (N.J. 1975) and subsequent cases.

278. See 1985 N.J. Laws 1935, 1940 (amending N.J. Stat. Ann. 2C:11-3). The amended statute required the appeal of all death sentences, even over the objection of the defendant, with representation by the public defender or other court-appointed counsel. This mandate was similar to action taken by other state legislatures after *Pulley v. Harris,* 465 U.S. 37, 50 (1984) held that the U.S. Constitution did not require proportionality review.

279. *State v. Ramseur,* 524 A.2d 188, 292 (N.J. 1987) ("While proportionality review is no longer mandatory, and shall be undertaken only 'upon the request of the defendant,' we assume that almost all defendants who are sentenced to death will request such review" (citation omitted)).

280. In *Marshall II* the court sidestepped the question of whether a 1992 legislative amendment limiting the universe of cases to death sentences only would violate the ex post facto clause of the U.S. Constitution:

> The Attorney General has filed a letter memorandum suggesting that the 1992 amendment be applied to this appeal. Were the amendment to be applied to pending appeals, we would undoubtedly be required to resolve whether, as applied to offenses committed before its effective date, the Act might constitute an ex post facto law . . . Because of the long pendency of this appeal, we decide this appeal under prior law . . . We therefore have no occasion to consider either its applicability or validity . . . Because there are several capital appeals pending under the prior law, we address the issues in sufficient detail to deal with those appeals as well. (*State v. Marshall,* 613 A.2d 1059, 1063–64 (N.J. 1992))

In both *State v. Martini,* 651 A.2d 949 (N.J. 1994), cert. denied, 116 S. Ct. 203 (1995), and *State v. Bey,* 645 A.2d 685 (N.J. 1994), the court found the death sentences proportionate and based its proportionality review on an analysis similar to that in *Marshall II,* using an updated and expanded data set prepared for each case.

281. Section 2C:11-3 was enacted in 1982—see *supra* note 196 and accompanying text—but the statute was not held constitutional until *State v. Ramseur,* 524 A.2d 188, 216–21 (1987).

282. For example:

> After the re-enactment in 1982, the majority of legislators expected executions to occur relatively quickly; they are disappointed that the statute has not been implemented as planned. "I expected that capital punishment would be the law of the state and that there would be executions. I had no idea the Supreme Court would thwart the will of the people," said [Assemblyman] Hardwick. The fault with the lack of complete implementation lies with a recalcitrant court, not with the legislators, says Hardwick. Other legislators expressed similar opinions. "I never imagined people would be languishing in jail while the courts fought it out," said [Senator] Orechio. Most of the legislators [interviewed] who supported the re-enactment expressed frustration at the "law in name only" that the death penalty statute has now become. According to Horan, Senator Dorsey thinks "it is a travesty that what the people want is not happening. It is almost like it was a waste of time to pass it." Dorsey would be bothered by the execution of another human being, but what has happened is "just opposite" from what he had expected. He never realized the legislation would be such an "exercise in futility. Why vote for something if nothing's going to happen?" said [Legislative Aide to Dorsey] Horan. The string of reversals has subsequently caused several legislators to accuse the New Jersey Supreme Court of legislating from the bench. (Chen, *supra* note 196, at 47–48 (footnotes omitted))

283. The Wilentz court era ended in 1996, when the chief justice resigned and died in July 1996. Deborah T. Poritz, the former attorney general and governor's counsel, was immediately appointed and confirmed as the new chief justice. Republican Governor Christine Todd Whitman also appointed the replacement for Justice Clifford, who retired in 1994. See Rocco Cammarere, "Coleman Passes Unanimously," *New Jersey Lawyer,* Oct. 24, 1994, at 1.

284. In California, Rose Bird was defeated in a retention election because of the unpopularity of the California Supreme Court's reversals of death sentences. See *supra* note 80. For a discussion of judicial election, selection, and accountability, see Joseph R. Grodin, "Developing a Consensus of Constraint: A Judge's Perspective on Judicial Retention Elections," 61 *S. Cal. L. Rev.* 1969 (1988); Gerald F. Uelmen, "Commentary: Are We Reprising a Finale or an Overture?" 61 *S. Cal. L. Rev.* 2069 (1988).

285. "'[The court] is looking for ways to circumvent [the death penalty statute] on a case-by-case basis, by splitting hairs . . . You can pass all the legislation in the world, but if the Court is going to move along this road, it doesn't mean anything.'" Tracy Schroth, "Gerald Nearly Fatal to Death Appeals," *New Jersey Law Journal,* July 5, 1990, at 1 (footnotes omitted) (quoting former New Jersey Senator John Lynch). See also Kathleen Bird, "Florio Faults Supreme Court on Death Penalty: Governor Challenges Justices to Enforce the Law or Strike It Down," *New Jersey Law Journal,* Dec. 20, 1990, at 3.

286. 549 A.2d 792 (N.J. 1988).

287. Following that decision in 1988, a number of other death sentences were set aside by the New Jersey Supreme Court on the grounds that the jury had not been appropriately instructed under the Gerald standard. Some of these cases went to penalty phase retrial, others were resolved with a plea to a non-death sentence. See Bienen et al., *supra* note 44, at 713 n.12.

288. See, e.g., Bird, *supra* note 285; Schroth, *supra* note 285.

289. See generally William J. Brennan Jr., "State Constitutions and the Protection of Individual Rights," 90 *Harv. L. Rev.* 489 (1977); "Developments in the Law: The Interpretation of State Constitutional Rights," 95 *Harv. L. Rev.* 1324 (1982); Jose L. Fernandez, "The New Jersey Supreme Court's Interpretation and Application of the State Constitution," 15 *Rutgers L.J.* 491 (1984); Stewart G. Pollock, "State Constitutions as Separate Sources of Fundamental Rights," 35 *Rutgers L. Rev.* 707 (1983); "Project Report: Toward an Activist Role for State Bills of Rights," 8 *Harv. C.R.-C.L. L. Rev.* 284 (1973); Robin B. Johansen, "Note, The New Federalism: Toward a Principled Interpretation of the State Constitution," 29 *Stan. L. Rev.* 297 (1977). The U.S. Supreme Court is "utterly without jurisdiction to review . . . state decisions" resting in whole or in part on state constitutional law. Brennan, "State Constitutions," *supra,* at 501. Justice Brennan uses as an example of this doctrine another highly controversial case decided by the New Jersey Supreme Court: *South Burlington County NAACP v. Township of Mount Laurel,* 336 A.2d 713 (N.J.), cert. denied, 432 U.S. 808 (1975).

290. See Phoebe C. Ellsworth and Samuel R. Gross, "Hardening of the Attitudes: Americans' Views on the Death Penalty," 50 *Journal of Social Issues* 19–21, 48–49 (1994). See also William J. Bowers et al., "A New Look at Public Opinion on Capital Punishment: What Citizens and Legislators Prefer," 22 *Am. J. Crim. L.* 77 (1994). The highest level of public support for the death penalty was in 1988, 79 percent, with a low of 42 percent expressing their support in 1966. Ellsworth, *supra,* at 48–49. After 1974 the polling question asked was: Are you in favor of the death penalty for persons convicted of murder? See James Alan Fox et al., "Death Penalty Opinion in the Post-*Furman* Years," 18 *N.Y.U. Rev. L. & Soc. Change* 499, 502 n.12 (1991). See also D. Milan, "Capital Punishment and Perception: Public Opinion and Its Influence," in 1992 WWS Final Report; Minhas, *supra* note 196; A. Southwell, "Life or Death? Analysis of the Current Public Opinion and Justifications: The Death Penalty and Its Alternatives," in 1992 WWS Final Report.

291. "When the Legislature originally enacted the death-penalty statute, they most likely operated under the misconception that the United States Constitution required proportionality review as an essential element of a valid death-penalty system. That assumption was proven incorrect by the holding in *Pulley v. Harris.*" *State v. Marshall,* 613 A.2d 1059, 1116 (N.J. 1992) (Garibaldi, J., concurring in part and dissenting in part) (citation omitted).

292. See *supra* "The Foundation for Proportionality Review in Capital Cases."

293. For example, the U.S. Supreme Court restricted access to the federal courts by (1) narrowing the procedural and substantive grounds for federal habeas review, while making those grounds much more technical; (2) interpreting the definition of incompetence of counsel so that only a very small subset of cases meet the standard for the appointment of counsel; and (3) tightening time requirements and strictly interpreting waiver questions. The goal of shutting down federal habeas review to capital defendants has been facilitated by the appointment of federal judges in favor of speeding up executions and limiting federal capital appeals. See *supra* "The Foundation for Proportionality Review in Capital Cases."

294. N.J. Laws ch. 5 (1992). The provision amended 2C:11-3e by adding the following language: "Proportionality review under this section shall only consist of a comparison of similar cases in which a sentence of death has been imposed under subsection c. of this section." N.J. Stat. Ann. 2C:11-3e (West 1995). Principles of ex post facto prevent this provision from having

a retrospective effect upon the *Marshall* case or upon any case in which the crime occurred prior to the effective date of the amendment. See *infra* note 298 and accompanying text.

295. N.J. Const., art. I, P 12 (amended 1992).

296. 549 A.2d 792 (N.J. 1988).

297. See Jerry Gray, "G.O.P. Is Told Not to Alter Constitution," *New York Times,* July 14, 1992, at B6. The article states:

> Blaming what he called "right wing extremists" within the Republican Party, the Senate Democratic leader, John A. Lynch, accused the Republican legislative majority today of trying to undermine the state constitution . . . Since the Republican-controlled 205th Legislature began its two-year session in January, legislators have introduced nearly 90 bills to amend the State Constitution, about a dozen of them sponsored by Democrats.

298. *Marshall II,* 613 A.2d at 1071–73.

299. Id.

300. As described by an observer:

> Surrounded by lawmakers, district attorneys and relatives of murder victims, Pataki used the pens of two slain police officers to sign the death penalty legislation into law shortly after noon Tuesday. It's a bill that backers have been trying to get a New York governor to approve for 18 straight years. "This bill is going to save lives. This bill is going to be a deterrent and it's going to allow us to have a system that imposes justice fairly and appropriately in New York state," Pataki said . . . Assembly Speaker Sheldon Silver, Senate Majority Leader Joseph Bruno and other lawmakers joined Pataki at the ceremony . . . "I think it's a deterrent. Maybe they'll think twice before they'll pull triggers," said Janet McDonald, whose police officer husband, Sean, was murdered last March execution-style after he came upon a robbery . . . Another murder victim's relative, who was featured in a campaign ad last fall for Pataki, said Tuesday's signing helped in the healing process. "It's an important day," said Carol McCauliff, whose stepson Thomas was killed last year allegedly by a repeat offender given early release from prison. McCauliff appeared in one of the campaign's more controversial ads, when, concerning her stepson's murder, she proclaimed, "I blame it all on Cuomo and his policies." (Tom Precious, "Justice Will Be Served," *Times Union,* Mar. 8, 1995, at A1)

301. Act of March 7, 1995, 1995 N.Y. Laws c.1.

302. See "Death Penalty Symposium," 23 *Hofstra L. Rev.* 627 (1995); R. Tabak, "Are Executions in New York Inevitable?" 22 *Fordham Urb. L.J.* 557 (1995). See also Mary R. Falk and Eve Cary, "Death-Defying Feats: State Constitutional Challenges to New York's Death Penalty," 4 *J.L. & Pol'y* 161 (1995); Robert Weisberg, "The New York Statute as Cultural Document: Seeking the Morally Optimal Death Penalty," 44 *Buff. L. Rev.* 283 (1996); Franklin E. Zimring, "The Wages of Ambivalence: On the Contexts and Prospects of New York's Death Penalty," 44 *Buff. L. Rev.* 303 (1996). See generally "The New York Death Penalty in Context: A Symposium," 44 *Buff. L. Rev.* 283 (1996). See also James R. Acker, "When the Cheering Stopped: An Overview and Analysis of New York's Death Penalty Legislation," 17 *Pace L. Rev.* (1997).

303. See *supra* tbl.2. Frank Zimring argues that the system's failure to execute a proportionate number of persons sentenced to death represents a societal ambivalence about the death penalty. See Franklin E. Zimring and G. Hawkins, *Capital Punishment and the*

American Agenda (1986); Franklin E. Zimring, "Ambivalence in State Capital Punishment Policy: An Empirical Sounding," 18 *N.Y.U. Rev. L. & Soc. Change* 729 (1991).

304. See Baldus et al., *supra* note 36, at 376–405. Section 4 of that article discusses the Racial Justice Act and the Fairness in Death Sentencing Act, both designed to "bypass *McCleskey* by relying on the legislative power granted Congress under the Enabling Clause of the Fourteenth Amendment." Id. at 377. The Fairness in Death Sentencing Act "would provide a condemned prisoner the opportunity to challenge his death sentence with statistical proof of racial discrimination and would also employ a risk-based model of proof." Id. at 379 (citation omitted). It is noteworthy that as this article went to press the American Bar Association's House of Delegates voted for a moratorium on all executions because of the persuasive disparities in their application.

305. The dispute between Governor Pataki and Bronx Prosecutor Robert Johnson is a highly publicized example of the different charging practices and the autonomy of local officials. Johnson refused to charge capital murder in a case involving the killing of a police officer. Pataki argued Johnson must be removed to reduce county-by-county disparities in the application of the New York statute.

306. For example, the provision requiring the prosecutor to give notice of the intention to seek the death penalty was the subject of litigation in New Jersey prior to the Supreme Court of New Jersey addressing the constitutionality of the death penalty statute as a whole. See *State v. McCrary,* 478 A.2d 339 (N.J. 1984). New York addresses this issue by presumably preempting litigation in New York if prosecutors adhere to the time limitations. See N.Y. Crim. Proc. Law 250.40 (McKinney Supp. 1996).

307. See Governor's Memorandum of Approval of L.1995, c. 1 (The Death Penalty). "Constitutional concerns and the infirmities in prior New York State law are fully met in this bill, which establishes a bifurcated trial procedure and sets forth clear standards to narrow the scope of the death penalty and guide the jury in determining whether to impose the death penalty . . ." As one commentator observed: "In one sense the New York law is itself a 'constitutional moment.' It might be read as the original MPC [Model Penal Code] law with constitutional annotations folded into it. Line after line, the New York law incorporates identifiable post-Furman Supreme Court cases. In its aim at being proof against constitutional attack, it not only acquires the constitutional wisdom of the last twenty years; it takes the most 'conservative' and prophylactic view of constitutional law possible." Robert Weisberg, "The New York Statute as Cultural Document: Seeking the Morally Optimal Death Penalty," 44 *Buff. L. Rev.* 283, 293 (1996).

308. During the Assembly debate Mr. Stringer expressed concern about the misuse of the potential publicity surrounding capital prosecution by prosecutors seeking reelection, commenting upon the fact that Robert Morgenthau, the district attorney for Manhattan, was known to be against the death penalty. See N.Y. State Assembly, Death Penalty Debate, Mar. 6, 1995, at 210 [hereinafter N.Y. Assembly Death Penalty Debate] (on file with the State Documents Collection of Northwestern University School of Law). There is now a controversy regarding Governor Pataki's assertion in December 1995 that he can remove a district attorney from a potentially capital case if that district attorney decided not to prosecute a case capitally. This raises the new issue of separation of powers and the autonomy of prosecutors.

The amount and disposition of funds appropriated for the defense of capital cases became, not surprisingly, both complicated and politically controversial. The Administrative Board of the New York Court of Appeals initially set the rates and requested comments. Differences arose in part because of large discrepancies in fee structures in various sections of the state. See Daniel Wise, "4 Panels Named for Death Penalty Cases; Assignments Include

Counsel Compensation," *New York Law Journal,* Aug. 16, 1995, at 1; Daniel Wise, "Panels Split on Legal Fees in Death Cases: Proposals Vary from $125 to $300 for Lead Counsel," *New York Law Journal,* Nov. 15, 1995, at 1, 4; Daniel Wise, "Comments Generally Favor Rates for Capital Counsel," *New York Law Journal,* Mar. 6, 1996, at 1; and Daniel Wise, "Pataki Urges Capital Cases Pay Cut," *New York Law Journal,* Mar. 13, 1996, at 1.

309. "Under the statute, prosecutors have the option of seeking the death penalty or life without parole. The Bronx District Attorney suggested yesterday he would seek the latter. 'The law is that district attorneys have the discretion,' Mr. Johnson said in a short statement." Ian Fisher, "Detailed Rules on Executions Released by New York State," *New York Times,* Sept. 2, 1995, at 1. See also Ellen Yan and Robin Topping, "Lawyers Dread Dealing with It but . . .," *Newsday,* Aug. 31, 1995, at A4:

> Nassau and Suffolk district attorneys' offices don't believe more than a few death penalty cases will be handled each year, because of the time and cost. Death penalty cases, which are appealed automatically, can drag on for years, possibly bankrupting counties and depleting state funds for the defense and prosecution of these cases . . . "I'm really dreading the first case I'm going to have to make the decision on," said [the Nassau County Prosecutor] . . . Like Nassau, the Suffolk District Attorney's Office has looked up their murder cases for the past few years to determine how many would have been eligible for the death penalty. About 20 to 25 cases met the criteria, said DA James Catterson Jr., and his prosecutors, in an informal survey, said they would be hard-pressed to recommend the death penalty in even three or four [of those] cases.

In addition, a *New York Times* article stated that:

> Prosecutors are discovering, however, that the state's first death penalty law in more than two decades, which covers a dozen categories of murder and appears to cast the widest of nets, is stitched so tightly that even the most heinous of September's murders may not qualify . . . There have been an estimated 65 homicides in New York City alone since the law took effect, and 26 just in Brooklyn—9 over the last weekend—Mr. Hynes said. So, he added, the absence of capital cases hardly implies that would-be killers throughout the state skidded to a halt over the Labor Day weekend. (Jan Hoffman, "Death Penalty Law Is Not Easy to Apply," *New York Times,* Sept. 22, 1995, at B2)

310. N.Y. Crim. Proc. Law 470.30(2), 470.15(2)(c) (McKinney 1994 & Supp. 1996) (courts can set aside a death sentence which is "unduly harsh or severe" as a corrective action).

311. Id.

312. The law provides:

> Court Set Aside of Death Sentence: Subdivision (d) authorizes the defendant upon written motion, in cases where a death sentence is imposed to have the sentence set aside upon any of the grounds set forth in section 330.30 of the Criminal Procedure Law including newly discovered evidence, improper conduct of a juror or jurors which may have affected substantial rights of the defendant and any ground appearing in the record which, if raised on appeal from a prospective judgement of conviction, would require a reversal or modification as a matter of law . . . In addition to ordering a new sentencing proceeding, the court may take any corrective action an appellate court could take upon reversing or modifying a judgment on the

grounds at issue in the motion. (Summary and Description of Provisions: D. Separate Sentencing Proceedings, N.Y. State Assembly Committee Bill Memorandum-L. 1995, c. 1. (available in Historical and Statutory Notes to N.Y. Correct. Law art. 22-B (McKinney Supp. 1996)))

313. 470.30(3). For an analysis of the most recent congressional enactments regarding federal habeas, see Larry W. Yackle, "A Primer on the New Habeas Corpus Statute," 44 *Buff. L. Rev.* 381 (1996).

314. 400.27(11)(d).

315. 470.30(3)(a).

316. Id.

317. 470.30(3)(b).

318. Id. The court is required to list all similar cases considered in proportionality review.

319. 211-a. The Court of Appeals set uniform rules for the Trial Courts in capital cases, effective Feb. 7, 1996. See N.Y. R. U. Trial Cts 218.1 et seq. These rules include the requirement of the submission of capital case data reports: ". . . in every criminal action in which the defendant has been *indicted for murder in the first degree (P.L. 125.27) including those actions resolved by pleas of guilty,* to assist the Court of Appeals in determining whether a particular sentence of death is disproportionate or excessive in the context of penalties imposed in similar cases." See Capital Case Data Report (available from Counsel's Office, New York Court of Appeals, Albany, N.Y.) (emphasis added).

Proportionality review in New York will necessarily confront county-by-county disparities perpetuated by different charging policies of prosecutors, different patterns in the incidence of homicide across jurisdictions, and the factors seen in New Jersey and other jurisdictions. See, e.g., Daniel Wise, "Prosecutors Want Death Penalty; Qualms Voiced About Costs, Time, Training of Lawyers," *New York Law Journal,* Mar. 3, 1995, at 1; Jan Hoffman, "Balancing Personal Beliefs and the Law," *New York Times,* Sept. 25, 1996, at B6. The existence of broad discretion in their decision to charge capital murder has and will continue to exacerbate county-by-county disparities.

320. 211-a.

321. See the criteria for research quality specified by the U.S. General Accounting Office:

> By quality we mean the strength of the design and the rigor of the analytic technique that leads to a level of confidence we have in the study findings. We judged a study to be high quality if it was characterized by a sound design that analyzed homicide cases throughout the sentencing process; included legally relevant variables (aggravating and mitigating circumstances); and used statistical analysis techniques to control for variables that correlate with race and/or capital sentencing. (1990 GAO Report, *supra* note 37, at 3)

322. See Governor's Memorandum of Approval of L. 1995, c. 1 (Death Penalty) and N.Y. State Assembly Committee Bill memorandum L. 1995 (A.4843), issued on Mar. 6, 1995.

323. On July 3, 1995, the court released Proposed Rules of the Court of Appeals in Capital Cases and Proposed Uniform Procedures for Appeals from Pretrial Findings of Mental Retardation in Capital Cases. On Aug. 31, 1995, the court released Proposed Uniform Rules for the Trial Courts in Capital Cases and Proposed Minimum Standards for Lead Counsel and Associate Counsel in Capital Cases. On Sept. 15, 1995, the court released the Proposed Uniform Rules for Capital Case Data Reports and the Capital Case Data Report Form, with a comment period ending on Oct. 16, 1995. See Richard R. Zander, public information officer, New York Court of Appeals, Statement Accompanying Release of Death Penalty Rules

for Public Comment (Sept. 15, 1995) (all on file with the State Documents Collection of Northwestern University School of Law).

324. Extensive comments were submitted to the court on the form and substance of the data collection, record-keeping, and certification of accuracy and reliability which the court has a responsibility to undertake. These are preconditions to the systematic analysis of racial and geographic disparities. Without reliable information on capital cases and similar cases in which the death penalty was not sought or imposed, the court cannot address the constitutional issues. See cases submitted on Oct. 16, 1995, by Professor David Baldus et al. (comments on proposed rules of the court in capital cases) (on file with State Documents Collection of Northwestern University School of Law).

325. Concerns for the execution of the innocent were expressed often in the Assembly debates. See, e.g., N.Y. Assembly Death Penalty Debate, *supra* note 308, at 165–75.

About the Author

Leigh Buchanan Bienen is a senior lecturer at Northwestern University School of Law. She has published numerous articles and books about crime, criminal law, and the capital punishment system, as well as fiction and essays on theater and other topics.